Cosima Wagner

Extraordinary Daughter of Franz Liszt

Cosima Wagner

Extraordinary Daughter of Franz Liszt

ALICE HUNT SOKOLOFF

ILLUSTRATED

DODD, MEAD & COMPANY

NEW YORK

Library of Congress Catalog Card Number: 69-13731

Printed in the United States of America
by The Cornwall Press, Inc., Cornwall, N. Y.

FOR BORIS

INTRODUCTION

SHE WAS BORN FRANCESCA GAETANA COSIMA LISZT, daughter of Franz Liszt and Marie d'Agoult. She became Cosima von Bülow, wife of Liszt's brilliant and favorite pupil. But it was as Cosima Wagner that she fulfilled her promise of greatness and realized the mission that she had felt was hers from her earliest days.

Richard Wagner was a strange man. In many ways and to many people he was a repellent man. He had a nature difficult in the extreme—violent, demanding, egotistical, pathologically self-centered. But he was a genius, one of those rare figures that tower over an age.

As a musician, he was a revolutionary. His whole concept of opera and of art was so startlingly original that for years he and his music aroused the most violent opposition. Performances of his works were savagely booed and hissed. But he aroused an equal intensity of devotion among his admirers, who worked unceasingly to help him and to further his cause. Wagner set his goals high, and artistic compromise was impossible for him. There were periods of hope, but they were soon followed by failure and despair again.

Wagner's personal life was as turbulent as his artistic one, and it is not surprising that such an intense personality as his would come more than once to the edge of ruin and collapse.

It was Cosima, and Cosima alone, who was willing and able to give this great and difficult artist the total, selfless devotion and understanding that he required. She knew that she could save him. And she did. Without her he never would have completed the *Ring,* nor written *Parsifal,* nor brought into being his dream that became Bayreuth. A measure of her greatness is that Cosima above all others cut through the dross and ugliness in Wagner's nature straight to the radiant core.

From birth Cosima was surrounded by extraordinary circumstances and extraordinary people. Her father, Franz Liszt, is still spoken of as the greatest pianist who ever lived. His fabulous artistry, combined with his striking appearance, his charm, and his showmanship made him one of the most talked-about figures of his time. He has been called everything from genius and saint to hypocrite and libertine. The stories of his love affairs fill volumes. At the same time he was a profoundly religious man with a belief that was almost childlike in its simplicity. He had great tolerance toward others and a rare and true generosity. In all the annals of music, there has never been a man who did so much to further the careers of his fellow artists—Schumann, Berlioz, Wagner, and a score of others. And yet there was something demoniac in him too, a restless, wild *zigeuner* aspect. The magnetism of his personality and his genius has not faded and even today the aura of Liszt the man and Liszt the musician is legendary.

Cosima inherited a good deal from her father. She had the same idealism and nobility of feeling that he showed in so many of the circumstances of his life, and she had some of his wild, ironic spirit too. Her physical resemblance to him was startling and often in the heat of argument something of his demonism would flash across her face. From her father, too, she inherited an unusual musical talent, a talent so extraordinary that her playing was once compared to that of Liszt himself.

Cosima's mother, the Countess d'Agoult, half-German, half-French, was a woman of unusual beauty and gifts. Through her father, the Count de Flavigny, she belonged to the elite of the French aristocracy and was brought up in the most exclusive circles of the old nobility. But into this rarified atmosphere of the Faubourg Saint-Germain, Marie d'Agoult brought something of the strong traditions of her mother's German family: an independence of spirit and an ardent romanticism. The life of the salons was not enough for this beautiful woman, in spite of the many admirers who surrounded her. She needed more than a social life or even a passionate attachment. Under the pseudonym of Daniel Stern she wrote, and wrote prolifically, publishing innumerable books and articles on a vast range of subjects.

Had she wanted, Cosima could no doubt have followed in her mother's literary footsteps, for she showed a genuine ability in that direction. Her intellectual gifts were like her mother's, too, a delight in using her mind and the highest standards of taste and culture.

It was a wild, passionate, and often stormy union between Liszt and the Countess d'Agoult, two gifted and strong-willed people who defied convention and courted scandal by their open liaison. This famous pair, completely absorbed in each other and in themselves, had very little time for their children. After the inevitable rupture, when the pendulum of their feelings swung from passionate attachment through coldness to a final and violent hostility, the children became helpless victims of their bitterness.

In view of her early life it would have been easy, and in

the light of present day psychology logical, for Cosima to have grown resentful, introspective, and incapable of loving or being loved. But the reverse is true. Cosima's nature was and always remained essentially a loving one toward all who were close to her throughout her long life. It was through love that Cosima found herself and her destiny, a love rarely equaled in its degree of intensity, devotion, and self-sacrifice.

Cosima's life has too often been looked upon as an adjunct to that of Wagner. To a great extent she herself was responsible for this through her dedication to him. But Cosima is far too complex, too vivid, too fascinating a subject to be put under the shadow of anyone—even a Wagner. Here is the story of a woman who was challenged to the limit by the circumstances and events of her life. It is the hope of this book, through an exploration of the people and influences around her, to illuminate the personality and development of this extraordinary woman and the times in which she lived.

ILLUSTRATIONS

Following page 112

Cosima Wagner

Extraordinary Daughter of Franz Liszt

CHAPTER I

It was an April evening in Vienna in the year 1823. The large audience in the Redoutensaal fell silent as a strong, stocky figure with a leonine head made his way slowly down the aisle to the very front row. It was Beethoven. He had come out of his isolation to hear the eleven-year-old prodigy Franz Liszt play.

The boy, slender, graceful, with enormous deep-set eyes, bowed low to the composer before taking his place at the piano. It was a Hummel concerto that he played and he followed it by an improvisation of his own.

The applause burst forth. Beethoven slowly rose to his feet, climbed the few steps to the stage, took the boy in his arms and kissed him on the forehead. Then, without a word, he pushed his way through the cheering throng, and left the hall to return once again to his lonely studio.

This is a charming and impressive story, no doubt, but one wonders how much Beethoven could hear of the playing of this young prodigy. It was only four years before his death, and he must have been, by then, nearly stone deaf. This fact, however, lends credence to the story that Beethoven had heard the young Liszt earlier, in his own studio, where he would have been able, with his ear trumpet, to have judged the young pianist. Beethoven's appearance at the concert, in spite of his well-known dislike of child prodigies, was a public tribute to this boy who was to become the greatest pianist of his, or perhaps of any, time.

Franz Liszt was born October 22, 1811, in the small Hungarian village of Raiding where his father, Adam, was steward on one of the estates of Prince Nicholas Esterhazy.

Adam Liszt felt lonely and miserable in this isolated village, cut off from the music and society that he enjoyed. His only pleasure was to play the piano to his wife Anna in the evenings and to dream of the musical career that he had missed. It was when Franz was six years old that Adam realized that his dreams might be fulfilled through his son, and he set about teaching the gifted boy with ever-increasing excitement. Franz made unbelievable progress, sopping up with ease all that his father taught him. His ear and his memory were remarkable, and by the time he was nine years old he was ready for his first public appearance.

One can imagine with what pride Adam Liszt took his son to Ödenburg, where the boy played with such effect that Adam knew the time had come to present him to Prince Esterhazy.

A concert was arranged at the Esterhazy Palace in Pressburg. All the wealth and power of the Hungarian aristocracy were present, a brilliant gathering that could easily have overawed the child from the simple country village of Raiding. But Franz seemed to feel perfectly at home and won everyone not only by his talent but by his beauty and charm of manner. A subscription was taken with the result that for the next six years Franz's future was assured with an annual stipend of six hundred florins.

The family moved to Vienna where lessons were arranged with Karl Czerny in piano and Antonio Salieri in theory and composition.

As one can imagine, from the hundreds of exercises and études which have come down to us, Czerny was a hard taskmaster. It must have been an ordeal for young Franz, who under his father's rather light hand had been allowed to follow his own musical inclinations, to have submitted to the endless technical grind that Czerny demanded. He often felt rebellious but nevertheless worked so well that Czerny refused to take any payment for the lessons. To the end of his days, Franz Liszt was grateful for the rigid training Czerny had given him.

During all this period, Franz continued to play in concerts and in the salons of aristocratic Vienna, where he was adored and spoiled by everyone. The next step was logical—foreign tours and, above all, Paris.

Franz Liszt was twelve when he arrived in the French capital, after a triumphant tour through Germany. In Paris he became the darling of the salons almost overnight. Everyone was talking about *"le petit Litz,"* as he was called, but Adam's hope that the boy, now twelve years old, could enter the Paris Conservatory for further study in composition with the famous Cherubini was doomed to disappointment. No foreigners were allowed to study at the Conservatory.

Adam Liszt was not reputed to be a worldly man; nevertheless, during the next four years young Franz was exploited as a prodigy. He was even prevailed upon to compose a full-length opera, *Don Sancho,* a work which fortunately has been consigned to oblivion. He performed continuously, in fashionable salons, in recitals, before the crowned heads of France and England, touring both those countries and Switzerland, but always again back to Paris. The growing boy began to loathe the adulation accorded him as a youthful prodigy.

Franz had received very little education apart from his musical studies. In his little village of Raiding he had been taught the rudiments of Hungarian by the village priest. The language at home was German, not only because his mother, Anna Liszt, was Austrian, but because it was the language of society in Hungary at that time. Franz picked up French with no trouble at all, and it remained his language of choice throughout his life. He also learned English with remarkable success.

By the time he was fourteen, Franz began to question more and more the empty life of a traveling virtuoso. His mother had returned to Austria, for she never felt at home in the grand salons and aristocratic society which delighted his father. Everything seemed empty to the young Liszt, no longer a child, but still being exploited as one. He was physically exhausted by the strains of his life. He was emotionally lost and desperately seeking his way.

From his earliest years, Franz Liszt had a deep, abiding and childlike religious faith. It was natural that during the difficult period of his early adolescence his thoughts should return again and again to the comfort and security of the Church. He read the Bible, the lives of the Saints, the *Imitation of Christ* of Thomas à Kempis. He attended Mass daily, seeking solace and solitude. Finally, he poured out his heart to his father, begging permission to enter the Church. The answer was a categorical: "No."

Franz's health deteriorated still more after this and his father grew anxious about him. The doctors suggested a holiday by the sea. The boy's health improved, but Adam Liszt was taken suddenly ill and died at Boulogne-sur-Mer within a few days. The year was 1827. Franz was always to remember what his father told him at the end, prophetically: that he had a good heart and did not lack intelligence but that women would trouble and dominate his life.

Kindly and well-meaning as Adam Liszt may have been, he had ruled his son strictly, never leaving him alone, guiding and directing his every move. One might have imagined that the sixteen-year-old boy would have been completely helpless without him, but that was not the case. The strength and fineness of his character were shown at once. He assumed all the debts incurred by his father's illness, even though it meant that he had to sell his beautiful Erard grand piano. He sent for his mother, from whom he had been separated for more than two years, to join him in Paris, where he rented a simple apartment on the rue Montholon. Years later, when he was a very old man, he chided one of his pupils, Alexander Siloti, for neglecting to write to his mother. "Now, my dear boy," he said, "don't do this again, because your mother has written to tell me she is anxious about you. You are young, and there is one thing you should remember. I am seventy-three years old, and have lived my life happily enough, but it is entirely owing to the fact that I have always been a good son to my mother." [1]

Liszt was a good son to his mother. Exhausted and weary of the endless concert tours and wanting to be with her as much as he could, he withdrew from the concert stage. In order to support himself and his mother he gave piano lessons, long hours every day, to the aristocratic daughters of Parisian high society. And soon the inevitable happened. He fell in love with one of his pupils, Carolyn de Saint-Criq, the daughter of one of his patronesses.

It was an innocent first love between this seventeen-year-old pair, which came to a sudden and shattering close when Carolyn's mother died. She had looked on the budding romance with a tender complaisance, but her husband did not. The Count de Saint-Criq informed Liszt in no uncertain terms that he was no longer welcome, and Carolyn was married off to the man her father had chosen for her, the Count d'Artigaux.

Throughout his whole life Liszt retained the tenderest regard for this young girl and in his will, drawn up more than thirty years later, he requested that some talisman of his be made into a ring for her. It had not been a casual feeling that he had for Carolyn, and his brusque dismissal threw him into a frightful depression. His thoughts again turned to the Church, but his confessor, Abbé Bardin, persuaded him that his true vocation was music.

During eighteen months, Liszt was in a state of deep melancholia, withdrawn from music and from the world. A mysterious illness, undoubtedly psychosomatic in origin, attacked him and brought him, as once before in his childhood, almost to death's door. In fact, announcements of his death were circulated around Paris.

Liszt's recovery was slow. Necessity forced him to take up his teaching again, but for a long time he remained apathetic and withdrawn, reading, when he did not have to teach, everything he could lay his hands on: history, poetry, religion, science, novels.

Paris was in ferment. Liberalism was on the march again. Social, political, and religious freedoms were in the air. The Revolution of 1830 brought the liberal Louis Philippe to the throne after a brief uprising when the streets of Paris were filled with barricades and echoed to the sound of gunfire. The effect on Liszt was electric. His mother later said that it was the cannons that cured him. His depression and ill health were forgotten, and he entered into a period of enormous productivity.

He met Berlioz and Chopin. He heard the fantastic violinist Paganini and through him was led to a complete rethinking and reconstituting of his piano technique and his concept of the potentialities of the piano. He was swept up in the social and artistic theories of Saint-Simon. The ideas of socialism, art, and religious freedom of Lamennais fired his heart and his imagination, and he became one of the Abbé's most fervent disciples. He re-entered the world at a gallop: the world of music, of ideas, of liberalism—and the world of the Paris salons. But now it was no longer as a child prodigy that he came to the silken drawing rooms, but as a young man already taking his place as the first pianist of Europe.

The position in society of a musician had long been a thorny one. There had been a time, not long before, when musicians entered and left the great houses of the aristocracy by the servants' entrance and were looked upon as semi-superior domestics whose role was to entertain their patrons. It had been pleasant and amusing to pet the boy prodigy, but the young man was a different matter. The new wave of liberalism, the weakening of the power of the ancient aristocracy, but most of all the emphasis on the individual that was the hallmark of the romantic expression in the arts and literature, all these influences combined to break down the old mores. But not completely, as the following letter to Liszt from the Countess d'Agoult will show. "I saw the Duchess . . . I told her that people had found it very ridiculous the footing on which we have established you in our salons, this familiarity, etc., etc., at which she lifted her ducal head superbly to make me realize that she would never cede an inch to the stupid clamor of these frogs and that, with her, agreeable people are always in the right." [2]

Liszt's fiery nature was not one to submit easily to any show of snobbism. He had a consciousness of his own value, as an artist and as a man, and he bitterly resented the position of the artist in society. Later he expressed his feelings of that period vividly: "There came over me a bitter disgust against art, such as it appeared to me: vilified and degraded to the level of a more or less profitable handicraft, branded as a source of amusement for distinguished society. I felt that I would sooner be anything in the world than a musician in the pay of the exalted, patronized and salaried by them like a conjuror, or the learned dog Munito." [3]

Liszt took his art seriously. He threw himself into work, hard technical work at the piano, determined to improve his already brilliant mastery. "Here is a whole fortnight that my mind and fingers have been working like two lost spirits—Homer, the Bible, Plato, Locke, Byron, Hugo, Lamartine, Chateaubriand, Beethoven, Bach, Hummel, Mozart, Weber, are all around me. I study them, meditate on them, devour them with fury; besides this I practise from four to five hours of exercises (thirds, sixths, octaves, trills, repeated notes, and cadenzas). Ah! provided I don't go mad, you will find an artist in me! Yes, an artist such as you desire, and such as is required nowadays!" [4] Creatively too, Liszt began to catch fire at this time.

His success was phenomenal. His superb artistry was responsible for most of it, but there was a good deal of the actor in Liszt too. His concerts were masterpieces of showmanship and he used every trick in the trade, and many outside it, to produce his effect.

Liszt's explosion into the artistic life of Paris after his years of withdrawal caused many a feminine heart to flutter. The wound of his separation from Carolyn de Saint-Criq had healed and Liszt found himself not at all unresponsive to some of the ladies who flocked around him. But his fateful meeting came in 1833, when he was twenty-two years old, with Marie Catherine Sophie, Countess d'Agoult.

Who was this Marie d'Agoult who was to become the mother of Liszt's three children? What kind of woman was she? There is a mass of contradictory opinions.

"Both beautiful and original, not only did she move, as befitted her many talents, on the highest human plane, but, thanks to these very talents, it was her lot to play a part in French literature, and that no ephemeral part, but a lasting one," says Count du Moulin Eckart.[5]

"Madame d'Agoult is said to have possessed great beauty and literary talent, though there is no evidence extant of either quality. She was 'highly temperamental'—in other words she had a violent temper—there is ample evidence of that, and she can hardly be said to have justified her existence in any way," Frederick Corder states categorically.[6]

Hans von Bülow's reaction was very different. "Daniel Stern (Madame d'Agoult) has made an impression on me that is as great as it was unexpected. Still marvelously beautiful, and noble in form and feature . . . In addition, dignity and nobility of bearing without the least effort—a fine elegant *laissez-aller* that sets those who are in her company perfectly at their ease and stimulates them intellectually, leading them to bring out what is best in themselves." [7]

Balzac, in his novel *Beatrix,* in the character of Madame de Rochefide gave an almost libelous picture of the Countess d'Agoult. "Women like Madame de Rochefide, cold, fragile, hard and thin . . . have souls as pale and colorless as their pale gray or green eyes." [8] And he sums her up as "a pattern of those vain natures, devoid of energy, but flirts out of vainglory . . . a woman devoid of heart and brain, frivolous in wickedness. Madame de Rochefide loves no one but Madame de Rochefide." [9]

Marie d'Agoult, in one of her moods of "extraordinary candor" analyzed her own nature: "My mind is not vulgar. It forms, with my imagiation and my feelings, an unusual temperament where the qualities of both French and German are combined in an unexpected manner. There is a gentleness in me, an even disposition and kindness, with a manner of being, of thinking, of speaking where loyalty is the most evident. Of pedantism I have none; of vanity, even less; neither pretensions, nor affectations, nor nonsense of any sort. A candor which one could call extraordinary . . . As a rule my feelings, no matter what they are, are deeply hidden; they are concentrated; they shine out only in flashes, pale and rapid; they are silent, in the fear of showing too much. I must appear to possess a glacial coldness; 'six inches of snow over twenty feet of lava,' someone said of me, and not without justice." [10]

Where is the truth in all these opinions? That the Countess d'Agoult possessed real beauty is apparent not only in her portraits but in the many tributes to her beauty by her contemporaries. She was a tall, slender woman, with very blond hair and a skin like snow. As for her intelligence, her writings attest to a mind of wide range of interest and activity. They cover every subject from Emerson, contemporary German writers, *Power and Liberty,* Mary Stuart, *War and Public Opinion,* Petrarch, Bismarck, Titian, *History of the Revolution of 1848* in three volumes, to novels and her *Memoirs.* A woman capable of writing and publishing as much as she did could hardly be said to possess an insignificant, undisciplined, or superficial mind.

That she had a gentle, even disposition, as she sometimes liked to pretend to herself, even she realized was not always true. Pride and love were her two great passions, she admitted, and neither one could succeed in driving out the other.

Marie d'Agoult was a patrician to the tips of her fingers. Her consciousness of rank was born and bred into her, and all her liberal ideas and romantic longings for a world where only the individual counted could not alter this basic substratum.

Her father, the Count de Flavigny, had been a page to Marie Antoinette, and she never forgot this. Emigrating to Frankfurt, he met and fell in love there with a young widow of eighteen, a daughter of the Bethmann banking family. Her parents opposed the match with this handsome but penniless aristocrat, but the young woman's inflexible determination and strength of will, qualities which she passed on in great measure to her granddaughter Cosima, overcame their scruples. Two children survived of this marriage: Maurice de Flavigny who held various important government positions in later life, and Marie Catherine Sophie.

Marie was born during the night of December 30–31, in the year 1805. The fact that she was born at night made a strange impression on her and she attributed to it all sorts of mystical and emotional influences that she felt ruled her life. Her first years were spent in Germany, but in 1809 her parents moved to France where they acquired a property in the Touraine. Loyal to the Bourbons, the Count de Flavigny stayed completely away from the court of Napoleon. He rode and hunted and enjoyed to the full the life of ease of a French nobleman of that period who had married an adoring wife possessed of a very substantial fortune. Marie idolized her father and was his constant companion. With her mother she felt all her life a certain constraint. "I do not know why," she wrote, "but her presence was not at all agreeable to me." [11]

She was baptized a Protestant according to the custom of mixed marriages where the daughters adopted the religion of the mother and the sons that of the father. Religion, however, in the Flavigny family seemed to have been regarded rather casually. It was Marie's paternal grandmother who approached the whole idea of Protestantism from a practical view point and found it rather ridiculous, as she said it would impair the girl's chances for marriage. So Marie became a Catholic, and just as for a long time she felt both French and German, or neither, so she felt both Protestant and Catholic, or neither.

Her father's sudden death when she was ten was a great shock and grief to the child. Soon afterward her mother took her for a long visit to Frankfurt, and it was there in her uncle's garden that she met Goethe. She was never to forget this meeting and the memory of his hand upon her head, a "hand of benediction," which always brought her a feeling of strength and purity.

The next six years she spent at the Convent of Sacré-Coeur where she learned "everything, absolutely everything that a young girl of my rank should know." [12] Her musical education was thorough too, mainly under the tutelage of her mother, who was a serious musician and who taught her piano, *solfège,* harmony, and composition with German thoroughness. The composer Hummel found her very gifted for composition and she later regretted that she had not applied herself more to this art.

Shortly before she was seventeen, Marie left the convent. She was beautiful, noble, and wealthy, and many suitors presented themselves. But Marie dreamed of something more than an arranged marriage, a marriage of convenience, a typical French marriage where, as she described it, there was neither love, nor fidelity, nor divorce, nor companionship, where, after the first year, the wife was free to do as she pleased, and so was the husband. She was not interested in a brilliant marriage. Her romantic German blood dreamed of eternal love.

At last Marie thought she had found this love. It was Count Auguste de Lagarde, a man more than twenty years older than herself, who inspired this tender feeling in her. But he was shy and she even more so, and when the moment came that she could have said to him "Stay," her tongue faltered and she let him go. By then she was twenty-one years old, and in her confusion and unhappiness she determined that she would accept the next man who presented himself. That man was Count Charles d'Agoult. He came from one of the oldest families of France, a colonel of cavalry in the service of the Dauphine. It was a *grande alliance* in all ways. They were married on May 16, 1827, in the presence of King Charles X, the Dauphin and Dauphine, Louis-Philippe d'Orléans, and other members of the French Court.

Charles d'Agoult has always been a rather misty shadow among the colorful figures who played out the drama that was to affect his life so profoundly. Considerably older than his wife, he felt almost from the very beginning that his marriage had been a mistake. He found Marie spoiled and cold, with little or no sense of duty or obligation. Her dreams were undirected. She did not know what she wanted—the life of an aristocrat, a brilliant salon, or success as a writer.

Certainly for a time Marie enjoyed the elegant life of the aristocracy. Years later she could still describe it in almost voluptuous terms—the six months at the country chateau, the six months in Paris; balls, concerts, weddings after Easter, a minimum of theater going, no travel at all, and cards all the time.

Marie d'Agoult moved in this elite circle with calm assurance. Always conscious of her aristocratic heritage, she nevertheless possessed an enormous intellectual curiosity, a desire to learn, to explore.

The Revolution of 1830 temporarily broke up the salons of the Faubourg Saint-Germain. As they re-established themselves, no longer under the eagle eye of the Dauphine, there was a greater freedom than before. Marie d'Agoult felt delivered from a kind of surveillance which had, up till then, not allowed her to open her salon fully to new people, to men who were not of the highest rank, to artists and writers whose fame had aroused her curiosity.

Under the new regime it was not long before she had drawn around her the leading figures of her time in the arts and literature. Alfred de Vigny was one of her most devoted admirers. There were Victor Hugo, Alfred De Musset, Chopin, Berlioz, Rossini, Henrietta Sontag—endless discussions, readings of poetry and plays, musical soirées at which the talented young hostess herself would often perform. It was a brilliant circle, and there was a whole ferment of new ideas, new feelings. They discovered Shakespeare, discussed Ossian, were inspired by Werther. Goethe and Byron were dissected, the revelations of Lamennais produced a tremendous effect.

Marie, however, grew more and more restless, searching for something, somewhere, that would satisfy the longings that she felt stirring within her turbulent heart and that were not satisfied in her loveless marriage. She was fond of her two little girls, Louise and Claire, but motherhood was not the answer either. "It is not true," she wrote, "that motherhood can be the only vocation of a woman. Profound or exalted as she might be, the love for her children cannot, to the exclusion of all other loves, absorb all her power of being, nor can it fulfill her destiny." [13]

Nevertheless, for a woman of society, she spent a good deal of time with her children. The two little girls, however, were a further source of estrangement between their parents, who did not agree about anything that concerned the children, neither their education, nor their pleasures. Madame d'Agoult found only a kind of bitter regret in the caresses of her little girls.

It was on her honeymoon that she had first discovered in herself what she describes as a "passable" ability to write. It was her mother-in-law who enjoyed the many descriptions that Marie sent her of the monuments and chateaux, the entertainments and parties that she attended. From that time dated her passion for writing and she never went anywhere without trunkfuls of papers, another source of irritation to her husband.

But Marie d'Agoult found in her German blood two tendencies: "In my intelligence, the thirst to know everything; in my heart the imperious need to love and to be loved." [14]

In spite of her patrician tendencies, this woman had a very real inclination toward the democratic ideal, toward a concept of human liberty and individual value. She was consumed with desire to discover an ideal way of life. The turbulent times of the recent past had shaken the establishment to its foundations, and although the Court and the aristocracy were again in the ascendency, the façade was full of cracks. There was a sense of anxiousness, of the unknown. Marie felt herself suffocated by the narrow boundaries of the Faubourg Saint-Germain. In spite of the brilliance of her position, her marriage, and the freedom she enjoyed to see her many friends, to amuse and occupy herself, she claimed that since the day of her marriage she had never had a single hour of joy. Her relationship with her husband, whose nature was opposed to hers at every point, brought her nothing but sorrow, and she found the pleasures of the brilliant life into which she threw herself, empty and vapid and false. Religion brought her no real consolation, although she tried to draw from it a spirit of resignation. But the more she read, the more she explored, the stronger grew her questions and doubts, so that she found progressively less and less consolation.

This is how Marie d'Agoult pictures herself, a woman suffering in silence, longing for the true and the beautiful and finding nothing but dross and emptiness around her.

How true was this picture that she drew of herself years later in her *Mémoirs*? How much of poetry did she allow to enter into the truth?

Undoubtedly there is a good deal of exaggeration and literary license in this melancholy self-portrait. Marie d'Agoult would not have been human had she not colored the period of her married life in more somber hues than the reality. However, we cannot dismiss all that she says. For certainly there was in this brilliant and passionate woman a deep frustration, an unsatisfied force that was strong enough so that when she found the courage to seek its fulfillment she was thrown, and this time did not exaggerate, "outside of law, in revolt against opinion, against everything that the people of my time and of my country held for certain, necessary and sacred." [15]

When Liszt and Marie d'Agoult met, each had arrived at a point in their lives when all that was needed was a spark to set the smoldering fires aflame. Liszt, after his unnatural childhood as a child prodigy and his later withdrawal from the world, was ready to explode into life and into love. Marie d'Agoult, bored and frustrated, felt her dreams could be fulfilled only in an ideal life where she would become the inspiration and companion of a man of genius.

CHAPTER II

IT WAS AT A FASHIONABLE SOIRÉE in the year 1833 that Liszt and Marie d'Agoult met. Her first impression of him was electric: "The door opened and a wonderful apparition appeared before my eyes. I say an apparition for there is no other word to describe the extraordinary sensation produced in me from the beginning at the sight of the most extraordinary person I had ever seen. A tall and extremely slender figure, a pale face with large eyes of sea green which radiated brightness like a blazing wave, a suffering yet powerful countenance, a hesitating step that seemed to glide rather than tread on the ground, a distracted and restless impression like that of a phantom for which the bell is about to sound the hour of return to darkness, that is how I saw before me this young genius whose retired life aroused at that moment a curiosity as lively as his triumphs had not long ago excited envy." [1]

Liszt was twenty-two, Marie d'Agoult twenty-eight at the time of this meeting. He started at once to talk to the young Countess with an assurance, an impetuosity, a directness to which she was hardly accustomed in the mannered world in which she lived. His ideas, his judgments, his look, his smile, sometimes sweet, sometimes caustic, disconcerted her. And then he played and after playing did not approach her again. That night she slept badly and had strange dreams.

A few days later, she decided to invite him to call on her but she tore up several notes before she found the proper way of addressing him. Already at this early moment in their relationship she was aware of the difference of name, of blood, and of fortune which they owed to the hazard of birth. She was embarrassed by her apparent superiority in her relationship with a person of his immense talent and what she believed she already knew of his character.

The relationship moved very rapidly after Liszt's first visit. They talked endlessly, about everything—about themselves, about the uncertainty and sorrows of human destiny, about the soul, about religion, about politics. Liszt's adventurous mind, his involvement with the revolutionary ideas of Lamennais and Saint-Simon, his detestation of convention, of injustice, of an aristocracy not based on genius or virtue—all these ideas, spoken always with vehemence and passion, opened a new and exciting world to the young Countess. Marie d'Agoult enjoyed the serious exchange of ideas and books, the elevated discussions, the intense, exploratory *conversations à deux*. Liszt later said of her that she was always most vulnerable to the attractions of the intellect and heart. There was something cold and analytical about her mind, and she had a horror of anything that was not of top quality, anything that was frivolous or vulgar. But under that six inches of snow we must not forget the twenty feet of lava. In spite of her intellectualism, in spite of her lifelong training in artificiality and restraint, in spite of her very apparent feelings of superiority in social position, Marie d'Agoult fell passionately, blindly, jealously, completely in love with Franz Liszt. And he with her.

They met often in a little apartment that Liszt had taken—the Rat-hole, they called it jokingly. When summer came and Marie went to her beautiful estate at Croissy, the young pianist visited her there. In between were letters, written almost daily, filled with news of their doings, their thoughts, and most of all, their love and longing for each other. It was a love affair carried on at fever pitch with intense emotionalism on both sides. They adored each other and gloried in being in love.

Marie d'Agoult recognized in herself that the need to be loved exclusively with no sharing of feeling at all dominated her emotions always, and gradually this need of exclusiveness made itself felt in her relations with Liszt. She was jealous of his past affairs; she wanted to know everything he did. Reproaches, explanations, began to fly back and forth between the two lovers. Some of his early letters to a youthful flame fell into her hands. He explained that they dated from a period two years before he had even met Marie. "Must I still justify myself to you? . . . You evidently did not understand my first words to you: This is to be! You have not understood that since that moment no past exists for me . . . In the name of heaven, give up these lovely discoveries of yours, they are simply too grotesque." [2] And he said: "Oh, how little you understand me sometimes." [3]

In the second year of their relationship, they came very close to the breaking point. "You say that you are already completely absorbed in the moment when we will see each other again!" Liszt wrote her. "Oh! that is how I too used to feel morning and evening the first days. Why did you destroy that hope in me? Now, I will tell you, since you wrote that unhappy letter to me which reopened all my wounds, I no longer dream of it, no longer desire it." [4]

When they would meet again, however, the bitterness was

forgotten, at least for a while. But then an event occurred which changed everything. Little Louise, Marie d'Agoult's older daughter, a child of six, fell desperately ill, probably of meningitis. Nothing helped, the child's condition grew steadily worse, and in December 1834 she died.

In her *Mémoirs,* Marie d'Agoult described the period after the death of Louise with considerable flight of imagination: that she and Liszt did not see each other or write for six months and that when they did meet she was confused and amazed when he declared with calm assurance that they could no longer live apart, that they must go away together. "Great God," she answered him. "Your God is not my God," said Franz, putting his hand on her mouth; "there is no other God but love." [5]

Actually, she wrote him on the day of Louise's death. "You thought constantly of me during the last two days, you tell me," Liszt answered her. "You thought of me by Louise's bed, yesterday, today . . . Forgive me, Marie, if I forget all your sorrows and all your griefs and speak to you only of myself, and of these words, 'I thought of you all the time.' " [6]

The death of Louise served only further to estrange Marie from her husband. Her grief was such that she could not bear the presence of her younger daughter, Claire, and the child was sent, at the age of four, to boarding school. Marie's affair with Liszt grew more and more intense.

The final decision to leave home and husband and break completely with her past life came in June of 1835. Liszt wrote her: "The day that you can tell me with all your mind and all your heart and all your soul, 'Franz, let us erase and forgive for always all that which was incomplete, distressing and even perhaps miserable in the past; let us belong completely one to the other for now I understand you and forgive you as much as I love you.' That day (and let it be soon) we will fly far from the world, we will live, we will love and we will die alone." [7]

There was another reason which may have influenced their flight together. Marie d'Agoult was already carrying Liszt's child.

For two months the young pair traveled in Switzerland. Alone, cut off from the world in simple Alpine villages, it was an idyl of discovery, of work, and of love. In the autumn they moved to Geneva and took an apartment on the rue Tabazan. It was a modest apartment compared to the grandeur of Marie's former Paris or Croissy establishments, but it suited her. The days were devoted to study and reading and endless conversations. Liszt composed, and Marie watched every movement of his pen, of his mobile expressive face.

At first they saw no one and Marie was happy in the complete exclusiveness of their life where they worked and lived only for each other. But the world could not be kept out forever, especially from the life of the young artist whose mature career was only beginning.

Even rigid, Calvinist Geneva was excited by the presence of the famous pianist in their midst and in spite of the scandal of his relationship with Marie d'Agoult, sought him out.

Marie felt keenly the different positions of the man and the woman in a relationship such as theirs where the burden of blame and of ostracism was placed on the woman. Liszt was invited and welcomed. Liszt had an adoring class at the Conservatory. Liszt had pupils who followed him from Paris. Liszt triumphed in public concert. She felt that he was strangely insensitive to her position, and when he asked that she attend his first concert, it was an ordeal for her. The crowds, the bright lights, the gossip, the public display confused her after the months of solitude. And when she saw Liszt at the piano, he seemed almost like a stranger to her.

The idyl was broken. The world, "that vulgar world," as Marie wrote, "from which we had fled and which we had forgotten, forced us to become involved with it and brought us down to its level." [8]

Gradually a small group of intimates began coming to the apartment on the rue Tabazan. The young woman enjoyed the long discussions on history and politics with Simonde de Sismondi, the serious pronouncements of Adolphe Pictet, the fascinating discoveries of the orientalist Alphonse Denis. During the day she wrote, articles of all sorts, and she worked with Liszt on a series of stinging essays for the *Gazette Musicale* of Paris on the position of the artist. And she waited for the birth of their child.

Blandine was born on December 18, 1835. On her birth certificate her parents were listed as Franz Liszt, professor of music, and Catherine-Adéläide Méran, a lady of property. The ages of both parents were given as twenty-four, a gallant gesture on Liszt's part toward his thirty-year-old mistress.

Spring brought their first real separation. Marie d'Agoult's income scarcely sufficed for a woman accustomed to the opulence of her former life. Liszt had his mother to support. And besides there was now Blandine.

In April, Liszt left for Lyon where he gave a series of concerts with great success and, fortunately, some financial reward too. But while in Lyon he felt an irresistible desire to go on to Paris. Since he had left there, a new pianist, Sigismond Thalberg, had appeared on the scene, and it was rumored that the fickle French public had forgotten Franz Liszt. Marie, understandably, did not want him to go, and he assured her that he would not, at least not without her full consent. His letters to her were filled with tenderness and love, but it was clear that this blazing talent could not be satisfied, as she had dreamed, by an idyllic life of isolation. In the end, he did go to Paris, and it must have been hard for Marie to remain alone in staid Geneva while Liszt walked the boulevards of the French capital, caught up in all the fascinating, active, busy life of that great city, surrounded by friends and admirers, feasting on a whole world of interest and excitement. He heard Meyerbeer's ever-popular opera, *Robert le Diable,* and the new production of *Les Huguenots.* He gave a splendid dinner for his friends at the Café de Paris. At Les Frères Provinciaux he entertained Delacroix, Boulanger, Meyerbeer, Barrault, Théophile, Ballanche, and a whole company of young artists and intellectuals. His constant companion day and night until the early hours of the morning was Chopin. Even his continual protestations to Marie that all this was boring and monotonous and that all he longed for was to be with her again could not obscure the excitement and interest he was feeling.

And Marie? She closed her doors even to their intimates and waited for his letters. Thalberg had left Paris before Liszt arrived, so the gauntlet that Liszt had been ready to throw down had to be held for another time. Nevertheless it was the end of July before Liszt returned to Geneva and to Marie.

A few months later Liszt went back to Paris, but this time Marie accompanied him. She did not stay there long, however. George Sand, with whom they had spent a delightfully gay vacation at Chamonix, invited Marie to her country estate at Nohant. It must have been quite a contrast for Marie after the arid life of Geneva to enter into the full, active, Bohemian, untidy, exciting life of the free-thinking and free-living George Sand, this tiny woman who smoked cigars incessantly, worked at her novels until nearly dawn every night, and loved a house filled to overflowing with people and talk.

Liszt stayed on in Paris, for this time his rival, Thalberg, was there, and it was time that the gauntlet be flung down. Thalberg played first, to a small, select audience at the Conservatoire. Liszt countered by playing at the opera house. The musical duel was the talk of Paris with everyone taking sides and arguing the merits of the two pianists. The Princess Belgiojoso was determined to settle the arguments once and for all. She invited both Liszt and Thalberg to play at one of her soirées, and after that there was no question at all. The laurels went to Liszt, hands down, and a *bon mot* went the round of the Paris salons: "Thalberg is the first pianist of Europe. Liszt is the only one."

After his triumph Liszt joined Marie at Nohant where George Sand's irrepressible and gay nature made for a very lively time. It was all rather alien to Marie, whom we can suspect of having not much sense of humor, and for a time she was jealous of George Sand's relationship with Liszt. And indeed, there is good evidence that he enjoyed a flirtation that was perhaps more than casual with this gifted young woman. By the end of the visit, however, Marie felt a growing confidence in herself and tried to laugh at her former fears that George might be the right woman for Liszt.

It was of Italy that Marie d'Agoult dreamed, and it was to Italy that the lovers went next, stopping on the way to see Blandine, who had been left with a nurse in Switzerland all this time. Marie found her little daughter enchanting, a serious and intelligent child with the promise of great beauty.

Italy was everything of which Marie had dreamed. She found that the customs were freer than in France, and certainly than in Geneva, and her liaison with Liszt did not exclude her from social life to the extent that it had in other places. Liszt too felt a happiness and freedom in Italy. Lake Como remained for him the happy place of two lovers.

They stayed at Bellagio, which nestles along the shore of the lake. Daily they walked together in the beautiful gardens of the Villa Melzi. Here Marie would read aloud to him in the little pavilion with the waves lapping gently below and the distant mountains across the lake veiled in soft light. Marie was overjoyed that Liszt was gay and cheerful in this intensive life *à deux,* in spite of what she recognized as the strong pull of his artistic nature, a nature which needed activity and engagement. For a while again she felt he was wholly hers, and was free from the inner conflicts which tormented her when she had to share him with the world, or indeed with anyone. But the idyl could not last forever. Marie was expecting another child, and they moved to the city of Como to wait its arrival.

An official search of the Parish records of the Cathedral of Como disclosed that "on the day 26 December, 1837 was baptized by the Priest Pietro Cavadini the baby Francesca Gaetana Cosima, born 24 December, 1837 at the Hotel dell' Angelo in Como, of Caterina de Flavigny, of Noble birth, and Francesco Liszt, Professor of Music, who, in the presence of two witnesses, has identified the child as his own daughter, the two not being married." [9] In spite of her imposing array of names in honor of her father, of Italy, and of St. Cosmas, the child was always to be known only as Cosima.

For several months after Cosima's birth, Liszt traveled back and forth between Como, where Marie stayed, and Milan, where he was establishing himself in the artistic life of the city, winning his audiences with programs that did not please him, a bag of tricks he called them, but that at least relieved the financial pressures. Marie was desolate again at the need to share him, and he did what he could to encourage her. "Love me always," he begged her, "and most of all try to be a little satisfied, a little gay, a little happy if it is possible." [10]

In March he took her to Venice, that romantic city that has stirred the hearts of so many. But Marie did not like Venice. She was bored and irritable there. The bookstores, she felt, had books worthy only of chambermaids. She claimed it was a modern Carthage, a false and materialistic city. And as always, her moods of uncontrollable depression worried her. She compared herself to Liszt and blamed herself for the sorrow and discouragement she brought to his life. He was patient with her, encouraging her, pouring out his love to her in a moving and sincere way. Only on rare occasions did he allow a note of irony and irritation to appear toward her for her unceasing doubts of his affection.

It was while they were in Venice that Liszt read the news of terrible floods in Hungary. It was a major disaster and the flood victims were in frightful distress. Scenes of Hungary, of his little village of Raiding, of his homeland that he had not seen for so many years flashed through his mind. Help was asked for the homeless, subscriptions for aid were taken up everywhere. Liszt's mind was made up in a minute. He must do what he could, and what he could do was to play as many concerts as possible for the benefit of the victims. And where else should he do this but in Vienna, the city of his earliest triumphs. Within days he set off. Marie stayed in Venice, alone again.

Vienna was a turning point in many ways. Liszt had long felt frustrated as a musician. He was tired to death of trotting out his bag of tricks, of playing superficial and unworthy music, of catering to uninformed and light-minded audiences. "Will my life be forever tainted with this idle uselessness which weighs upon me?" he wrote to Lamennais. "Will the hour of devotion and manly action never come? Am I condemned without respite to this trade of a Merry Andrew and to amuse in drawing rooms?" [11]

Certainly there was much of the showman in Liszt, but there was another side too, that of the dedicated, high-minded disciple of his art. Vienna was the city of Beethoven, whose music he placed above all others. It was the city of Mozart, of Schubert. It was the city of music.

Liszt's triumphs in Vienna are hard to imagine. Not even the popular singers of today arouse a greater frenzy than did this brilliant, handsome young pianist. Even Liszt, accustomed as he had always been to adulation and, without question, enjoying and capitalizing on it, was amazed at the effect he produced. Here at last he was able to play the music he respected and loved —Weber, Berlioz, Schumann, Chopin, Mendelssohn, but always, first and foremost, Beethoven. He brought the works of Scarlatti out of obscurity and electrified his audiences with them. All the musicians were there: his old teacher Czerny, who must have been touched when his former pupil played one of his sonatas; Clara Wieck, the young pianist who was to become the wife of Robert Schumann; even his old rival Thalberg.

The aristocracy was there too, in full force, and Liszt found himself the center of endless lavish entertainments in princely houses.

Liszt's letters to Marie, however, in spite of the excitement and enthusiasms that they contained about his Vienna successes, were filled with longing for her. He urged her to join him. "My God," he wrote, "how happy I would be to see you . . . I love you, yes, I love you with all my force. I belong only to you. You alone have the right over my whole being, for you alone have the secret of my life, of my joys and of my sorrows." [12]

Vienna for Marie too was a turning point. Years later, in her *Mémoirs,* she could not help writing with incredible bitterness of that time. She described herself, alone and abandoned in Venice, with only their new friend, the young Count Theodoro, as her companion. All they talked of was Liszt, and they counted the days till his return. But Liszt's letters were short, and they contained the names of several women. One day, returning from the Lido with the Count, she felt overtired; the next day there was fever. Count Theodoro wrote immediately to Liszt in Vienna, as he felt that Marie's illness was caused by worry and that Liszt's arrival would cure her. They calculated how many days before the letter arrived in Vienna—how many days for Liszt to reach Venice, for they were sure that he would leave immediately on receipt of the news that she was ill. Instead, a letter from Liszt arrived for Theodoro, thanking him for all he was doing, apologizing that he could not leave Vienna at once, and suggesting that Theodoro bring Marie to Vienna instead. Theodoro was mortally pale when he brought her the letter, and at that moment Marie fainted. When she finally revived, Theodoro flung himself at her feet in a passionate declaration of love. "Where is Franz?" is all she said.

According to her description, during the next eight days she hovered between life and death. Finally she revived enough to write an emotional letter to Liszt full of reproaches. "Franz, Franz, is it really you who has abandoned me like this?" By the time that Liszt arrived, the May sun and the brotherly attentions and tender solicitude of Count Theodoro had restored her strength. She found Liszt very changed. He had abandoned her not for a great work or patriotism or devotion but for trifling successes in the salons of princesses and to be the hero of cheap publicity. She could not forgive what she termed his abandonment and neglect of her. His conversations about his Vienna successes, into which the names of several women entered, outraged her. In her anger and hurt and jealousy, Marie was replaced by the Countess d'Agoult. "I took on," she wrote, "all my pride of a woman, of a great lady, of a republican, to judge him from above." And then she hurled unforgivable words at him, calling him "a parvenu Don Juan." [13]

It was typical of their relationship that she gave him this whole story in her journal to read. He added these lines below it: "You remember my words but perhaps those which you said to me in these various circumstances have left no trace in your memory. For my part, I have not forgotten them, no matter how much effort I have made to do so. When you are able to remember them, they will explain many things to you which seem inexplicable." [14]

From the earliest months of her relationship with Liszt, Marie d'Agoult had been jealous and possessive and as time went on she was able to control herself less and less. She could not hold to her resolve to stop her reproaches and yet she knew the harm her endless scenes were doing. Liszt grew increasingly caustic and dry, and his reserve produced only more reproaches from her. Yet the bond between them was still very strong, and underneath all the quarrels and griefs there was a deep feeling of real tenderness.

Marie d'Agoult suggested that it might be better if they separated. Five years was perhaps long enough, and she knew that he felt hemmed in. "If I did not love you so religiously and did not place you so high, I could not speak this way, but I have a profound respect for your liberty," she wrote him.[15]

Did she really mean it or was it simply another way in which she tried to bind him more closely to herself? Something of both, perhaps, but his answers to all such suggestions that they should part or that he would be happier with someone else were still what she wanted to hear.

"Oh, never tell me that I should have had another than you!" Liszt replied. "Do not tear out all the flower and root of my heart." [16]

And so, for another year they stayed on in Italy, going again to Como, which had held such magic, traveling about to Florence, Milan, Lugano, Genoa, trying to recapture the spell of the past. They were together most of the time with Liszt absent only rarely for concerts in Italy. Marie was expecting their third child, Daniel, who was born in Rome on May 9, 1839.

The two little girls, as was the custom among aristocratic families of that time, had been placed with nurses soon after their birth, Blandine in Switzerland and Cosima in Italy. But now Blandine was three years old and it was time that she rejoin her parents.

Liszt was delighted with his little daughter and amused her and himself by playing to her Schumann's *Kinderscenen.* "As to the *Kinderscenen,*" he wrote the composer, "I owe to them one of the greatest pleasures of my life. You know, or you don't know, that I have a little girl of three years old, whom everybody agrees in considering *angelic* (did you ever hear such a commonplace?) Her name is Blandine-Rachel, and her surname *Moucheron.* It goes without saying that she has a complexion of roses and milk, and that her fair golden hair reaches to her feet just like a savage. She is, however, the most silent child, the most sweetly grave, the most philosophically gay in the world. I have every reason to hope also that she will not be a musician, from which may Heaven preserve her.

"Well, my dear Monsieur Schumann, two or three times a week (on fine and good days!) I play your *Kinderscenen* to her in the evening; this enchants her, and me still more, as you may imagine, so that often I go over the first repeat twenty times without getting any further. Really I think you would be satisfied with this success if you could be a witness of it!" [17]

Marie started the first lessons with the tiny girl, as she had done with her two older daughters, Louise and Claire, at the same age.

In spite of Liszt's pleasure in his daughter, Marie found him depressed at this period. Not only did he chafe under her emotional demands, but the thought of being the father of three children affected him strongly. He knew that he must provide for them, for their education, for their future. The financial burden was a heavy one, and Liszt decided to make arrangements for an extensive tour for the winter of 1839, one that would take him through most of Europe and, hopefully, earn him enough money to support his family. It was impossible even to think that Marie could accompany him.

Was she to remain once more alone in a foreign land? She

could not face it. She could not bear to read of her lover's brilliant concerts, his travels, his successes, the women who surrounded him, and to be not only far away from him but isolated from anything that was her own too. She began often to sense more pity and irritation than love in Liszt's attitude toward her and if there was one thing that the Countess d'Agoult found unendurable it was pity. Anger, yes. Jealousy, even delightful. But to be an object of compassion was intolerable. In spite of all the histrionics she indulged in to touch his heart, to feel that she might be treated as a pathetic woman by her lover, as someone to whom he was obligated because of the sacrifices she had made for him, was a position she was determined to avoid.

It was a hard decision to make and in a way a humiliating one for the proud woman who had cut herself off from everyone and everything more than four years before to follow her dream. The decision was that Marie d'Agoult return to Paris and that she try to re-establish herself there with her mother, her brother, and her friends; that she reconquer the world of the Paris salons.

Marie d'Agoult had thought sometimes of suicide, but in an unreal, romantic fashion. Her nature was far too proud, her intellect far too analytical for that. It was not in self-destruction that Marie d'Agoult sought her salvation, but in a carefully planned, well-thought-out self-realization. It was in the autumn of 1839 that Marie returned to Paris to start the long climb into the sun again, but this time it was to be on her own terms and in her own way.

The final break with Liszt did not occur for another five years but the seeds of the rupture had been sown and they grew, hidden sometimes for long periods, but inexorably.

They were both aware of it and it is a witness to the reality and depth of their love that they fought against it for so much longer. The day after their parting in Italy, Liszt wrote to her: "Adieu and adieu again. Do not ask me to speak to you today of anyone or anything, I know and feel only one thing, that you were here and are here no longer. So adieu, and let me always be yours and only yours." [18]

Marie, too, expressed her feelings. "How can I leave this dear land of Italy without sending you a final adieu? How could I see these two years, so beautiful and so full, leave my life without regretting them. Oh! my dear Franz! Let me tell you once again from the depths of my soul that you created a profound feeling, an unalterable one . . . a feeling of gratitude without limit. A thousand blessings on you!" [19]

Liszt spent most of the next six months in Vienna and Budapest where he aroused, if possible, an even more frenetic adulation than on his previous visit. There were the usual rounds of concerts, luncheons, suppers, parties of all kinds with the highest members of the aristocracy and all of important Vienna in attendance. Marie could not help feeling that the misfortune of being only his mistress and not his wife was more than ever apparent to her now, when she thought that she had to stay far from him during these splendid days.

Liszt was the first to give an entire evening's program alone. Until he dared it, concerts were usually made up of a potpourri, quite often enormously long, with several artists appearing on the same program, interspersed with interludes of orchestral or chamber music. Liszt was determined to give programs that had unity and quality throughout. He felt strongly the right of the artist to impose music that was beautiful and of the highest quality on his audiences. The public adored it, and him, and flocked to hear him play whatever and however he wanted. *"Le concert—c'est moi,"* he said, paraphrasing Louis XIV.[20]

Liszt's position was impregnable now as the most brilliant virtuoso of Europe. When he learned that the subscription for a monument to Beethoven to be erected in Bonn had been miserably unsuccessful, he did not hesitate a moment to offer to make up out of his own pocket the entire sum and he asked in return only that he be allowed to name the sculptor. He had been sincerely shocked at the lack of public response to the planned monument and looked upon it as a disgrace and a dishonor to Beethoven's memory. His generous gesture earned him even greater popularity. Through all this, however, he remained in close contact with Marie, and his letters to her were full of warmth and tenderness.

Before returning to Paris, Marie had gone to Genoa where she took Cosima from the nurse who had been keeping her, and the two little sisters saw each other for the first time. "I am in possession of Mlle Cosima," she wrote Liszt, "for which I had to come to Genoa. Mlle Cosima resembles the adorable Mouche feature by feature, except that she is a great deal less beautiful and especially less distinguished. Her training is the same. Her nurse says that one must give her everything she asks for at once or else she will die. I will try to teach her to live differently." [21]

Liszt was enchanted at the thought of the two little girls. He wanted to know all about them. How did they get along together? How did Blandine react to her younger sister? Did she still speak of him? Which of the two was the more affectionate? He hoped that Marie would dress them alike. And how he longed to take them in his arms and kiss them!

When Marie finally arrived in Paris with the two girls she found that her brother was very favorably disposed toward her and ready to help her to re-establish her position. Maurice de Flavigny told his sister that the most important factor for a reconciliation with her mother was that her children by Liszt should not live with her. Liszt was in complete agreement with this and urged her not to delay or hesitate to send them to live with his mother. He wanted to do everything he could to undo the harm he felt he had done her and to help her regain her position in society and the world.

Marie did not seem at all reluctant to follow the urgings of her brother and of Liszt. Daniel was still safely in Italy with a nurse. Cosima and Blandine were taken to the home of Anna Liszt in Paris, where that good woman received them with open arms. It was here with their grandmother that they found a home and a tender, indulgent love without which their childhood would have been far more difficult than it was.

Marie d'Agoult set about rebuilding her position in Paris. Her days were busy, and her letters to Liszt were full of the concerts, the operas, the scandals, and gossip of Paris. In revenge for the stories that came to her of his entanglements with various women, she spared no detail about the men who were paying court to her. One of the most serious was Henry Bulwer-Lytton, brother of the author, and she obviously enjoyed discussing with Liszt whether she should have an affair with him. These were very different days from the ones she had spent so bitterly alone in Venice. She was in her element—busy, admired, and flattered. The little girls were prospering, she wrote Liszt, but she saw them rarely.

Nevertheless, in spite of the separation, in spite of their different activities and entanglements, in spite of the discords of the past, the bond between them was not yet broken. Marie could still write of the power that Liszt had over her, so that all her joy and all her sorrow came only through him. Liszt declared that he would finish by living entirely for her and for music.

Liszt advised and encouraged her in all her efforts to rebuild her life. He was delighted at her growing success as a writer. It was Émile de Girardin who published her articles first under the name of *Un Inconnu* and later under the pseudonym she was to use for the rest of her life—Daniel Stern. She claimed that she was strongly attracted to Girardin, whom she saw every day, describing him and their meetings in great detail to Liszt, who found in all this still another reproach for his own defects.

During the first three summers after they left Italy, they spent several weeks together on a lovely little island of the Rhine, Nonnenwerth. There were still moments of joy and of hope. But there were jealous scenes too, and Liszt grew increasingly bitter over her reproaches.

"You have often accused me of being tyrannical in my affections. Would it not be that you have never believed in the tyranny that you exercise over me? The need to dominate, even tyrannize, is it not the most inherent aspect of your nature? I believe it is." [22]

For ten months of the year Liszt traveled, giving concerts in England and Ireland, France, Germany, Belgium, even as far as Russia. The financial burden of his three children, his mother, and Marie oppressed him, in spite of the fact that Marie's mother was now letting her have a considerably larger share of her inheritance. Liszt sometimes traveled like a prince, with a whole retinue and special carriages, with great fanfare and color. Yet he was often exhausted, having to play after hours of uncomfortable journeying and then leave wearily the next morning for another town.

The stories of his conquests grew, and his conquests were not only musical ones. Wherever he went women flung themselves at him and he no longer felt any guilt about his numerous affairs. Marie was deeply hurt and as time went on became more and more outraged by the stories of his amours, especially with the notorious Lola Montez. To be his mistress was one thing. To be one of his mistresses became intolerable. In the spring of 1844 when Liszt returned to Paris, Marie d'Agoult told him that all was over between them.

In spite of everything, Liszt had not anticipated the break, and though Marie's endless preachments were supremely irritating to him, he still had for her a deep feeling.

"I am very sad and profoundly grieved," he wrote her when she told him of her intentions to break finally with him. "I count one by one the sorrows that I have given your heart and nothing and no one can ever save me from myself. I do not want to talk to you, nor to see you, even less to write you. Did you not say that I was a comedian? Yes, in the manner of those who would play the dying athlete after he has drunk the hemlock. No matter. Silence must seal all the torments of my heart." [23]

Marie took the step in the "profoundest sorrow." Years later in her *Mémoirs* she gave her reason for it this way: "Had he been what he should have been, I would have stayed." [24]

CHAPTER III

"WHOM ALONE DO I THANK for life's delights? Who approached me so lovingly with tender glances? I feel it and will never forget it. For you are all my happiness," [1] Cosima wrote to her grandmother in a verse celebrating her name day.

Anna Liszt was a plump, plain, comfortable-looking woman who loved all three of her grandchildren without favoritism. Cosima could not have helped sensing, in the way that even the smallest children do, that Blandine was very much her mother's favorite. Marie d'Agoult thought Blandine beautiful, intelligent, responsive, and full of charm. She found her infinitely superior to Cosima in every way and did not hesitate to express her partiality for this child. "I feel that I will love this child," she wrote of her, "with an excessive passion for already I would like not to love the others in order to love only her." [2] The summer before her rupture with Liszt she had even taken Blandine with her to Nonnenwerth for the vacation weeks with Liszt. Cosima was not included.[3] As for Daniel, Marie's only wish was to think of him as little as possible.

Although the children lived at their grandmother's home surrounded by her warm and protective affection, the high points in their little lives were visits with their father and mother. Accustomed as they were to long separations, at first they felt few effects of the final rupture between Liszt and Marie d'Agoult. It was not long, however, before they became pawns in the growing bitterness between their parents.

Liszt left Paris almost immediately after the break and at first he was willing to leave the decisions in regard to the education of Blandine and Cosima in the hands of their mother, while continuing to carry the full financial burden of their care himself. Nine-year-old Blandine was to be sent to the boarding school of Madame Bernard, and Liszt asked that Cosima and Daniel be left with his mother. But this facile solution was not to last long.

Liszt became more and more angry, not only at the continuing reproaches and attacks concerning his past and present way of life with which Marie bombarded him, but at the way she did not hesitate to talk of him in the most disparaging terms to others. Did she really believe, he asked, that he would allow Blandine to live with her when she maintained such a violently hostile attitude toward him? His proud and fiery nature was touched to the quick, and he determined to remove his children from her influence at any cost, even if he had to move them to Germany. He took steps to legitimize them and bring them under his exclusive control.

Anna Liszt and Marie d'Agoult had never liked or understood each other, and there had been a good deal of conflict between them over the years. Marie found Liszt's mother undistingushed, a cardinal sin in her book, and the warm-hearted grandmother could hardly be expected to understand a mother who left the care of her children to others. So Anna Liszt was a strong ally to her son in his fight to remove the children completely from their mother's influence.

Marie d'Agoult has often been called an unnatural mother who accepted and even welcomed the estrangement from her children without a moment's regret, a woman so occupied with herself and her career that she felt only relief at shedding any burden or responsibility for them.

Marie herself claimed, however, that she had fought for her children "like a lioness" and when she could fight no more she wrote Liszt: "I recognize that I am vanquished, Monsieur, in a hopeless battle where I could invoke only your heart, your mind and your conscience. But I protest before God and man, and before all mothers against the violence which has been done to me . . . One day, perhaps, your daughters will say to you: Where is our mother? You will answer: It did not please me that you have one." [4]

Liszt would have answered that these were mere words, a flowery, empty expression without any real emotional or practical truth in them. In spite of his notorious love affairs, in spite of their quarrels, he still believed that he had given Marie a serious and passionate devotion which she willfully and wrongfully had severed because of her lack of understanding of him. Obviously, too, there was an element of vindictiveness in his actions, a retaliation for her attacks against him.

Marie accepted the separation from her children with considerable philosophy. Certainly the maternal instinct was not very strong in her, especially toward very young children. Once the die was cast and she was no longer allowed to have anything to do with them, she accepted the fact gracefully and did not continue in any efforts to see them. Yet it is hard to believe that she did this as casually as has sometimes been stated. Her letter of renunciation may have been flowery, but such words could not have been written without some emotional validity behind them. On the other hand, two years later, Liszt wrote her on the occasion of Blandine's first communion and suggested that perhaps she would attend it. She did not.

If Marie took the separation from her children without much unhappiness, the same can hardly be said for Cosima and Blandine. Daniel, who had now joined his sisters in Paris, scarcely knew his mother at all, but the two girls felt a growing bewilderment and sadness at her prolonged absence. In their letters to their father they told him that they remembered their mother every day in their prayers and were very sad at never seeing her nor even knowing where she was. If Liszt would send them her address they wanted so much to write her, for they missed her terribly. It was not long, however, before any mention of their mother vanished from their letters. It was not that they had forgotten her or resigned themselves to her absence. It was because Liszt forbade them to speak of her to him. Neither did Liszt come to see his children. He was determined to avoid Paris and any chance of an encounter with Marie d'Agoult.

The three children had a very close and tender relationship with each other, an extraordinary bond that Cosima described in later years as having been forged by the difficult and unusual circumstances of their childhood. Cosima, especially, adored her little brother, a handsome boy who bore a startling resemblance to his father, with deep-set eyes under straight, strong brows. He had a loving and affectionate nature, open and responsive, and he was full of mischief too. From the start Cosima felt protective toward him and took the greatest delight in him. Of them all, Blandine resembled her mother most and already gave promise of great beauty. She was extremely feminine, very emotional but with a fine mind. Cosima was a delicate child and for many years her health was a subject of great concern. She was almost excessively thin and grew rapidly. Her thick blond hair framed a slender face, strong-featured, with the prominent nose and generous mouth she had inherited from her father. Already as a child the fire and force of her character were apparent.

When Blandine was sent to Madame Bernard's boarding school in Paris, Cosima was desolate. She begged to be allowed to join her sister. Anna Liszt was reluctant to let her go, partly because of her delicate health but also because she was not yet quite eight years old. The tender grandmother had hoped to keep Cosima with her for at least another year so that she could supervise her health and feed her the strong beef tea and other nourishing foods with which she tempted the girl's finicky appetite. Cosima, however, had made up her mind and when she saw that pleas and entreaties did not work, she made such a scene, stamping and screaming, that her grandmother finally gave in. Poor Daniel felt abandoned with both of his sisters gone, and he suggested that he be allowed to go too. Was it a school only for girls? Well, could not Grandmama dress him in one of Cosima's dresses and a hat and then he could join his sisters? Instead a tutor was found for Daniel and now all three children embarked on their formal education.

Their schooling in no way interrupted their close relationship with their grandmother, whom they visited each week, and of course she was always going to see them. Cosima and Blandine liked the school very much and grew to love Mlle Laure, the sister of the directress, as though she were a second mother to them. But in spite of the love and attention of their grandmother and Mlle Laure, as well as their devotion to each other, they missed their father bitterly and longed to see him. From time to time his letters indicated that he might come to Paris, and then their spirits would soar. Even a letter from him was a joy to them and brought tears to their eyes, and the prospect of actually seeing him again seemed the happiest and most exciting thing in the world. But he did not come, and the months passed with only occasional letters.

They wrote him about their courses, quite serious and advanced: ancient history, mythology, style, botany, cosmography, the *Iliad* and the *Odyssey* were among the subjects they were studying. Both girls, but especially Cosima, were intensely interested in music and made fine progress with the piano. Cosima was determined, as the daughter of Liszt, to be as worthy of him as she could, and when she was given Weber's *Invitation to the Waltz* to learn, a piece she found difficult, she declared that she would take the greatest pains to play it without a mistake. Soon she was playing Mozart sonatas and loving them. But in spite of all her activities, nothing could make up for the emptiness in her heart caused by her father's long absence.

Nearly three years had passed since she had seen him. All the combined pleas of the three children had been to no avail. And then suddenly for several months they did not receive even any letters from him. Liszt's activities were well reported in the French newspapers and the *Gazette Musicale,* so they knew that he was on an extended tour in Russia. But he had been to Russia before and had still written them. Had something happened to make him silent for so long? Something had happened, something that was to affect their lives and their relationship with their father deeply.

It was February 1847 when Liszt arrived at the city of Kiev, on the banks of the river Dnieper. He at once organized a concert for the local charities, as was his custom. His program that evening was one he had played often before: Chopin, Weber, Schubert, and some of his own pieces. There was the usual wild success, the applause, the after-concert party—things that he had experienced a thousand times before. There was nothing to indicate that this was the turning point in his life, that after tonight nothing would ever be the same again.

A young woman attended the concert, and she was to preserve the program for the rest of her life. The next morning she sent Liszt a hundred-ruble note as a donation to the charities and he promptly called on her to thank her for it.

She was the Princess Carolyne Sayn-Wittgenstein, a brilliant, passionate, dark-eyed young Polish woman of twenty-nine, the daughter of a wealthy landowner, Peter Ivanovsky, from whom she had inherited vast estates. As a girl she had been wild and intractable, with the full arrogance of the daughter of a man who owned thirty thousand serfs. But she had an eager and searching mind, too, and threw herself into her studies with the same violence and totality that she brought to everything she did, so that she soon earned for herself nicknames such as Miss Cato and Miss Scipio. At the age of seventeen she had been married to Prince Nicholas Sayn-Wittgenstein, a member of the Russian branch of that distinguished family. The marriage was not a success, and she separated from her husband soon after the birth of her daughter, Marie, born in 1837, the same year as Cosima. She retired to her large estate at Woronince, on the Podolian steppe, between Kiev and Odessa, and there she devoted herself to intense study and the education of her little girl.

The Princess Sayn-Wittgenstein was not a beautiful woman, as Marie d'Agoult was, nor did she have the highly developed feminine art of the French Countess. She was small and dark with great flashing eyes, and like George Sand, she smoked endless cigars. She had an immense will and determination and a self-confidence and habit of command that was bred in her as the spoiled daughter of a powerful, autocratic father.

It was love at first sight between Liszt and the Princess, or perhaps it was an immediate, unconscious recognition of a psychological need that each would find fulfilled with the other—she to dominate, guide, and direct an artist of rare talent, and he to be saved from himself. Three years earlier he had written

Marie that no one could do that, but here on the lonely Russian steppe he found a woman whose will and strength were such that he gave himself up to her completely.

Within a few days of their first meeting Liszt accompanied the Princess to her estate in Woronince, where they spent intense weeks discovering each other. The Princess talked endlessly of all she had learned and read and thought during the years of her isolation—the philosophy of Hegel, which so attracted her, Dante and Goethe, the musical ideas of Berlioz and Wagner. Years later Cosima wrote that Liszt and the Princess had found common ground in the breadth of their outlook, their generosity, their detestation of small and narrow ideas and, above all, in their strong religious beliefs. The Princess was a challenging, demanding companion and absorbed all of Listz's attention and interest with a totality he had never experienced with anyone else. Liszt felt that here at last he had found a woman beside whom all others seemed pale and insignificant. Small wonder that under this potent spell he forgot for a time his mother and his children in Paris. A whole new life began for him, and he wanted to break completely with the past and everything it contained. He told the Princess that nothing he had done during his life until he met her was worth even five minutes of her attention. From almost the first moment of their meeting it was clear to both of them that their lives would be joined from then on, unconditionally and unreservedly.

Liszt had long since begun to tire of his endless concert tours. He had built up sufficient capital to assure the future of his mother and his children, and the idea of settling down permanently somewhere became more and more appealing, especially as there was no question that the Princess would go with him wherever he went. The logical place seemed to be Weimar where, since 1844, he had spent three months of every year as conductor. The prospect of Weimar, the city of Goethe, of Schiller, where there was a brilliant court and an atmosphere in which Liszt felt he could live and work freely, filled their minds with all sorts of wonderful plans to create there a great musical center. Liszt was eager to devote himself to serious composition and he found in the Princess the most ardent champion of this plan. Although she was a devout Roman Catholic, she was confident that she could win an annulment of her marriage on the grounds that she had been forced into it against her will at a very early age. And then she and Liszt would marry.

Liszt went ahead to Weimar and the Princess soon followed him, with her daughter Marie. It was 1848, and revolution was on the march again. The Princess barely managed to cross the frontier of Russia before it was sealed off. Liszt took her to the Altenburg, an opulent house that he had found for her in Weimar, and after a brief period of living separately at a hotel, he abandoned all pretense and moved into the Altenburg where he occupied two rooms in one of the wings.

Anna Liszt was hardly enchanted with this new liaison and when she learned of it she understood the weeks of silence which had so disturbed her and the children. The Princess at once made her position clear, addressing her as "Mother" and writing regularly to her. Anna Liszt was polite but she complained to her son that though she often had news of him through the Princess, she would prefer to hear directly from him occasionally. Realizing the force of the Princess' character and her enormous influence over Liszt, she wanted to make sure that the three children would not be forgotten or neglected. She wrote often to the Princess about them, stressing their devotion to their father and telling of their achievements. "You see, noble Princess," she wrote meaningfully, "that I am not afraid of boring you with my chatter about the children, because I have entire trust in your tender heart and am confident that it cannot be unpleasant to you to hear about all that concerns me or my son." [5]

In the meantime, the girls' education was progressing by leaps and bounds. They studied German and English and the literature of both countries and read prodigiously. They had a dancing master, too, no less a person than the brother of Johann Strauss. Cosima was making great strides with her piano and was already being introduced to the music of Beethoven, the composer she knew her father revered. She was deeply pious and had been profoundly moved by her first communion. It was a day of such importance to her that she longed to share it with all those whom she loved, her father above all. "I am very anxious for you to be present," she had written him, "and in the interval I shall expect you impatiently." But in her heart she must have known that her hope would not be realized, for she added, "but we have been disappointed in our expectations for so long past." [6]

Liszt, of course, did not come. He was still in Woronince at the time, lost in the wonders and delights of his new love. Grandmother Anna was present, however, and Daniel and Blandine and Mlle Laure, the young teacher whom Cosima loved and who had prepared her for the great event, but it did not compensate in Cosima's heart for the absence of both father and mother.

In spite of the new arrangements of Liszt's life with the Princess and her daughter at the Altenburg in Weimar, Cosima and Blandine never ceased hoping that he would find time to visit them. Every letter to him spoke of their longing to see him and they counted the years that had passed without him with infinite regret. His letters caused them joy and pain. They wept at his tender words and at the endless waiting for his visit.

Liszt's letters, however, were not always entirely tender. He supervised their education strictly, criticized their writing and way of expressing themselves, and exhorted them to be always obedient, modest, and worthy of bearing his name. Cosima's one thought was to please him in every way she could.

One day, however, when Cosima was thirteen and Blandine fifteen, they showed an independence and daring which is hard to imagine in view of the restricted life they led. It was by chance that they overheard someone speaking of their mother and learned her address. The next day, when they were out walking, the idea of going to see her suddenly came to them. Without telling a soul, they found their way. Marie d'Agoult was at home, and for the first time in nearly six years mother and daughters were reunited. They dared stay only a little while but it was a visit surcharged with emotion. Marie was overjoyed to see them and to find that they still loved her with all their hearts. They did not dare tell even their grandmother what they had done, and it was only after several weeks, when their grandmother was visiting the Altenburg in Weimar, that they finally wrote their father and confessed their escapade. They admitted that they had had further visits with their mother, and Daniel had too. They described in the most touching terms the great joy it was for them to see her again after the pain of such a long separation and how much it meant to them in every way. They assured him of their loyalty and love for him and declared that their happiness would be complete only when they could give their caresses to both their father and their mother.

Liszt exploded. His answer was harsh and uncompromising. He accused them of ingratitude, and wrote that it was he who alone had cared and looked out for them and that they had betrayed him. He told them that his motives in not letting them see their mother were real and serious and that they owed him a respectful and total obedience. He ordered them to stop at once any visits, correspondence, or relationship with their mother. "As precious as your affection for me is," he wrote in closing, "I tell you in all sincerity that I value it only in so far as you are truly daughters after my own heart, whose upright will, sound judgment, cultivated talents, noble and firm characters are such as to bring honor to my name and some consolation for my old age." [7]

Cosima and Blandine were desolate, not only at being once more deprived of any contact with their mother, but at having incurred their father's wrath. They begged to be forgiven and announced themselves ready to submit entirely to his dictates.

This immediate obedience, however, was not enough for Liszt. There is no question that his uncompromising attitude was encouraged by the Princess. The annulment of her marriage and the possibility of regulating her relationship with Liszt had not advanced at all. In fact, her position grew steadily more bleak. She had counted a great deal on the intercession of the Grand Duchess of Weimar, a sister of the Czar of Russia, to plead her cause. However, the Sayn-Wittgenstein family had more influence at the Russian court than anything she could summon, and the Czar not only refused her pleas but confiscated her property in Russia, giving half of it to her estranged husband and keeping the rest in trust for her daughter. Moreover, he demanded that his sister refuse to receive the Princess any longer, and the society of Weimar, which had initially given her at least a token acceptance, followed suit. And so the Princess' life was more than ever centered on Liszt and all he did. She read every letter he received, even before he did, and more often than not dictated his answers. She even advised and made suggestions about his musical compositions. She watched over him with an authority and exclusiveness that made Marie d'Agoult seem like the most gentle and understanding of companions. It is hard to credit the degree of dominance that the

Princess exerted over every facet of Liszt's life and even more difficult to understand the manner in which he seemed not only to accept but to welcome it. She possessed a fascination for him that was quite out of the ordinary. His letters to her are veritable poems of love breathing a rare devotion. Also he was always conscious of the fact that she had abandoned everything for him—home, fortune, friends, position, and he was never to escape this burden of responsibility.

It is small wonder that this possessive woman should regret not being able to possess Liszt's past as well as his present and that she should feel the greatest jealousy toward Marie d'Agoult and her children.

In the meantime, Marie had taken her own revenge in typical fashion. She wrote and published a novel, *Nelida,* which was a thinly disguised story of her romance with Liszt, written, needless to say, entirely from her own point of view. Although Liszt in his letters to her, which surprisingly continued for a time even after he met the Princess, pretended to her that he did not see himself in the book at all, actually he was outraged at the derogatory public picture of him that she paraded for all the world to see. And so, surely, was the Princess.

As soon as Liszt learned that the children had visited Marie once more, he withdrew his daughters from Madame Bernard's school and returned them to his mother's house where he ordered that they be strictly supervised so that they would not be able to see their mother again.

It was a double grief for the girls to be deprived not only of their mother but also of Mlle Laure to whom they were so attached. Blandine wrote begging to be allowed to stay with Mlle Laure, who many times had dried her tears and comforted her in the sorrow she felt at being separated from her father.

Cosima felt the separation just as acutely, perhaps even more so, but she showed great pride and a reserve about expressing too much of her deepest feelings. She already had that sense which was to grow so strongly in her that she must bow uncomplainingly to her fate. "I want to make up for the injustice I did you in thought by an entire submission to your will," she wrote her father. "The letter you wrote caused me pain, but it also made me feel to the full how wrong I was. I am of course full of grief at leaving Mlle Laure, whom I love dearly and who has taken such a great interest in me. But since I know that you have a motive for separating me from her, I submit to my fate." [8] Liszt was pleased with Cosima's response. He required that his children show unquestioning obedience to him in everything. A more permanent solution, however, had to be found for the girls' future, and Liszt and the Princess were not long in discovering what seemed to them the perfect answer to all their problems.

As a wild, untamed and untamable girl, Carolyn Sayn-Wittgenstein had run through a whole series of governesses until one was summoned from Paris. She was Madame Patersi de Fossombroni and she succeeded in controlling and directing the hitherto uncontrollable girl. Why not bring her from Russia and put her in charge of Cosima and Blandine? It seemed perfect. That Madame Patersi was already in her seventies, that she was rigid, severe, and old-fashioned in her outlook did not matter at all. She was a disciplinarian who would command total obedience. In addition she was completely loyal and devoted to the Princess and would keep her informed of everything that went on with the children.

Letters were dispatched, and Madame Patersi soon set out on her long journey from Russia to Weimar. Since during the entire trip she sat bolt upright in the railway carriage, not thinking it correct even to lean back in her seat, she arrived in Wiemar thoroughly exhausted and ill and had to spend two months there with her Princess in order to recover. Years later, when

Cosima was already a very old lady herself, someone spoke of her habit of never leaning back in her chair. She smiled one of her ironic smiles and remembered Madame Patersi who would, she said, turn over in her grave if one of her pupils ever dared to relax against the back of a chair.

Liszt wrote to his mother advising her of his plans for the future of his daughters. "I should have preferred that these lines could be delivered to you by Madame Patersi, to whom I request you to hand over both my daughters, since I desire to entrust her with their education from now onward. I thank you with all my heart for all the love with which you have taken charge of the children during the last few months, and they too, as well as myself, will always be grateful to you for the care which you have bestowed upon their early childhood. Unfortunately, Madame Patersi fell ill immediately on arriving here and cannot reach Paris for a fortnight to come. But since you are moving, her sister, Madame Saint Mars, who will live with her and my daughters at No. 6 rue Casimir-Périer, Faubourg Saint-Germain, will be so good as to fetch the children away and keep them with her until the arrival of Madame Patersi. On receipt of this letter, therefore, will you hand over Blandine and Cosima to her care? . . . I hope that you will often give my daughters the pleasure of joining them at their meals, and I wish Daniel, too, to visit Madame Patersi's house frequently . . . I have requested Madame Patersi to call upon you frequently with my daughters, and to escort them everywhere. I am sure that on closer acquaintance you will esteem her, and even be fond of her, when you see that she has a good influence on the children. It is for her alone to decide what they are or are not to be allowed to do. She knows my ideas on their education and future, which are in complete accord with her own. Under her influence I hope that the evil effects of their education as directed by Madame Bernard, which are so distressing to me, will soon disappear." [9]

Cosima was very sad at this news but was determined to make the best of things. "Madame de Saint Mars has produced the effect on me that you had reason to expect," she wrote her father. "She is a woman full of good feeling and virtues and is nicer to us every day, but I tell you frankly that I felt great grief at leaving Grandmamma. It seems to me that it would be a great ingratitude to feel no grief at leaving a grandmother who has shown us so much kindness. But Madame de Saint Mars is so kind that I am already quite accustomed to her and am really fond of her. I am perfectly ready to feel the same toward Madame Patersi, whom you praise so highly." And she closed by telling him, "And now, dear Papa, I hope that you will not be dissatisfied with this letter. I am very depressed. All my life long I will always do everything to give you pleasure, and I hope that you will always find in me a daughter who comes up to your expectations." [10]

Blandine was less tractable and continued to complain and to beg her father to let her return to Madame Bernard's school. She accepted Liszt's authority fully only after he wrote her that if she did not give up her fanciful dreams he might have to punish her more cruelly than she could imagine by leaving her to herself to make her own difficult way in life. And so, as was inevitable, both girls had to accept this new life, each in her own way. Cosima was too proud to beg for anything. With her deeply religious feelings she responded to the concept that a woman's life should be one of sacrifice and dedication to others. She idolized her father and recognized that he was a great and famous personage and she wanted to be worthy of him. Her anomolous position had been made repeatedly clear to her from her earliest years, and Liszt had emphasized more than once that his affection for her depended on her obedience to his will. It was not, however, in an effort to curry favor that Cosima tried so hard to please him. In spite of the independence and fire of her character, Cosima wanted to be dutiful, to submit uncomplainingly to whatever fate had in store for her.

The adjustment to Madame Patersi was not an easy one. She ruled every facet of the girls' life with a rod of iron. One of the most painful of the new rules was that their letters to their father were limited to one a month. Besides, every letter had to be read and approved of by Madame Patersi before it was sent, so that they felt less free than ever to open their hearts to him. Sometimes that lady was busy with other things and found it too much trouble to censor the letters, which occasionally had to wait weeks before they could be dispatched. Madame Patersi sent constant reports to Liszt and the Princess of her pupils' progress, both intellectually and morally. Everything was strictly supervised and everything was reported on. There was not a single moment or area of the privacy which is so necessary to an adolescent and the absence of which is more painful at that age than at any other.

Madame Patersi had an absolute veneration for her former pupil, the Princess Sayn-Wittgenstein, and she never ceased talking about her and extolling her virtues. Cosima was told again and again how fortunate she was to have the affection and interest of such a person as the Princess and that the possibility of having her for a mother was something that she could never be sufficiently grateful for. Obediently, Cosima wrote: "I hope that God will hear our prayers, and that we may soon be able to call the *Frau Princesse* mother, for she already occupies a place in our hearts." [11]

Undoubtedly too, Madame Patersi spoke often of the Princess' daughter, Marie, who was almost exactly Cosima's age. Princess Marie lived at the Altenburg with her mother and Liszt and how fortunate her life seemed to Cosima. She who longed for even a single day with her father must have thought often of the girl who saw him every day. Liszt's relationship with

Princess Marie was everything that Cosima could have dreamed of. During his occasional absences, Liszt wrote the young Princess endless letters full of an ineffable charm. "Your letters are for me not something to read," he wrote her, "but rather stars that rise in my heart." [12] Liszt felt none of the burdens of parenthood with the young Princess that so dominated his attitude toward his own children. There is a great contrast between his relationship with her and that with Cosima. To Cosima he would write exhortations and criticisms, continually telling her how she must improve and study and make life easy for those around her. His tender words were few and far between. But to Magnolette, as he called Princess Marie, there were nothing but loving, uncritical letters. The little girl teasingly called him her fiancé and there was a delicate almost flirtatious note in Liszt's letters to her. He signed himself her humble slave and kissed her hands with reverence. "I can never stop saying to you, dearest Magnolette, that you are grace, kindness, *wisdom,* and even *perfection* itself. My happiness is to accompany you with heart and soul and ever to delight in you unreservedly." [13]

Cosima's interest in music was developing rapidly. She read avidly about her father's activities at Weimar in the *Gazette Musicale,* but what would she not have given to have had news from him directly of what he was doing and planning at Weimar, to have been able to share in his activities. Here again, his letters to her were completely bare of any word of himself or his music whereas to Magnolette he wrote every detail of what was going on in Weimar during her absences and everything he did. Toward the girl in Paris Liszt seemed to feel all the responsibilities and none of the joys of parenthood. How grateful Cosima would have been for just a small corner of the free and open heart that he gave so charmingly and unreservedly to her almost-twin at Weimar.

Unquestionably, the Princess here, too, played a role and Liszt's flattery of her daughter sprang to some extent from their strange and overwhelmingly intense relationship. Liszt was almost forced to put her child first. She supervised and probably often dictated his letters to his own children and her jealousy of anything to do with the past and with Marie d'Agoult exerted an iron control over his relationship with Cosima and the two other children. Cosima recognized this and in later life she wrote of an incident toward her brother which illustrated the role the Princess had played in controlling Liszt's relationship with his children. Daniel was a brilliant boy and won many first prizes at school. On one occasion, after the news of his successes had reached Liszt at Weimar, the letter that Daniel received from his father was like a dash of cold water, and Cosima, who from earliest childhood had had an almost maternal love toward her brother, was hurt and shocked. Two years later the same circumstances had a very different result. This time, Liszt was in Vienna, far away from the Princess, and he wrote a charming, warm, and delighted letter to Daniel. Cosima drily commented: "We can understand from this how the Princess was intent to allow no harmful weakness toward the son to prevail." [14] With the Princess in Weimar and Madame Patersi in Paris it was sure that no indulgence would touch Cosima either.

Madame Patersi's role, however, was not limited only to that of disciplinarian. She was an able educator and she soon set up a course of study and training of the highest standard for the girls. Languages played an important role, and Cosima could already write very acceptable letters both in English and in German. She found special interest in the works of Schiller. She read Shakespeare and learned parts of *Macbeth* and *Hamlet* by heart, performing various scenes with Blandine.

Cosimo and Blandine were devoted, sharing all their thoughts and feelings. They found great comfort in each other in all the difficult circumstances of their lives and each consoled the other in their sorrows. They did not always agree, however, and Blandine complained that Cosima had different opinions on everything. Blandine preferred the plays of Corneille while Cosima found the tragedies of Racine far superior. As Cosima became more and more fascinated with history, here too she took issue with her sister. Blandine was impressed with the grandeur of Rome and especially with the great ladies whom she described as being full of virtue, dignity, and noble disinterestedness. She complained that in spite of all her arguments Cosima simply would not agree with her and found infinitely more value and interest in Greece. In reading Thierry's *Conquest of England by the Normans,* Cosima was definitely on the side of the Saxons, although she did not like King Harold at all. She felt that he had been at fault to swear to free his country and then to fail in doing it. There were many lively and stimulating discussions between the sisters and their differences of opinion served to sharpen their observation and attention.

Madame Patersi saw to it that the girls visited museums, the porcelain factory at Sèvres, Versailles, the Hôtel de Ville, where Cosima recalled all the exciting events that had taken place there, and the wonderful historic and art treasures of Paris and its environs. They attended sessions of the Assembly and followed the debates there with lively interest.

Music as always played a dominant role, and Cosima continued to advance rapidly in her piano under the able teaching of Jean-Baptiste Seghers, a distinguished musician and friend of her father. They were taken to important concerts and to the opera. Cosima enjoyed her studies and was immensely interested in them, especially in history, but music came more and more to be important in her life. She had a striking talent for the piano and must have found release and comfort for her ardent nature in her increasing ability to express herself at the keyboard. She was already playing many of her father's compositions, which produced an enormous effect among her companions and were a great source of pride and inspiration to her.

Religion was a very important aspect of Madame Patersi's tutelage, as was natural in view of the Princess' almost excessive piety and absorption in Catholicism. The slightest sign of intransigeance in the girls would bring forth a visit to the priest, who would exhort them to blind obedience to their father. They were taken to hear all the great preachers of Paris, and the necessity for good works, piety, and sacrifice was constantly emphasized to them.

Madame Patersi, however, who had served as governess to several girls of aristocratic birth in Paris, was not unaware of the importance of the social arts and graces, in spite of her piety and severity. The apartment on the rue Casimir-Périer had occasional visits from some of Liszt's friends and fellow artists, among them Monsieur Erard, who presented one of his famous grand pianos to the girls. Every Thursday the girls dined with their grandmother, and on Sundays she came to them. Through her Cosima had some of the news of her father that she was so eager to hear, and when Madame Liszt went to Weimar for a visit she was begged to send "a long letter, Grandmother dear, and tell us all the details, so that we can associate ourselves with our father's fame from afar. This is our greatest joy, and our consolation for being so far away." [15]

Cosima never ceased longing to see her father in spite of the fact that she had not a free moment in the day to indulge her feelings. Madame Patersi was a firm believer in the saying that "Satan finds mischief still for idle hands to do." If there were not lessons, or practice on the piano, or concerts to attend and museums to visit, the girls learned to sew and embroider, to take care of their own clothes, and to run the house.

It was in 1853, three years after they had been turned over to Madame Patersi, that the great news arrived. Liszt was coming to Paris at last! Cosima was now a young lady nearly sixteen years old. She had not seen her beloved father for nine years.

CHAPTER IV

WHEN LISZT LEFT PARIS in the late spring of 1844, he did not imagine that so many years would pass before he returned to that city, the scene of his early triumphs. The years had brought about many and profound changes. His children, whom he had last seen still in the nursery, were almost grown up. Blandine and Cosima were already young ladies, and Daniel a gangly adolescent. Liszt himself was no longer the almost ethereally beautiful youth of his Paris days. At forty-three his hair was heavily streaked with grey. The prominent jaw and nose were no longer masked by youthful softness, and there were grim lines that gave a severity to his face in repose.

Liszt had left Paris as the most famous virtuoso of his time. He returned to it as a musician who had, in effect, abandoned the career of concert pianist and entered the ranks as composer and conductor. The change was not an easy one. As a composer he met with hostility that was in total contrast to the adulation he had aroused as a pianist. In his post as music director at the Court of Weimar, Liszt was becoming more and more involved in the controversial advocacy of the music of his great contemporaries, especially that of Wagner. The greatest change of all, perhaps, was the fact that he had tied himself heart and mind to a woman who dominated every aspect of his life.

Liszt arrived in Paris in October 1853. Accompanying him were the Princess and her daughter, Marie, and Richard Wagner. They had all been together visiting Wagner in Basel where Wagner had begun reading aloud to them his *Nibelungen* drama. He and Liszt had planned to go on to Paris alone, but Princess Marie begged so hard to be allowed to hear the rest of the reading that her mother changed their plans and all four of them went on to Paris. And so Cosima, Blandine, and Daniel not only saw their father, but they met for the first time the woman who was all in all to him, and her daughter whose life, in its daily proximity to Liszt, seemed to them the most enviable on earth.

As for Wagner, there was not the slightest presentiment on his part of what Cosima was to become for him. He described several visits that he made with Liszt to the children. "It was quite a novelty to me to see Liszt with these young girls, and to watch him in his intercourse with his son, then a growing lad. Liszt himself seemed to feel strange in his fatherly position, which for several years had only brought him cares, without any of the attendant pleasures." [1] Wagner found Daniel especially attractive, not only for his brightness, but for his amazing resemblance to his father. Of the girls he merely said that he found them "very shy."

Daniel was the most easygoing and unself-conscious of the three children. Spoiled and adored by his sisters, he had an affectionate nature, and great charm and enthusiasm. He was a fine, even an outstanding student at school, and his sisters took great pride in his achievements. Blandine had already begun to fulfill her early promise of beauty. Her nature was essentially gentle, somewhat sentimental, and she fell easily into moods of romantic daydreams and emotions.

Cosima was much more complex. Many years later, Princess Marie wrote of her impressions of this first meeting with the sixteen-year-old Cosima. Her words give, perhaps, as good a picture of her own character as of her impressions of Cosima. "I was older than the two girls who were still rather unpolished and who looked out at the unfriendly world with timid doe eyes. The elder, Blandine, was prettier, plumper, more pleasing —though in no way heaven-storming, and she was already rather pleased with herself. Poor Cosima, however, was in the worst teen-age stage—tall and angular, sallow, with a wide mouth and long nose, the image of her father. Only her long golden hair, of unusual sheen, was of great beauty. In the poor child's heart there raged a volcano. Dark stirrings of love and overweening vanity pulsated in her little heart. Now and then her thin lips would curl mischievously with the inborn mockery of the Parisienne. Her brother Daniel was the youngest—a pale, sad-looking boy with dreamy eyes . . . After a simple meal at the house of Liszt's children, in the small, plain salon of the rue Casimir-Périer, Wagner read us the end of the *Nibelungen*. The children understood scarcely enough German to grasp the meaning of the words. Still, even they were gripped by our emotions. Daniel's laurel wreaths which, according to the French custom, he had received at school, were hanging on the wall. Half in jest I took one down in order to crown Wagner with it. I can still see Cosima's rapturous expression with the tears running down her sharp nose. At that time, Wagner had no eyes for the ugly child." [2] Princess Marie goes on to say that Wagner later presented her with the copy from which he had read, with a charming verse dedicated to the "clever child." Princess Marie was obviously a young woman of the world and one who was accustomed to being flattered and admired.

It was a heady week of excitement for the three young people with a dinner given by Liszt at the Palais Royal, and a musical evening at the Erards in addition to Wagner's reading at the rue Casimir-Périer. Twenty-two years later it was still vivid in Cosima's mind, and she described, in a letter to a friend, the occasion when she and Wagner had seen each other for the first time. "It was the same day on which I saw my father again after eight years—there suddenly appeared in our quiet home my father, the Princess Carolyne, her daughter Marie, Berlioz, and Wagner, who read us *The Death of Siegfried.* This was a great deal to happen all at once to three children who thought themselves cut off, not only from the world, but also from family life. That day has remained deep in my memory . . . on that occasion I did nothing but look at the floor, my weak eyes and shy disposition made me unable to do anything but snatch at everything by stealth, as it were, though I knew that, strictly speaking, it did not exist for me." [3]

Listz's charm and fascination were as potent as ever and his children fell even more completely under his spell. Almost the most wonderful of all, especially for Cosima, whose musical gifts were developing rapidly, was the opportunity at last to hear the incomparable Liszt at the piano.

A poignant footnote to the visit was added years later by Cosima in a letter to her oldest daughter. "My whole youth was a staying at home! For example, when after eight years my father saw us again for eight days, we were taken nowhere with him and we found it quite natural that he went out with Carolyne and Marie." [4]

The week, filled with so many impressions, so many longed for experiences, ended only too quickly and the young people were plunged once more into the dull routine of their lives—Daniel at the Lycée and the girls under the strict and uncompromising eye of Madame Patersi. It was ten days after Liszt's departure before that good lady saw fit to allow them to write to their father. He was much too busy at Weimar, she told them, to have time to be bothered by letters from his children. Their letter, when the restriction was finally lifted, must have been graded at least satisfactory by the censorious Madame Patersi, whose sun rose and set with the Princess' pleasure.

"Finally the orders have been revoked and we can tell you how happy your presence in Paris made us; not only because we had the happiness of seeing you again, but because it brought about an immense change in us. We understand better what is good. Added to our gratitude in bearing your name is an inexpressible desire to see you made happy through us. Madame Patersi has often told us this, and she was right. She knew more than we did on this point, as on many others and we own that your attitude, the tender way that you welcomed our expressions of joy, the maternal goodness of the Princess, and her daughter who treated us as sisters and Daniel as a brother, all this, our dear father, gave your three children an immense sum of happiness. We like to repeat it to you. Tell the Princess that we already love her like a mother and that she said things to us which we will never forget. This letter is for both of you from the three of us. Bless us both together, my very dear father. From our side, we pray that God will leave you nothing more to desire, and that we may be able to give the name of mother to her who will receive all her happiness from you as you will receive all yours from her, above, it goes without saying, that part which your children will bring." And they signed it, "Your submissive and respectful children who love you." [5]

In spite of Princess Marie's condescending feelings toward the children, they succeeded in making friends with her and soon a correspondence started between them which was to continue for several years. Although obviously spoiled, Marie was a girl of charm and sensibility and she evidently succeeded to some extent in overcoming the feelings of jealousy that Liszt's daughters felt toward her and toward the fortunate circumstances that brought her into daily relationship with their father. On the other hand, it is probable that they were eager to find any road at all that would bring them closer to Liszt and to life at the Altenburg. Often through the light and gay tone of their letters runs a forlorn and lonely undercurrent. "In spite of all the charms of Paris," Cosima wrote, "the Altenburg seems much more beautiful and more enviable to me, and often we find ourselves transported there in our wishes." [6]

Events, however, were to move more quickly now for the three young people in Paris. Blandine was already eighteen, and the question of marriage began to be thought of with growing frequency. Indeed, during the months following her father's visit to Paris three offers were made for her hand, and here we see the generous aspects of Liszt's nature come to the fore. In discussing his hopes for the marriage of his daughters, he writes: "What I want above all for them is a husband who is intelligent, active, honest, and capable of inspiring in his wife a feeling which the first years will not threaten with decay . . . The questions of family, of position and of money are secondary for me." [7] Liszt was determined to allow his daughters to choose husbands after their own hearts without pressure or direction from him. When, therefore, Blandine refused the offers made to her, there were no reproaches from Liszt.

More important than anything at this period, however, was the re-entry once again of their mother into their lives. It was by chance that the two girls met their mother at a concert. Marie d'Agoult was quick to take advantage of the occasion and arranged for the girls to visit her two days later.

At the age of forty-eight, Marie d'Agoult had lost none of her beauty or elegance. Her appearance, her dress, her walk, her charm, her intelligence, her skill as hostess and conversationalist were finely representative of the arts and graces of the best of French aristocracy and culture. Her reputation as a writer, and as a liberal, was firmly established, especially since the appearance of her book, the *History of the Revolution of 1848.*

Marie's mother had died some seven years earlier, in 1847, and she was now in full possession of a considerable fortune. Her relationship with her eldest daughter, Claire, had long since been re-established. Although Claire did not possess her mother's beauty, she had inherited many of her intellectual interests. Claire's marriage with the Comte de Charnacé was not happy and she found great interest in trying to follow a literary career, like her mother, writing under the pseudonym C. de Sault.

The house to which Marie d'Agoult invited Cosima and Blandine was called the Maison Rose. It was an exquisite, Renaissance-type house situated within view of the Arc de Triomphe and surrounded by open fields. A fountain in the garden was encircled by rhododendron, gardenia, mimosa plants, and colorful summer flowers. The interior was artfully decorated. It is not difficult to imagine the effect on Cosima and Blandine of such a setting and of the woman who reigned there who was their mother.

Marie d'Agoult set out to charm and win her daughters. What her motives were in doing this is difficult to estimate. Certainly she was flattered by their gifts and their intelligence. Daniel's brilliance and success at school and his remarkable resemblance to his father were very agreeable to her. Having so long been deprived of any contact with these children and having had not the slightest say in regard to their education must have been a source of frustration to a person of the intellectual force of Marie d'Agoult. Unquestionably she resented the woman who had supplanted her in Liszt's affections and felt bitterly that this interloper, as she viewed her, should have more to say about her own children than she did. In spite of the years that had passed and the finality and bitterness of the rupture with Liszt, Marie was never able to forget him and she may even have dreamed sometimes of a reconciliation, if only the dreadful woman at the Altenburg could be eliminated. One of the first things that Cosima and Blandine noticed at the Maison Rose was the bronze medallion of Liszt and the portrait of him by Ingres which hung in their mother's study. Whether or not Marie's feelings were deeply maternal, certainly at this period she threw herself heart and soul into a mother's role toward these three children.

Liszt was hardly pleased by this renewed relationship, and the Princess even less so, but they realized that it would be impossible any longer to forbid any intercourse between mother and children. Liszt managed, however, to surround the resumption of the relationship with so many matters of protocol, of restrictions and demands that it must have cost Marie d'Agoult all her self-control to comply with them. Long letters passed between Liszt and her and Liszt and the children as to the exact way everything must be done. Marie had first to invite Madame Patersi to visit her alone. Then she had to return the visit to the apartment on the rue Casimir-Périer. Only after these formal visits had been carried out could the girls be invited again to the Maison Rose. Liszt required that either Madame Patersi accompany Blandine and Cosima, or else that Marie come and fetch them herself in a "carriage of the highest quality." They were not to be allowed to make the trip alone, nor could anyone else accompany them, not even their married half sister Claire. And on the occasions that Madame Patersi was with them, Liszt made it clear that she was not to be treated as a governess and banished to the next room. Only if Marie showed proper respect toward Madame Patersi could her relationship with the girls be allowed.

The fine hand of the Princess can be seen in all these fussy demands and it is another example of how completely she dominated every aspect of Liszt's life down to the smallest detail. She was determined to wring from Marie d'Agoult a respect and recognition for Madame Patersi, her personal emissary, and by inference the respect and recognition she felt was due herself, as the woman who would be Liszt's wife.

Marie wrote Liszt of her desire to contribute to the dowry of Cosima and Blandine. He replied that he had nothing against it and then launched into a sermon, on the subject of "Seek first the Kingdom of Heaven," expressing the hope that his daughters would not be materialistic but would share his religious feelings. As for his own contribution to their future, he stated that each would receive at the time of marriage a capital of sixty-thousand francs or the interest therefrom. Marie d'Agoult hinted to Madame Patersi that she was considering adding one hundred thousand francs to that.

While all these tedious and long-drawn-out arrangements were being made, Liszt invited Cosima and Blandine to meet him for a few days' visit in Brussels. It was barely nine months since they had last seen him in Paris, and they could scarcely believe their good fortune. Even the inevitable presence of Madame Patersi could not spoil their pleasure. Liszt himself, in the absence of the Princess, was a great deal more attentive and affectionate with his daughters. He took them to the Zoo, to the museum to see the Rembrandts, and talked endlessly with them, or rather, as he said, "to them." After their regretful return to Paris without him, they wrote to Princess Marie that the habit of happiness which they had found in being with their father was hard to do without. They were trying hard to conquer their feelings; they wrote, "but often we look about us to see if some inhabitant of the dear Altenburg is not there. And then our soul is filled with sorrow which we dispel only by the hope that we will all find ourselves together soon." [8]

Finally, however, all the requirements for seeing their mother were met, and after the aridity of the restrictions under which they had lived until now, Cosima and Blandine were swept off their feet by the interest and excitement that Marie d'Agoult brought into their lives. She took them everywhere—to museums, to the opera, to the theater. She directed their taste in discussions of architecture, of literature, of painting. She discussed Plato with them and Greek tragedy. They were present at her receptions and listened, fascinated, to the conversation of the brilliant company there. And she taught them invaluable lessons in the arts of society, of elegance, of taste. Marie brought magic into their lives, and she herself felt rejuvenated in her relationship with these three children.

Liszt, and especially the Princess, grew more and more disturbed at Marie d'Agoult's obvious influence, although both Cosima and Blandine wrote again and again of their complete devotion and loyalty to their father. They insisted that their mother in no way tried to influence them against him and that nothing or no one could ever make them forget all that he meant to them or their desire to obey him absolutely in everything. Nothing that they could write, however, tempered the irritation and suspicion with which Liszt and the Princess viewed the re-entrance of Marie d'Agoult into the lives of her children.

It was in the summer of 1855 that Liszt decided on a step which was to shape Cosima's life fatefully. Prodded by the Princess, with whose plans he always voiced complete agreement, more and more suspicious of the effect that Nelida, as he called Marie, was having on Cosima and Blandine, he determined that he would end her relationship with them. Since he realized that he could not forbid them to visit her, he fell back on a plan he had thought of once years earlier when he first had made up his mind to keep his children away from their mother —he would simply move them from Paris, and distance would solve all his problems.

Germany was the logical place and Liszt considered two cities —Dresden and Berlin. The latter won out when he persuaded Madame von Bülow, the mother of his favorite pupil and disciple Hans, to take the girls into her home and assume full charge of them. It was the Princess who actually made all the arrangements and decisions in this situation. She went to Berlin and stayed there several weeks. Not only did she spend a great deal of time with Madame von Bülow, with whom she got along famously, but she entered extensively into the literary and artistic circles of Berlin. Determined to counterbalance the effect of Marie d'Agoult, she made her influence and ideas felt both with the woman who would be in charge of Cosima and Blandine and also with the people whom they might be expected to meet.

It was a wily Liszt who wrote to his children inviting all three of them to visit him at the Altenburg in Weimar. He said not a word about his latest plan for the girls, and in all innocence and joy they made ready for this trip of which they had dreamed for so many years. Although Liszt arranged that Madame von Bülow was to go to Paris to fetch them, Cosima and Blandine had not the slightest suspicion of what was in store for them.

They arrived in Weimar on August 21, 1857. The Princess and her daughter had chosen that time for a visit to Paris and so the three children had their father to themselves. Not completely so, of course, for there was Eduard Liszt, their father's cousin, Miss Anderson, Marie's English governess, and various other friends who were constantly dropping in, but at least there was no Madame Patersi to hamper them and no Princess to bring out the disciplarian in Liszt. The visit was almost as perfect as they had always dreamed it would be. The children laughed and joked, took up two-thirds of their father's time, upset all his routines, chattered incessantly, and quite charmed and bewildered him. His only rule was that he simply would not have breakfast with them. It was a very different and a gay Altenburg with these three young people in charge.

When Liszt finally got his courage up and broke the news about his plans for Cosima and Blandine, the effect was predictable and the two girls argued and begged and pleaded not to be sent to Berlin. "The girls do not much care about settling in Berlin," Liszt wrote a friend in a considerable understatement. "I hope that having duly sent them to all the thirty thousand devils for their illusive and illogical arguments (which has already happened several times during these three days) they will end by being completely convinced of the sincerity and wisdom of my solicitude for them . . . for they have a great fund of tenderness for me." [9]

Anna Liszt, when she heard the news, was blunt. Her letter is worth quoting at length as it gives a clear summing up of many of her feelings past and present in regard to her granddaughters. "I am so upset since hearing the latest decision about Blandine and Cosima ten days ago. The Princess told me about it with the greatest indifference, that they were to be sent to Berlin under the charge of Madame de Bülow, who is to be with them always and direct them. I could find nothing to say but that the children are too big to make another change. The Princess replied that otherwise there would never be an end to Madame d'Agoult's scribbling, as she had been very impertinent in her letters to you for some time past. But consider, dear child, to hand these children over to strangers in a strange land, where they do not know anyone, is certainly no indifferent matter for them, and I am afraid that if this happens, one or the other of them will fall ill. It would have been better if the Princess had left Madame Patersi in Poland or in Russia and not entrusted these children to a woman who was, moreover, already in her seventy-second year when they were handed over to her charge. She was already too tired . . . I was sad for the children, and perhaps you may still remember that I cried a good deal. But when I got to Paris I saw that I must resign myself and God gave me the grace to do so. I prepared the children for their new residence and had to say a great deal that went against my feelings—and it went all right. They became reconciled to this old lady, who never felt any affection for them, for when she arrived here she had been prejudiced against their mother by the Princess; she had an antipathy for Blandine and greeted her with the words 'She is her mother's daughter' in that tone of hers which you know. To Blandine, who had been under the gentle guidance of Madame Laure Bernard, this seemed very unfriendly. She cried a great deal, and the only reply was 'Tears are only water' and more to that effect. Oh, my dear child, it was a good thing I was here too. I talked to her and in time things went fairly well. Now these two ladies have taken a dislike to Cosima because she has the misfortune to be like her mother . . . The children are good and must be guided by love, for they have proud, sensitive hearts. Madame de Bülow seems to me to be a kindly disposed woman, but to send the children away to Prussia on account of their mother! Look into the matter if you think it necessary and if you fear any bad influence over the children. You have them with you now, they will listen to you and take things from you that they would not take from others because they love you and feel that they, too, are loved by you. Do not believe all the bad things that have been told you . . . Ask the children; they will tell you the truth. You will see whether they are not better than they are painted. I have received a letter from all three of them, full of happiness and joy at being in your society. I am embarrassed when I write to them, since I know what is before them." [10]

In spite of his mother's opinion and the continued entreaties of the two girls, Liszt remained adamant in his decision. Although Blandine, when they were already all en route to Berlin, managed to wangle a return to Weimar for a few extra days, the moment of departure finally came and the girls, accompanied by Madame von Bülow, set out with obvious reluctance for their new home. It was less than a week later that still another bombshell fell.

In her excitement at leaving Paris and the impending visit to Weimar, Blandine had left three letters from her mother, who had been sojourning in Holland, in the apartment on the rue Casimir-Périer. Needless to say, these letters did not escape the eagle eye of Madame Patersi, who undoubtedly profited from the girls' absence to go through their things with more than her usual thoroughness. She did not delay in sending the letters at once to the Princess who, in turn, forwarded copies of them to Liszt.

Marie d'Agoult, caught in the full flush of enthusiasm for her new-found role as mother, had reacted as might be expected when she heard from Blandine of the proposed visit to Weimar. Her feelings of hostility toward the Princess, her realization of the threat to her own position with her children that this visit implied made her expend every ounce of her persuasive literary and dramatic talents in her answer.

Liszt's letter to Blandine and Cosima in Berlin was like a whiplash. He was obviously in a rage and he did not mince any words. He took their mother's letter phrase by phrase and demolished it. Marie d'Agoult had been consternated at the visit to the Altenburg, which was "contrary to honor," she claimed.

She was horrified at what she called their youth, inexperience, and blindness. Liszt was outraged at the implicit castigation of the position of the Princess in his life and home and pointed out acidly the many "honorable" people who found it an "honor" to visit there. The remark about the girl's innocence he considered an attack on their feelings for him. "You will eat the bread of a stranger, a stranger who is not and never will be the wife of your father!" Marie wrote. "I would rather see you work for a living, or even beg, than this last affront . . . Tell your father that you would prefer to give lessons and to return to your grandmother rather than stay—not at his home—but at the home of a stranger." Liszt answered that their mother had been more of a stranger to them than anyone else and that he alone had furnished them with bread for nineteen years. "Oh! my proud children," Marie exclaimed, "always remain proud." Liszt exhorted them to be gentle and humble. Their mother, he told them, wished to harm him at any cost and at all times and, unable to attack him either through his position or through his conscience, she was trying to hurt him through their affection for him, and through his respect and love for the Princess. He ended by heaping coals of fire on their heads. "I will not undertake to dispute for the heart and affection of any of my children, a task both repugnant and beyond my forces. If you find, in the end, that the share of affection should be equal between him who fulfills his obligations with devotion and conscientiousness and her who forgets them, I will make no objection and, when you are of age, you can freely make the choice which suits you." [11]

After the delights of their visit to Weimar, where they had gained so much in closeness with their father, this letter came as a terrible blow. Daniel, who was still at the Altenburg, spoke indignantly of the "espionage" and the "police procedures" of Madame Patersi which he found disgusting. The girls too were particularly outraged against their former governess who had violated their privacy by her "vile and base action" in sending their mother's letters to the Princess. Letters flew back and forth between Weimar and Berlin. The girls at first struggled under what even Liszt admitted they must have felt were his "tyrannical demands," but the habit of a lifetime coupled with their veneration for their father won the day with amazing speed. Liszt once again wrung from them total obedience to his wishes, and they wrote the letter that he required of them to Madame Patersi expressing their gratitude to her for all she had done for them. Exactly one week after his first explosion, Liszt was able to write to Blandine that he approved and thanked her for doing what had to be done.

Once more, Liszt had succeeded in winning his daughters wholly to his side. Marie d'Agoult did not accept this turn of events easily, as one can well understand. She recognized that the move to Berlin was in reality an attack against herself and that it was a tactical victory for Liszt and the Princess.

It was not long before she was forced to realize that it was all of that and more. In effect, she had lost her influence with her daughters once again, in spite of what even Liszt sensed were the "poetic feelings" of the girls toward their mother. Her attempts to salvage the situation only made matters worse, especially as far as Cosima was concerned. Blandine described the situation to Liszt: "Maman wrote a rather stiff letter which displeased Her Majesty the theatrical one (Cosima) who wrote an even stiffer one: second letter from the Avenue Sainte-Marie arrives. The theatrical one, faithful to her principles, writes one that is even more steely and since then, no more letters from Maman to her." [12] Cosima, soon to be eighteen, was maturing rapidly. She was no longer the shy, timid little girl whom Wagner had scarcely noticed two years earlier.

CHAPTER V

WHEN COSIMA AND BLANDINE ARRIVED at the home of Madame von Bülow in Berlin, they found the way had been well paved for them. The Princess, during her long visit in Berlin, had had many intimate talks with Madame von Bülow about the girls and her ideas for their future. Liszt, too, wrote with his usual frankness about what he considered was unfortunate in the characters of his daughters, urging Madame von Bülow to spare nothing that would improve their "presumptuousness and feverish vanity." Although Madame von Bülow was not Madame Patersi, and they were free at last from that tyrannical governess, she was an extremely difficult and demanding person. But the two girls were accustomed to adapting themselves to thorny personalities. The most important thing was that they were together. Cosima's mischievous sense of humor and Blandine's gift of mimicry helped to lighten many lonely and difficult moments.

Lessons, which included Italian and music theory, were begun almost at once. Liszt had asked that Hans von Bülow take over the musical education of his daughters, a task he hoped would not prove too boring and irksome for his young disciple. He must have been startled to say the least when he received Bülow's first letter describing his reaction to the girls and to their abilities. "You ask me, dear Master, to give you news of Mesdemoiselles Liszt," Bülow wrote. "Until now it would have been impossible for me in view of the stupefaction, admiration and even exaltation to which they have reduced me, especially the younger. As to their musical dispositions, it is not talent, it is genius that they possess. They are certainly the daughters of my benefactor—completely exceptional beings. I busy myself rather consistently with their musical education in so far as they are not too superior to me in force of intelligence, delicacy of taste, etc. . . . How moved and touched I was to recognize you, *'ipsissimum Lisztum'* in the playing of Mademoiselle Cosima when I heard her for the first time!" From the first, Bülow showed not only an enormous admiration of Liszt's daughters, but a sympathy for them, and he was quick to defend them even to Liszt. "They are not amusing themselves too much, as you seem to fear, in Berlin," his letter continued, "but they are acclimating themselves, nevertheless, little by little to their—Jersey.* [1]

Cosima knew something of Bülow's struggles and the difficulties he had surmounted in entering a musical career against the wishes of his parents. Although his musical talent had been apparent at a very early age, his parents had never looked on it as anything more than a hobby, something that would be a pleasant resource and diversion for a man who would, of course, follow some serious and important career such as the law. Bülow was an affectionate and loyal son to his difficult and dissimilar parents. His father, Eduard, was a man of charm and talent, a student, a writer of modest attainments, and totally impracti-

* Jersey: where Victor Hugo lived during his exile.

cal. His was a gentle nature basically, but he was temperamental and nervous and not very strong-willed. His wife, Franziska, was a very different person. She had a will of iron and a dominating, passionate nature. Highly conservative in inclination, in spite of her musical and intellectual gifts she laid great stress on position and appearances. It was not strange that this pair did not get on at all, and when Bülow was nineteen, his parents were divorced. His father remarried shortly, the daughter of Count von Bülow-Dennewitz, a cultivated, witty woman who soon produced two sons, half brothers for Hans. This left Bülow and his sister, Isa, even more at the mercy of the demands of their mother, who was determined that he continue at the University and give up any idea of music as a career.

Bülow was twenty when he visited his father and stepmother in Switzerland. He had spent two years at the University, dutifully following his parents' wishes. His letters, however, were filled much more with music than with anything else, and it is easy to see from them where his heart lay. It was on a rainy September day in 1850 that Bülow made his decision and declared his independence. In company with his friend, Karl Ritter, he set out on foot from his father's house on a two-day journey to Zurich to see Richard Wagner. "I was forced to act as I did," he wrote later to his sister, "and I do not repent it, and trust I shall never do so. I had almost let myself be over-persuaded by Papa to travel back to Berlin without even seeing Wagner, when Ritter brought me a letter from Wagner which made me instantly resolve to go to Zurich and there to fill the post of musical conductor under W's direction. We did the trip on foot in two days: firstly in order to escape any possible pursuit on Papa's side, and also I wanted to test whether I had the energy to do that piece on foot in the most awful weather, amid ceaseless rain and storm." [2]

Since the age of twelve, when Bülow heard his first Wagner

opera, *Rienzi,* Wagner had been his idol, the man who represented his greatest source of stimulus and interest. There were two things, however, about which Bülow's parents agreed, in spite of all their disagreements: their opposition to a musical career for their son and their mistrust of Richard Wagner, the revolutionary both in music and in politics.

The year 1848 had seen the uprising in Dresden and Wagner's participation in it, as a result of which he had been banished from Germany. Bülow had been swept up in the revolutionary fever, though from afar, and his liberal political inclinations had terrified his archconservative mother. She was outraged at her son's decision on a musical career but even more so at his choice of mentor.

Wagner wrote her a long and persuasive letter from Zurich, setting forth his certainty of Bülow's talents and his plans for the young man's future. "I have observed that his love of Art, and especially of music, is based upon no mere transient excitement, but upon great, indeed uncommon, powers. It was with my special concurrence, and indeed at my suggestion, that he went on with his law studies with undiminished zeal . . . And now what is the result of all his pains and experience? Simply the outspoken and absolute conviction that the more he sets the one thing against the other the more he feels that it is Art alone—in other words Music—that he can love unceasingly. This one thing, my dear lady, stands first and foremost as an undeniable fact, and I cannot doubt that, when once you yourself are convinced of this wish of your son to devote himself entirely to music, you will make it your own wish also . . . If you will further permit me, on the ground of my own experience, to give advice which I trust you will not consider intrusive, but tendered from the purest human sympathy, it is this: give willingly and speedily your consent to this, so that your son may not go on living a moment longer in coercion against his well-founded and well-tested inclination; grant him permission to spend the coming winter season with me here in Zurich, so that, with his friend Ritter, he may learn under my direction the practical work of a musical conductor; wait with patience and see what further turn his life as a practical artist takes; have full confidence in whatsoever depends on my small powers of help, but especially in what our friend Liszt may be able to do to help him on; and in every case where trials await him, where trouble threatens him, where he needs help, do all that lies in your special power to sustain him with your self-sacrificing support! You will thus have the satisfaction of calling a worthy, perhaps a great, artist your son . . ." [3]

All of Wagner's persuasive powers, however, did nothing to move the inflexible Madame von Bülow. Indeed, his efforts on Bülow's behalf undoubtedly served only to stiffen her objections still more.

Barely, if ever, has a young musician entering his career had such powerful advocates. Liszt was an old family friend, and the year before Hans had spent several days in Weimar, basking in the delight of Liszt's personality and his playing which completely "enchanted and inspired" the young man. Liszt, too, wrote the mother, a tactful and diplomatic letter in which he apologized for meddling in such serious and delicate matters but stating his belief that: "Hans is evidently gifted with a musical organization of the rarest kind. His executive talent will easily place him in the front rank of the greatest pianists, and his essays at composition denote quite exceptional qualities of imagination, of individuality, and of concentration." [4]

Madame von Bülow was as unmoved by this letter as by Wagner's. Bülow had been a frail and sickly child, subject to attacks of nerves and violent headaches. Nevertheless, he possessed a firm will and strength of character and purpose. In spite of his distress at his mother's feelings, he stuck to his decision. "I have violated all the duties of a child toward you," he wrote his mother, "and am fully conscious of it . . . I do not, however, repent the act which, from the standpoint of my sacred duties toward you, is to be condemned, and I only fear that your just anger has won the day over your motherly love: I fear, and tears come into my eyes at this most terrible of all fears, that you might want to know nothing more about your son, who separated himself of his own accord from his mother, that you would not recognize him as such any more; that you would perhaps destroy his letters unread." [5]

Bülow dedicated to Wagner, that autumn of his twentieth year, his complete devotion and loyalty. He thought him "the noblest, the most lovable and honorable man," [6] and he felt that he himself "recognized, as perhaps few others have done, the greatest artist who has appeared in our age." [7] Bülow wrote to his sister that Wagner "has been so fine, so noble, so fatherly toward me that I owe him eternal gratitude for it all." [8] The immense devotion that Bülow felt toward Wagner, both as man and as musician, became the prime moving force in his life and work. He made Wagner's cause his own; Wagner's struggles were his struggles. Highly strung, nervous, subject to constant attacks that were in part illnesses of psychosomatic origin, Bülow nevertheless was a born fighter. He was impetuous, fiery, and fought uncompromisingly for what he believed in. He made himself Wagner's champion in every sense.

After six months in Switzerland under Wagner's auspices, where Bülow acquitted himself excellently as a conductor, he moved to Weimar to pursue his piano studies under Liszt's direction. Madame von Bülow was somewhat mollified by this plan. She was more willing to agree to the career in music if only her son would remove himself from Wagner's influence. And so Bülow came to Weimar and to the second of his great loyalties—Franz Liszt.

Bülow moved into a small apartment at the Altenburg and plunged into intensive work at the piano, practicing often eight to ten hours a day, and building a solid repertoire. He appeared more and more often in concerts, no longer as an amateur but as a full-fledged virtuoso, and he acquired a few pupils. Liszt and the Princess occupied a good deal of his time when they were there. Bülow was impressed with the force of the Princess' mind, especially her very apparent powers of argument, but he was not drawn to her as a person at all. Quite to the contrary. Liszt, on the other hand, he loved and admired in all respects. Bülow willingly did all the myriad commissions of copying, letter writing, arranging of music, and a host of purely secretarial duties that came his way not only from Liszt but from the Princess too. Liszt shaped and guided his pianistic work, and Bülow felt a growing confidence in his own musical worth. It was not long before he was Liszt's obvious favorite, and indeed Liszt spoke of him as the one who would inherit his own mantle as a virtuoso.

Bülow's parents were erratic in their response to the development of their son's musical career, most especially his mother. She was willing to help him out financially, but she could not restrain herself from making constant reproaches, from expressing critical opinions on much of what he was doing and in general keeping him in a constant state of nerves and tension. "The letter you have just written to me after your long silence has made me very sad," Bülow wrote her, "for it proves pretty clearly to me that the events of the past year have greatly shaken, if not enfeebled, your love and your motherly indulgence—a fact which I liked to think was not so . . . Let me beg you once more, my dear mother, to write to me some kinder words soon . . ." [9]

Bülow was devoted to both his parents and his letters to them overflow with affection. Their slightest displeasure was very painful to him. The death of his father in 1853 was a severe blow, especially as it came during a period of estrangement between father and son, the result of the father's irritation at what he considered Bülow's indiscretion at criticizing one of the most popular singers of the day.

Bülow was writing articles on music for various musical journals, and it was not long before the caustic opinions that he knew how to express in pure vitriol earned him a reputation for combativeness in which he delighted. His mother was anxious about his lack of prudence. "It amuses me to see how Hans carried on an interesting conversation with as much ease as sublety; he is altogether very remarkable; he has on the one side an incredible self-command, certainty and aplomb, and then again a boundless imprudence, which may drag him into the worst of quarrels, and there are more of contrasts in his character." [10]

The fight into which Bülow plunged himself with such energy was that of Wagner, and Liszt too, against what they called the Philistines. By 1850, Wagner was the most talked-about musician in Germany. His political involvements and flight only served to heighten the attention that had already been aroused by his revolutionary musical ideas and by the mass of controversial articles that poured from his pen on a variety of subjects. Whether the ideas he expounded in *Art and Revolution* and *The Art-Work of the Future* were really understood or not, they nevertheless helped to draw the battle lines between the old and the new, between the "Establishment" and the ardent souls who saw in Wagner, his music and his ideas, a wave of the future that would bring new life and meaning to the musical scene. His operas *Rienzi* and *Tannhäuser* had been attacked brutally by the critics, but had met with considerable success with the general public nevertheless. It is hard to imagine today the violence of the pro and contra Wagner feelings. Lifelong friendships were disrupted, families quarreled, and the powerful intendents of the musical and critical world were lined in solid ranks against everything that Wagner stood for.

Wagner, however, had his cohorts too. Rarely if ever in the arts has a man been able to arouse the fanatical devotion to himself and his cause as did Wagner. Outstanding among his admirers was Liszt. The friendship and devotion between these two disparate men is one of the strangest in the annals of music. There was everything in them for disagreement, hardly anything for harmony. And yet, strangely, their devotion ran basically strong and true, in spite of the strains and stresses to which it was subjected and which brought it to the breaking point, and beyond, more than once. Wagner's music was a revelation to Liszt. "Your *Lohengrin* is a sublime work," he wrote, "from one end to the other: the tears rose from my heart in more than one place." [11] But even musically the admiration was not wholly one-sided and Wagner once admitted that "since my acquaintance with Liszt's compositions I have become a completely different man as a harmonist from what I was before." [12]

Liszt made himself Wagner's ally and supporter in every way. "Believe me, you have not for a moment ceased to be very near to my heart," he wrote Wagner. "The serious, enthusiastic admiration I have for your genius would not be satisfied with sleepy habits and barren sentiments. All that I can possibly do, either in the interest of your reputation and glory or in that of your person, you may feel certain will in no circumstances remain undone. Only a friend like you is not always quite easy and convenient to serve, for those who understand you must wish, before all, to serve you in an intelligent and dignified manner. I hope that so far I have not been wanting in these two essential conditions, and I do not mean to depart from them for the future. You may therefore have full confidence in me, and listen to me, and believe me as one who is frankly and without restriction devoted to you." [13]

"I must say," Wagner exulted in answer, "*you are a friend.* Let me say no more to you, for although I always recognized in friendship between men the noblest and highest human relation, it was you who embodied this idea in its fullest reality by letting me no longer imagine, but feel and grasp, what a friend is." [14]

Liszt devoted a great part of his talent, his time, and his purse to helping Wagner in an extraordinary display of generosity of one artist to another.

By Liszt's side was a whole group of young fighters, ready to do battle for Wagner, Liszt, and the Music of the Future. Bülow, with his facility for writing, with his mordant wit, with his courage and idealism, was in the front ranks of the battle. Article after article flowed from his vitriolic pen, attacking the hoary attitudes of the critics, the academic circles, and the opera managements with such flaming impetuosity that he made scores of enemies and left no doubt that this was a fight to the death in which the Wagnerians would give no quarter.

When Cosima came to Berlin in 1855, Bülow's years of apprenticeship were behind him. He had achieved growing recognition as pianist and conductor and held the position of professor at the Stern Conservatory in Berlin. Of all the many pupils of Liszt, he was the favorite and enjoyed a continuing relationship that went far beyond that of mere teacher and pupil. "I love him like my son, and I look upon myself as his father, and as it is today it will be in ten years," Liszt said.[15]

Bülow showed a warmth and understanding toward Cosima and Blandine from the start and in spite of his veneration for Liszt he could not refrain from reproaching him for his neglect of the girls. "Your daughters are sad that you pay no attention to them," he wrote to him in Weimar, "but sad with a resignation that is truly Christian. They have been waiting in vain for a week for letters from Paris. They lament their frustrated hopes. I asked them with as concealed as possible a bitterness why they do not complain at all of the absence of direct news from their father. Mlle Cosima replied that she never complained of that from which she suffered the most." [16]

It is not difficult to see why Cosima was drawn to this sympathetic young man. He was cultivated and talented, an aristocrat with sensitive feelings. He had an idealistic nature that strove for the highest in art. Through him, Cosima felt a part of the world of music and of her father's life and work. No longer was she the isolated stepchild, kept on starvation rations. Through Bülow she could take her place in her father's world and perhaps even contribute something to his cause. Bülow's admiration of her and her abilities was pleasant to a young girl who had received so little praise in her life.

Strangely, Bülow, reckless and opinionated as he was, was subject often to moods of great self-doubt and depression. "I am always in extremes," he wrote his mother, "at one time tremendously courageous, at another endlessly apathetic and dejected." [17] Bülow sometimes felt that Cosima had qualities of such obvious superiority that he wondered how he could be interesting to her. Cosima's strength and determination, the self-discipline that her early life had developed in her represented a source of stability to Bülow. Most of all, perhaps, she was the "Erlkönig's daughter" someone who, in bearing Liszt's name towered above all other women and evidenced many characteristics that were a true mirror of Listz's personality.

In her sheltered and arid life, Cosima had never before had the constant companionship of a young man, and the relationship between her and Bülow moved rapidly. It was only six weeks after her arrival in Berlin that Bülow conducted a concert at which he performed Wagner's *Tannhäuser* overture. It was a terrible shock to Bülow's hopes in his struggle to further Wagner's cause when the overture was received with boos and hisses. The violence of his reaction and the sensitivity of his nature are shown by the fact that he fainted dead away after the performance. Liszt, with a group of other artists, took the young conductor out later, and tried to console him for the debacle. Cosima and Blandine, accompanied as usual by Madame von Bülow, went straight home where Cosima announced her intention of staying up until Bülow arrived, no matter how late it was. The others went to bed, but Cosima waited until two in the morning when Liszt, without coming in himself, delivered Bülow home. The emotion and stress of the evening broke down all barriers, and the two young people declared their love openly. Many years later Cosima remembered that evening and thought of the words of Othello: "She loved me for the dangers I had passed / And I loved her that she did pity them." [18]

Liszt, of course, was informed at once. Although he was not opposed, nevertheless he felt that Cosima was too young and that the pair had known each other too brief a time for any decision on their marriage to be possible at that moment. Liszt had once expressed himself against musicians as husbands for his daughters, although he admitted there might be exceptions to this reservation.

Six months later, Bülow wrote, formally asking for Cosima's hand. It was an extraordinary letter in which his admiration for Cosima and his own modesty are clearly apparent. He assured Liszt that he had done nothing to raise himself in Cosima's eyes or to bind her to himself; he had given her full freedom to change her mind, but she had not done so. He swore to Liszt that, although he himself felt completely bound to Cosima by his love, if she should ever change her mind about him, he would set her free.

Liszt still hesitated to give final permission although he wrote to his mother that he was determined to leave his daughters "entirely free" in their choice of husbands. That wise old grandmother had not been at all surprised at the news of the proposed marriage. Knowing only too well the deprivations that Cosima had been through, she realized that the daily companionship with a young man, who was also her teacher, could easily lead to friendship and through that to love. She found it not a brilliant marriage, but felt that often marriages which do not appear brilliant are the happiest. She knew Bülow to be intelligent, for which she was glad, and she was confident that he would make his way in life successfully. Her letters to Cosima were full of encouragement and affection as always.

Marie d'Agoult was not so sanguine about the idea of a marriage between Cosima and Hans von Bülow. In spite of the disagreements that had occurred, she continued to write to the girls often, sending them dresses and books and all sorts of small gifts. She was troubled about Cosima's engagement. The girls urged her to come to Berlin and to judge the situation for herself. Instead, she sent her oldest daughter, Claire de Charnacé. Cosima was not at all pleased by what she considered this unwarranted interference. She insisted that she would discuss the whole affair only directly with her mother and not through anyone else.

Bülow, in the meantime, had long since moved to another apartment while Cosima and Blandine remained under the ever-nervous eye of Madame von Bülow. Life with that peculiar lady could hardly have been easy, but Cosima's mischievous sense of humor could always find something to laugh about. They called her "Lady Perhaps," probably because that was the answer she gave to so many of their requests. Madame von Bülow remained the overanxious, overprotective, and domineering mother, and Cosima gives a hilarious picture of her in a letter to Princess Marie which was faithfully sent on to the Altenburg and must have caused quite a sensation there, especially in view of Liszt's complacent opinion that there was "the most perfect union" between Cosima and Madame von Bülow.

"I promised to send you the account of a pathetic, moving, touching and sympathetic scene, in a word, our return to Berlin . . . I must tell you that an hour and a half before our arrival, Lady Perhaps began to groan: 'Oh my God! Pooooor Henns. He will be ill. That article and that fire-spouter will kill him.' " (An article had appeared in the humorous magazine *Kladderadatsch* with a caricature of Liszt and Bülow as Don Quixote and Sancho Panza.) " 'And what a dishonor for him to appear in *Klaaderadatsch!* With his name and his talent! I will never console myself!' 'But, Madame,' I answered her, 'my father is there too!' 'Oh, your father, that is something else!' Followed a series of monologues in this style. Harassed, I beseeched God to shorten the trip. Here at last the whistle of the engine that announces the capital, the train stops, and we get off. Lady Perhaps gets off and approaching a cab, cries to the coachman that her son being at death's door, she had the right to the first carriage. But coachmen are beings without heart who do not stop for inner feelings and take care of first arrivals without considerations of name, or rank, of illness or of motherhood. After having run about for five minutes like a poisoned rat, she suddenly saw her son and almost fell over backwards with surprise. 'Good evening, Mama,' said Hans. 'My son, my dear son (all this before embracing him of course), are you not then ill? I thought you would be in bed. Oh! that Wagner!! . . . 'Why should I be ill?' 'But, that article . . . Everyone in Leipzig is laughing about it . . . Ah! your poor aunt, and Livie . . . Ah! my God, my God!' . . . Then, remembering that she has not seen him for ten days, she throws herself on his neck, winding her little self like a serpent around him. Hans, already completely morose from this sympathetic reception, turns to us and welcomes us to Berlin." And Cosima adds pointedly: "I have not yet made my *'epousailles'* with Hans' mother! I would like to be able to fling my ring like the doge, but am waiting for an occasion where I can 'make an occasion.' " [19]

Madame von Bülow had gradually resigned herself to her son's choice of a musical career. From her initial position of total hostility, she had come to recognize what she called his "transcendent talent." Nevertheless, she found it impossible to accept the fact that a 'von,' a baron, would give lessons for money. She continued to loathe Wagner and to resent her son's espousal of his cause. "If only he becomes reasonable at last!" she wrote to her daughter. "He won't take any advice from me." [20]

It was especially the things in which Cosima and Bülow believed ardently that Madame von Bülow was against. The overbearing mother hardly took kindly to her prospective daughter-in-law, and Cosima felt her own nature very much hemmed in by that domineering woman. As always, she found resources within her own nature, most of all in music. "My only salvation is to become a great artist!" she wrote. [21] Bülow was not at all against a career as pianist for Cosima, in fact he favored it, as did also Marie d'Agoult. Liszt, however, was unalterably opposed.

The engagement dragged on, with no firm date set yet for the marriage. The summer of 1856 saw the girls once more in Paris, where they were warmly welcomed by their grandmother. Marie d'Agoult too was overjoyed to see her daughters and hoped to spend a great deal of time with them. Needless to say, the subject of Cosima's engagement was discussed heatedly. Her mother asked Blandine whether Cosima really loved Bülow and was assured that she did. Marie then stated that she could not forgive Cosima for having acted without her consent. She declared the proposed marriage to be absurd and she took Cosima with her for four days to the country so that they could discuss the whole situation without interruption. Cosima listened to all her mother had to say but was immovable in her decision to marry Bülow, not because she was obstinate, she stated, but because she loved him.

Whether Marie openly voiced her ideas on marriage or not, Cosima could not have helped sensing them and, with her passionate heart, could hardly have felt in sympathy with them. Women, Marie thought, should learn to live through and by themselves alone. Most of all, they must learn to love men as they deserve to be loved, "very little and with perfect selfishness." [22] She admitted that this was not a sublimely moral point of view but an eminently practical one. No matter what arguments her mother presented, however, Cosima was completely unmoved and it was Marie d'Agoult who finally gave in saying that nothing would make her break with her daughter even if she were opposed to what Cosima did.

It was proposed that Blandine remain in Paris and not return to Berlin. Cosima had already made clear that her heart was in Berlin and that she would go there as planned in September. The idea of a separation was a sad one for these two sisters who were so close and who had never been separated before, and they appealed to their father for advice. But Blandine felt infinitely more at home in Paris, and so, with Liszt's consent, the decision was taken that Blandine would remain there while Cosima went back to Berlin and her new life.

Before they parted they wrote a letter together to Liszt. "Before separating, Cosimette and I want to join our voices and send you the expression of our souls intertwined for a last time; we call for your blessing on our heads and we ask you to keep your love for us who have no joys except in your joys, hopes except in you, happiness except through you. No matter what comes, whether we live tranquilly or whether we will be put to the test, it is always to you that we will lift our eyes, it is to you that we will call to strengthen us in the good through your example, to encourage us with your sainted and adored voice!" [23] Liszt still remained for them both the father whom they idolized.

Another winter was to pass before Liszt finally agreed that Cosima was ready for marriage and that the nearly two years of their engagement had sufficiently tested the feelings of the two young people for each other. After further postponements to allow for Bülow's necessary naturalization as a Prussian, the date was finally fixed. Not, however, without Liszt making sure that the Princess had no objection.

The marriage took place on August 18, 1857, at the Hedwigskirche in Berlin. Although Bülow was a Protestant, he did not want the ceremony repeated in the Lutheran Church, as he said he felt a higher regard for the Catholic ceremony, which considered marriage as a sacrament. Liszt was the only member of Cosima's family who was present. Three days before the wedding, Bülow wrote his father-in-law to be. "It is impossible for me to express to you fully the feelings of gratitude and devotion which I have in thinking of the further happiness that I will owe you, as I already owe all the happiness that has come to me in my life which I date from Weimar." And he tactfully asks to be allowed to present his respects to the Princess to whom he is also grateful for the happiness of his life, since it was she who had the idea to bring Liszt's daughters to Berlin, where I found "that angel of heart and mind who is named Cosima." [24]

Cosima, like many a bride before and since, "wept twelve hours long the night before my marriage . . . It seemed to me that I was going to make a great sacrifice whereas I was only joining my own destiny to a being whom I loved with all my soul and through it I was giving a meaning to my own life!" [25]

CHAPTER VI

COSIMA'S LONG ENGAGEMENT had given her an insight into the needs and character of her husband, and she was well aware of the problems presented by his nervous, irascible temperament and his moods of depression and self-doubt. The difficult and often painful years of childhood and early youth were over, but they had left an indelible imprint on her character and personality. She had learned to put up with hardships without complaint and not to let circumstances deflect her from her purpose.

Her love for her father, which for so long had fed on dreams, remained as strong as ever and she was happy at the affection and pride in her that he began to demonstrate more openly. Liszt admitted to his mother at the time of Cosima's marriage that she had always been his favorite and he spoke of his pleasure in the progress she had made in bearing and intellectual distinction. She had been "so sickly, so ailing in her childhood that I favored her over her sister," he once wrote, "and I believe that basically I have preserved a special weakness for her." [1] He was pleased and surprised to find that, as a young married woman, she was becoming "completely sensible, alert and even practical." [2]

Marie d'Agoult looked a little more deeply into her youngest daughter's nature. "Cosima is a girl of genius," she wrote, "very like her father. Her powerful imagination will lead her away from the beaten path; she has an inner demon to which she will resolutely sacrifice everything." [3] She felt that Cosima was a most unusual personality with a great deal of talent, someone "who could please or displease greatly according to the hour or the day." [4] Marie sensed a kind of duality in this "child of passion and liberty. There is both goodness and grandeur in her. She is often lacking in judgment but that will develop, perhaps even too much, alas, with the sorrowful experiences of life." [5] Marie remained concerned about Cosima's marriage in which, she feared, there would be happiness for no one.

The honeymoon plans were to take the young couple to Switzerland. For months before Bülow's marriage, Wagner had been urging him to come to Zurich for a visit—married or unmarried, with Cosima or without her. He felt exiled and bitterly lonely in Switzerland and he longed for the companionship and understanding of his friends. When Wagner wanted to be persuasive he could be very persuasive indeed. Bülow too was eager to see his friend and to show off his young wife. As Blandine and her mother were also in Switzerland, Cosima looked forward eagerly to a reunion with them. So the newlyweds set off, by way of Baden Baden, for Geneva.

Cosima was disappointed to find that her mother and Blandine had already left Geneva for Italy. But Blandine too was in love now and was soon to be married to a young French lawyer, Émile Ollivier. Wagner, however, was awaiting the young couple impatiently and so, after spending a few days on the lake of Geneva with Bülow's old friend Karl Ritter and his wife, the young couple journeyed to Zurich.

There they found Wagner, and his wife Minna, in the small house he called the Asyl—a charming house situated on the estate of the Wesendoncks in a suburb of Zurich. Otto Wesendonck was a successful silk merchant whose generosity toward Wagner had shown itself in the financial help he gave the composer not only for his musical plans but also for his personal expenses, all done with enormous tact and understanding. Much as Wagner profited from Otto Wesendonck's friendship and open purse strings, it was Mathilde Wesendonck who furnished the prime attraction for the composer. Fifteen years younger than he, cultivated, emotional, totally swept up in Wagner's ideas and music, she was, as she described herself later, a blank page for him to write on.

Whether Wagner created *Tristan and Isolde* because he was in love with Mathilde Wesendonck, or whether he was in love with her because his mind and heart were stirring with that passionate love drama, is a debatable point. In any event, it was an emotionally surcharged atmosphere that Cosima and Hans found when they arrived in Zurich. The Wesendoncks had just moved into their large new villa, only a stone's throw from Wagner's Asyl where he and Minna had been living since the end of April.

One of their trunks, the one in which Bülow had placed all their money, was lost and then found. And then Hans was stricken with one of his painful attacks of rheumatism which kept him in bed for several days. Wagner was distressed at his friend's illness and as soon as he was recovered enough, carried him off to the Asyl where the young couple stayed for several weeks.

"We spent the month of September together most pleasantly," Wagner wrote. "In the meanwhile I completed the libretto of

Tristan and Isolde, and at the same time Hans made me a fair copy of each act . . . At last I was able to get them all together for a private reading, which made a deep impression on the few intimate friends who composed the audience. As Frau Wesendonck appeared to be particularly moved by the last act, I said consolingly that one ought not to grieve over it, as, under any circumstances, in a matter so grave things generally turn out in this way, and Cosima heartily agreed. We also had a good deal of music together, as in Bülow I had at last found the right man to play Klindworth's atrocious arrangement of my *Nibelungen* scores. But the two acts of *Siegfried,* which had only been written down as rough drafts, were mastered by Hans with such consummate skill that he could play them as if they had really been arranged for the piano. As usual, I took all the singing parts . . . Cosima listened silently with her head bowed; if pressed for an expression of opinion, she began to cry." [6]

Although Cosima was silent and shy, her agile brain was busy observing and judging all that she saw and heard. She noted in her husband the joyous mood that the presence of Wagner created in him and recognized the near idolatry that it represented. "I can think of nothing which can more bring me such a sense of blessing and refreshment as to be with this glorious, unique man, whom one must venerate like a god," Bülow wrote during this visit. "All life's miseries melt away in the presence of this Great and Good." [7] And not one word about the new bride!

Although Cosima admired Wagner as an artist and recognized his greatness, she felt a certain reserve about Bülow's utter devotion and selflessness where Wagner was concerned and of which she had ample proof during this honeymoon visit. She had not realized before how all-absorbing was Wagner's personality and how strongly he was the sun to Bülow's moon, lighting and warming and vitalizing the younger man. Much as she believed in Wagner's cause and wanted Bülow to be a part of it, she nevertheless did not want him to sublimate himself too much, to forget his own work and career in his devotion to Wagner. Wagner's readiness to accept, or rather compel any sacrifice from his friends was not lost on her, and she felt a certain resentment in the way that Wagner took for granted that Bülow would always put Wagner's cause ahead of his own.

It was the incessantly demanding aspect of Wagner's character which had affected someone else too: the Princess Sayn-Wittgenstein. For some time now there had been clouds appearing in the relationship between Liszt and Wagner which to some extent can be attributed to the Princess' feelings. She was irritated by the endless demands Wagner made upon Liszt—for help, for money, for encouragement, for advice, for literally everything. In addition to this, she was fearful lest Wagner's growing prominence overshadow that of *Le Grand,* as she called Liszt, and she was clearly jealous in this regard.

Wagner worried about Liszt and was growing ever more critical of the way he lived. Wagner could not understand a man who went constantly into society, was perpetually busy and surrounded by people, not the least by adoring women whom, in spite of his permanent liaison with the autocratic Princess, or perhaps in part because of it, the *Zigeuner* in Liszt was never able to resist. Wagner had written Bülow not long before this visit, and Cosima could hardly have remained unaware of the letter, criticizing Liszt's way of life in very strong terms. He did not moralize, but he pointed out the danger that this restless *perpetuum mobile* was to Liszt's health and to the man himself. He felt strongly that if Liszt did not withdraw from all excitement and effort he would soon be absolutely destroyed. In his usual forthright way, Wagner wrote all this not only to Bülow and to Liszt himself, but to the Princess, with the inevitable result that that good lady was even more irritated with him. At the time of Cosima's honeymoon visit to Zurich, there was a distinct coldness between Liszt and Wagner. It is true that Wagner's criticism of Liszt was meant for Liszt's own good, nevertheless it must have been somewhat painful for Cosima, who still saw her father through eyes unable to criticize or to accept criticism.

There was a third factor which played a role in Cosima's initial reaction to Wagner. He was a man with few inhibitions, a man who said what he thought and who could often be not only violently opinionated, but rather earthy and coarse. Cosima, with her discriminating Parisian background, was sometimes shocked by Wagner's too easy familiarity.

Wagner was aware that Cosima's reaction toward himself was not what he had hoped for, in spite of the fact that he was delighted with her and more than pleased that his favorite Hans had found such a remarkable wife. Wagner was a man who needed approbation. His concern at Cosima's diffidence continued to trouble him even in his correspondence with them after the young couple had left, and he finally wrote to Bülow seeking to understand and explain Cosima's feelings. "But first I must nevertheless still tell you that Cosima's reserve toward me really grieves me, since I believe that I can be sure . . . that she really feels embarrassed in my presence. Should my manner seem strange to her, should here or there a blunt expression, a little scorn have wounded her I would truly regret that I let myself go too far in my familiarity, something which I perceive and regret from my heart each time when I alienate from myself sincerely worthy people in this way. It is a matter, I well know, certainly only of a mistake. My whole inconsiderate familiarity toward people I am fond of has already resulted in many estrangements. May the estrangement of your dear young wife not be of long duration!" [8]

Cosima, who had long since learned to conceal her feelings,

did not let on to her husband how she felt about Wagner, and he attributed her reserve to what he considered very natural feelings of awe before such a genius. He was too much under the impress of Wagner's magic personality to dream that his young wife could have other feelings for the composer than he himself had.

Cosima was full of plans and hopes for the future, most of which centered on her husband's work and career. The first thing she wanted was to establish a home and a way of life that would enable Bülow to pursue his own work, to develop his own gifts to the fullest, and to realize his potential not only as pianist and conductor, but as a composer.

Bülow, with his restless nature, with his fiery temperament and generous disposition, was disseminating his efforts in too many directions, leaving very little time for composing. His many activities in regard to the Music of the Future, the cause of his two idols, Wagner and Liszt, the concerts he organized and directed, and the battery of articles and letters he was always writing—all this took a great deal of energy. Besides, he had his classes at the Conservatory, piano lessons which he found irritating and time consuming, but necessary nevertheless in order to earn a living. Financial problems seem not to have been clarified at the start between the young pair, for later Cosima spoke of having sold her watch those early months of her marriage because she was afraid to ask Hans for money; and he once suggested that the dowry she had brought from her father and mother represented, to a man who was proud and sensitive about the fact that he was poor, the first stumbling block in their marriage.

Cosima helped him rearrange his schedule so that he could devote mornings to his own work, and she created an ordered, peaceful, and harmonious atmosphere with the least possible external pressures.

Bülow had long wanted to compose and here again both Liszt and Wagner had encouraged him, assuring him that he possessed unusual gifts. Liszt had arranged performances of several of his compositions at Weimar, which had been well received. None of these were major works, however, and it was Wagner who constantly urged Bülow to attempt a large-scale work—an opera or a symphony. He suggested a symphony on the theme of the Greek tragedies, an idea about which Cosima was enthusiastic, so enthusiastic that she made a long synopsis of the *Oresteia,* which she gave to Hans. There is a strange parallelism between Cosima's interest in Hans' creative work and her mother's similar feelings about Liszt. Cosima herself even took lessons in composition, not with the idea of becoming a composer, but in order to deepen her understanding of music in general and the works of her father and her husband in particular.

The young couple plunged into the social and artistic life of Berlin. There had been a good deal of publicity in the papers at the time of their marriage, and everyone was interested in the young bride, this French daughter of the famous Liszt. The acid later comments of the Princess Marie are rather amusing here. She described Cosima as "an excellent housewife, efficient in every department, putting up cheerfully with her husband's morbid moods and his perpetual peevishness. Not that the fairies had endowed her in her cradle with mildness and gentleness. On the contrary, through her lofty self-confidence and her inborn sharpness she offended most women and many German men of her acquaintance, who complained that she was unfeminine." [9]

Du Moulin Eckart, however, gives quite a different picture of Cosima's position in the early Berlin years of her marriage. "This Parisian now adapted herself to Berlin conditions in an absolutely brilliant fashion and, through her French education, succeeded in securing for her husband a position of his own in a world which was far from insignificant . . . It is attractive to follow these first beginnings, and the charm is greatly enhanced by the fact that soon absolutely everything was at her feet." He says that she was a "pattern for all women, combining in herself all the good German qualities." In short he describes her as a "social star in the firmament of Berlin," a figure of "universal fascination." [10]

There is some truth, perhaps, in both pictures of Cosima, exaggerated as they are, especially if we remember Marie d'Agoult's words about her daughter as someone who could "please or displease greatly according to the hour or the day." There is one thing about Cosima that was clear even then, she was not someone to whom people were indifferent.

Madame von Bülow remained a difficult individual and often sorely tried the patience of her new daughter-in-law. Cosima described her once as someone who could find a source of worry even in a subject of consolation. Bülow was accustomed to her constant scenes and reproaches, which experience had taught him to take with at least a show of calm. Cosima, however, found her many moods difficult, to say the least. "She is becoming sentimental and tender," she wrote Princess Marie, "which is almost as disagreeable as when she is sour and furious. There are really people for whom curses are more natural than caresses." [11] For the moment Madame von Bülow was living in Leipzig with her daughter and so at least her presence was not a continual one. In spite of Cosima's feelings about her mother-in-law, however, she always maintained toward her a correctness of manner which she believed she owed to the mother of her husband.

The winter passed rapidly in a welter of new impressions and new freedoms. Cosima was trying her wings in many directions and gained in skill and assurance every day.

Blandine and her husband came for a brief stay, and Émile

Ollivier was understanding enough to leave his wife with Cosima for a short while after he had to return to Paris. The two girls found that time and marriage had done nothing to alter their affection for each other. Cosima felt that "an angel" had visited her who made everything radiant with happiness. Liszt too came to see the young couple from time to time and his visits were the occasion for soirées to which Cosima invited the elite of Berlin artistic circles. She was in seventh heaven when her father was present and enjoyed enormously his obvious pride in her.

Although Cosima had not seen her mother since her marriage, she was in constant touch with her by letter. Marie d'Agoult, whose ideas of marriage in general and Cosima's in particular we know, urged Cosima to try some literary work of her own. Cosima set to with a will. Her first attempts consisted of translations and adaptations from German into French of various literary pieces for the *Review Germanique* in Paris. Cosima's excursion into professional writing caused her a certain amount of distress at first. She resented certain criticisms and suggestions that her mother made concerning the work and she found the changes made by the publisher in her manuscript simply silly. However, she took her literary work quite seriously and had her own little study in the apartment. Hans was pleased and encouraging about her efforts.

In the meantime, the news from Wagner grew more and more disturbing. The work with *Tristan* had progressed rapidly and by the end of the year the sketch of the first act was complete. He asked Bülow to do the piano arrangement, an intensely interesting but nevertheless time consuming and difficult task which was to cost Hans an enormous amount of effort. But Wagner's personal and financial affairs were once again in a state of crisis. The triangle, or rather quadrangle with the Wesendoncks had grown more and more tense. Wagner began to resent Otto Wesendonck's eternal presence and he longed for more time alone with his Mathilde.

Minna Wagner was a simple, pathetic, unimaginative woman whose youthful charms had long since begun to fade. Her little world and Wagner's touched only in the most rudimentary way, and she was never able to understand or even to recognize the existence of the soaring reaches within him. Her stormy marriage with this genius, who was four years younger than she, had taken its toll of her health and disposition. Wagner grew oppressively stifled and felt he must get away from his Asyl at any cost. He was, however, once again without funds and as usual he wrote Liszt frenzied letters begging for help.

Cosima's reaction was rather dry and she wrote about Wagner's position and Mathilde Wesendonck somewhat caustically to Princess Marie: "I reached the conclusion that the famous bankruptcy of Wagner is happily covered by this modern Beatrice who opens for her poet the heavens of material tranquillity and free and easy luxury, the only heavens in which he believes, perhaps. But I grow mean and will stop." [12]

Liszt rushed as always to his friend's assistance, and in January Wagner left for a brief trip to Paris where he saw a great deal of Blandine and Émile Ollivier and took great pleasure in their company.

The month's trip to Paris did not result in any miracles, however, and when Wagner returned to Zurich the situation was exactly as he had left it. He plunged at once into work on *Tristan* and by April had completed the full orchestral score of the first act.

Wagner tried desperately to maintain his balance between his poetical, mystical passion for Mathilde Wesendonck and his homely relationship with his wife, Minna, whose frightful jealousy had by now reached alarming proportions. Cosima and Bülow kept abreast of everything, not only through letters from

Wagner himself but from numerous other friends. Cosima's reaction continued rather cold toward Wagner, though she began to show a deeper understanding of him than heretofore. Her condemnation of Mathilde Wesendonck was uncompromising. "The situation of Richard, our very illustrious friend, afflicts me and surprises me to a certain degree. Although I have been informed of the sad scenes that have broken out between husband and wife, I did not believe that things would come to this point, and I see only sadness and prose in these conflicts about a love born of boredom, of vanity and of a need for money! Like you, I pity Madame Minna without being able to blame Richard who, consumed little by little by the need of the ideal and of rest at the same time, tired of the monotonous and incessant annoyances of his life, asked for a little happiness from a pale and weak nature, who is as incapable of living strongly a simple and upright existence as to break with her previous obligations in order to abandon herself to love and to the support of her lover." [13]

Bülow felt acutely the misery of Wagner's position and his need for the support and help of his friends. Wagner was devoted to Bülow in an extraordinary way. "You are so very right for me, and your fate lies as close to me as though it were my own. Keep well and take special care of yourself so that you remain healthy and steadfast for me." [14] As soon as the summer holidays made it possible, Bülow rushed to Zurich to be near and to help his troubled friend.

Hans and Cosima arrived a few days before Wagner's return from Brestenberg, where he had gone to bring his wife, who had been taking a cure there. Marie d'Agoult had come to Zurich and Bülow was enormously impressed with her beauty, her bearing, her intelligence, her taste—in short, Marie d'Agoult charmed her son-in-law totally at this first meeting and he could not help comparing her to Liszt's present companion, that caricature of a woman, as he termed her, who ruled the Altenburg and Liszt too. Cosima, as always, admired the skill with which her mother quickly surrounded herself with the most interesting people in Zurich, and the striking impression she made wherever she went. For her part, Marie was intensely interested to make the acquaintance of the son-in-law about whom she had such doubts.

As soon as Wagner arrived back at the Asyl, Bülow went to see him and, as chance would have it, arrived in the middle of a frightful scene between husband and wife. Shocked and distressed by what he had witnessed, Hans would have been ready to leave Zurich at once had it not been for the presence of Marie d'Agoult. The next day he received a note from Wagner regretting and explaining the circumstances of the quarrel and telling Bülow that their visit to him was heaven sent. But the scene had been set, and the moods remained tense and gloomy.

The whole sordid mess made a terrible impression on Cosima. She felt sorry for Minna; was coldly critical of Mathilde Wesendonck. But gradually, through the month that they were there, observing all the tension and conflict at first hand, a feeling began to grow more and more strongly in her, a sense of pity, of understanding and protectiveness toward Wagner and a plague on both your houses toward the two women who seemed to be tearing him to shreds between them. Cosima recognized more clearly than ever the genius of the artist and his desperate need for the peace and quiet to pursue his work. She saw the danger that life was for him, drawing him again and again to the very edge of destruction and she understood what her father had meant when he said that the only way was to accept Wagner as he was, to love him and try to help him as much as possible. Liszt, however, did not come to Zurich, much as Wagner had hoped for his presence. The Princess had done her work too well and the two friends no longer felt the old freedom in their relationship that had existed before.

Hans was deeply disturbed by Wagner's troubles and at his obvious distraught mood and was determined to stay by his friend's side until some resolution of the intolerable situation could be found.

It was during the month of July 1858 that Cosima became involved in a curious situation that might have been sparked to some extent by the cross currents of strain that surrounded her. When her mother was ready to leave Zurich, Cosima decided to go with her as far as Geneva. Karl Ritter, recently separated from his wife, had also been staying at the Asyl, and he offered to accompany them. It was in Geneva that a strange emotional scene between Cosima and Ritter took place. There is only a little information on the incident contained in a letter of Wagner to Mathilde Wesendonck in which he briefly outlines the following facts as told to him by Karl Ritter. One day at Geneva, Cosima suddenly became very agitated, nearly hysterical, and she begged Ritter to kill her. When he refused she threatened to throw herself in the lake and drown herself and was only dissuaded when Ritter swore that he would do the same if she carried out her threat. They parted in a state of mutual confusion and distress having decided to let three weeks pass and then to communicate how they felt and what they would do next.

Was Cosima in love with Ritter, as some people tried to make out, and even responsible for the break-up of his marriage, as Minna declared? It is more than dubious. Certainly Cosima was in a state of high agitation. The whole Minna-Wagner-Mathilde mess plus Ritter's separation, about which he undoubtedly poured out his heart to Cosima, was not conducive to a calm emotional state. Her own first year of marriage had not been easy, and as she admitted many years later, she had often thought of suicide during those months. Hans' nervous attacks, his explosive temper, his recurring self-doubt left her bewildered and frustrated. Most of all, she felt that Hans cut her off, kept her at a distance, so that often she did not know how to talk to him and she doubted her ability to make him happy. She did not feel the inner closeness with him, the uninhibited rapport that were so essential to a nature as highly geared as hers, capable of such intensity of feeling. "In the very first year of my marriage I was in such despair at our misunderstandings that I wanted to die," she wrote years later.[15]

Then, too, there was Wagner. Whether she recognized the emotions that were growing in her toward him for what they were or not, there is no doubt that already at this period the attraction was stirring between them. "I ought to have taken you with me to Venice that time in Zurich," Wagner told her long afterward. "Why did you not say to me in 1858, 'I will live for no one but you?' Then I would have known what to do." [16]

When Cosima returned from Geneva, Wagner was surprised at Cosima's "strangely excited state, which showed itself especially in convulsively passionate tenderness toward me. At our parting the next day she fell at my feet, and covered my hands with tears and kisses: astonished and alarmed, I gazed into this mystery without being able to find the key to it." [17]

Cosima's reactions were not so mysterious after all. Frustrated in the ardent stirrings of her heart, wanting desperately to love and be loved with totality and abandon, in love with love actually, she was in a state of extreme susceptibility to strong emotional appeal. The brief, abortive Ritter episode was an explosion of the volcano within Cosima's heart, aimless but indicative of the degree of frustrated passion within her. It is at just that moment that a woman is most vulnerable emotionally and can be led into situations and relationships that normally would be quite impossible for her. That Cosima flung herself at Wagner's feet in the over-wrought way that she did was an indication of the emotional strength he represented for her and of her need for it.

Three weeks later Cosima wrote Ritter telling him that she was ashamed of her impetuosity and begging him to forget the whole incident. Wagner described Ritter as "bitterly offended." It is not surprising that Ritter was confused about Cosima's feelings, when she could not understand them herself. Wagner was deeply troubled for his young friends. He had seen depths in Cosima's nature which were a revelation to him.

The last days of the visit were harrowing. Wagner had realized that life at the Asyl had become impossible. His dream of a "refuge" where he could live in idyllic peace and compose had been shattered and there was no mending it. Minna, half-crazed with jealousy, grew daily more uncontrollable and violent under the influence of the drugs she hoped would relieve her insomnia. Wagner, driven by the necessity to create, knew that he must find peace somewhere in order to bring *Tristan* to completion. The decision was a sad but necessary one: Minna would go to Saxony to her relatives where hopefully her health would improve; Wagner would go to Venice where he could work in peace and quiet; the Asyl would be left forever.

Cosima and Hans stayed till the bitter end. At their parting from Wagner, Bülow was in tears, Cosima gloomy and silent. Bülow, obviously blind to everything that had happened, to the subtle change in the feelings of Cosima and Wagner toward each other, was still worried about the impression that his young wife had made and soon after their return to Berlin, he wrote Wagner hastening again to try to explain her.

"My wife is again most amiable. I do wish you could one day get to know her in another way than heretofore at your house. With you her affability has thus far tended to become silent, her open, expansive way to draw back. There is a compliment for you in this, if somewhat ill-placed: 'Awe held her spellbound.' She is always afraid that you will find her childish and all too insignificant to be able to love and understand you. And yet she is one of the very few who are really capable of it." [18]

Wagner, who had seen below the surface of Cosima's behavior during this second long visit, was not concerned any longer about her reserve, or lack of it, toward himself, but about her own inner development, her relationship with her husband and the success of her marriage. He felt that Cosima was the higher nature of the two and that her marriage was not and would not be easy for her. Perhaps he was trying to open Bülow's eyes a little more toward the difficulties his young wife was going through when he wrote him: "Will Cosima indeed soon learn to grasp what misery lies in life and where the only redemption from it is to be found? One day, one hour matures us more than years." [19]

Cosima, however, after the emotional tensions and upheavals of the summer, returned to Berlin with renewed determination to build an interesting life and a satisfying marriage. She continued energetically with her literary work, sending contributions regularly to the *Revue Germanique* in Paris. As a first-rate housekeeper she knew how to create the kind of restful atmosphere that helped relieve some of the stress that so affected her high-strung husband. And she was more convinced than ever that he must have the chance to develop his creative talents and not be swamped by day to day work and cares, lessons, concerts, and too much selfless devotion to the Music of the Future.

For years, Bülow had been interested in the Merlin legend and had discussed with Wagner and Liszt the idea of using it for the subject of an opera. He had tried several times to find someone to prepare a libretto for him but nothing had come of it. It was Cosima who decided to surprise her husband for the second Christmas of their marriage with the libretto he had wanted for so long. She chose an amazing person to help her, none other than Ernst Dohm, editor of the humorous magazine *Kladderadatsch*. Bülow was in seventh heaven over the surprise and wrote to Liszt that it was a "jewel of a libretto." He was full of hopes of being able to send his father-in-law the completed first act within a few months.

But Bülow was busier than ever with constant appearances both as pianist and conductor, with lessons, and also with the piano arrangement of *Tristan*. Although he found this work full of "infernal, head-breaking difficulties," he was completely swept off his feet by the power and originality of the score. He often despaired of realizing its vast complexities for the keyboard and the work absorbed him to the exclusion of his own. "Last month I began and even finished some pieces for piano," he wrote Liszt. "I have about a dozen in mind, but all that is at rest now because of the domination of that *individualitätsregungenmörderischen* (murderous of individual stirrings) *Tristan*. God, how despotic that music is!" [20] In many ways *Tristan* was to prove more despotic for Bülow than he could have imagined and that music, which he described as "pushing the power of expression to its final limits," [21] would run as a *leitmotiv* through his own personal tragedy. Frustrated and dominated by the powerful *Tristan* music, it is small wonder that all Bülow was able to compose were a few piano pieces of his own. The *Merlin* libretto lay on his desk almost as a reproach.

In the early spring of 1859, after a trip to Prague where Hans played, Cosima and he went to Paris, the first time that she had been there since before her marriage. Bülow gave two concerts there during their stay and had an extraordinary success which was very gratifying, especially to Cosima who had not forgotten her mother's opposition to her marriage.

Marie d'Agoult's position vis-à-vis her children had taken another major shift during the period since Cosima's marriage. At first she and Blandine had been very close, and, indeed, it was only she who had been present at Blandine's marriage in Italy to Émile Ollivier. At the time of the marriage she professed great admiration and esteem for that young man. It was soon evident, however, that Ollivier did not return these sentiments. On his return, ahead of Blandine, from his first meeting in Weimar with Liszt, he was shocked by Marie's attitude, by the questions she peppered him with about the Altenburg menage, by what he clearly felt was pressure on him to distort the true picture of Liszt's relationship with the Princess, and finally by her then cult for Cosima which, with her usual exclusiveness, he felt left Blandine out in the cold. Questions and delays concerning the dowry she had promised Blandine did not help matters at all. By the time Cosima arrived in Paris, relations were strained, to say the least, between the young Olliviers and the Maison Rose.

Daniel too, had completely turned away from his mother. He had been again another source of conflict between mother and father. Marie d'Agoult had hoped that the brilliant boy would remain in France and study engineering on the completion of his studies at the Lycée. Liszt, on the other hand, was determined that Daniel should study law in Vienna. The outcome was predictable, although Daniel's hostility toward his mother was not. His letters from Vienna show that he and Blandine were in complete sympathy and unity against Marie d'Agoult and for their father.

Cosima tried to steer a middle course. She maintained her tremendous attachment toward her father, but she wanted to try to be fair toward her mother too. She was far from blind to the difficulties of Marie's nature and to the injustices in her behavior toward her children. Cosima refused to allow herself to be influenced by her mother in anything, least of all in her literary efforts. Indeed, she felt that her mother's attempts to criticize her work simply spoiled the whole undertaking for her. And her sense of humor could not help but mock many of Marie's poses. Nevertheless, she did not fall into total hostility, as did Daniel and Blandine, who separated themselves wholly from this woman who, they accused, had never been a mother to them.

Thus the conflict, the endless pulling and pushing and pressures between father and mother continued to make themselves felt on the three young people. Anna Liszt, however, that devoted grandmother, was her usual warm-hearted, indulgent self. There were no conflicts or tensions there. Émile Ollivier had, as Blandine described it, a real "cult" for the old lady who, on her side, simply adored him. Both Blandine and her husband showered her with care and attention.

Although Blandine was a little hurt that Cosima stayed with her mother and not herself, she and Cosima were far too close to let anything really come between them; Hans was delighted and impressed with Marie d'Agoult; Grandmother Liszt was adorable to everyone, and Hans had a resounding musical success which put him in very fine fettle.

CHAPTER VII

THE AUTUMN OF 1859 brought tragedy at first hand into the lives of Cosima and Hans. It was toward the end of August that Daniel arrived in Berlin to spend his vacation from his law studies in Vienna with his sister and her husband. Cosima was shocked to see how badly he looked—pale and with a persistent cough that worried her greatly. She and Hans hoped that he would soon improve under the tender care which Cosima planned to lavish on him. There was an affectionate bond between Daniel and his brother-in-law which was a delight to Cosima. Each enjoyed the other's company, ideas, and conversation, and Hans shared completely Cosima's concern for her brother.

Instead of the hoped-for improvement, however, Daniel continued to look badly and soon after his arrival fell seriously ill with consumption. Hans arranged to practice and do his work outside the house in order not to disturb the invalid, and Cosima dropped all her activities and devoted herself to caring for her young brother. Bülow spent every minute that he could spare

Cosima, Blandine and Daniel Liszt in 1855. The three children of Liszt and the Countess d'Agoult after a drawing by Frédéric Preller.

Young Franz Liszt from a portrait by Ary Scheffer.

Marie d'Agoult, Cosima's mother, after a painting at *Wahnfried*.

Franz Liszt at the piano with admirers including, seated from left, Dumas *père* and George Sand; standing, Victor Hugo, Paganini and Rossini; and, right, the Countess d'Agoult.

Cosima in her youth.

Hans von Bülow.

A cartoon showing Wagner, Cosima and Bülow. Caption reads: "In the Maximilian Strasse after the *Tristan and Isolde* rehearsal. Drawn from life 1864. M. Schultze."

Wagner's house in Triebschen at Lucerne (1866-1872).

The Bettmann Archive

Richard and Cosima Wagner at the time of their stay in Triebschen.

Cosima in 1878, the year of her visit to Triebschen.

The Bettmann Archive

The Bettmann Archive

King Ludwig II of Bavaria.

Richard Wagner.

The Bettmann Archive

Wagner in his family circle. Upper row (left to right), Wagner's daughter Isolde, Freiherr von Stein, Cosima and Richard Wagner, stage painter Joukowsky. Lower row: daughters Blandine, Daniela, Eva, and son Siegfried.

Wagner's house, *Wahnfried*, in Bayreuth.

Cartoon of Richard Wagner by André Gill.

Statue of Nietzsche by Max Klein.

Franz Liszt and his pupil Alexander Siloti with whom the author studied.

Cosima in old age. Photograph by Adolf von Gross.

with the boy, talking to him, encouraging him, and doing everything he could to lighten the burden of the illness, which grew more serious day by day. Daniel could scarcely bear to let Cosima out of his sight, and she expended every ounce of energy, of optimism, and of intelligence that she had fighting the disease step by step, as if she could hold death at bay by her own love and will. Inexorably, the malady progressed, and the three, Cosima, Hans, and Liszt, drew closer together than ever in their concern. Cosima did everything she could not only to keep from Daniel himself the gravity of his illness, but to spare her grandmother and sister as much of the burden she was carrying as she could. It was in mid-December that the Princess sent Liszt once again to Berlin to see his son. Two days later, December thirteenth, Daniel died. "He nestled into the arms of death as into those of a guardian angel, as though he had long awaited it," Cosima wrote her grandmother. "He did not strive against it: he was not weary of life, but he had longed with a burning heart for eternity." [1]

Bülow was inconsolable at the loss of this young man to whom he was so deeply devoted, and he treasured Daniel's memory as long as he lived. Blandine was grief stricken but her solicitude for her grandmother, her concern for Cosima and her father, helped to give her strength to accept the loss of her dearly loved brother.

Cosima, emotionally and physically exhausted, found little solace. "Sometimes I feel that my heart will burst or that my poor mind will be reduced to madness; and then I think that he did not love life, that he suffered every moment and that he came only to touch it lightly, so to speak, and to fly to those regions which our hope makes us imagine! Then I feel a kind of consolation and there is a great silence within me." [2] But the new year brought consolation to Cosima and new meaning to her life.

On October 12, 1860, a daughter, Daniela Senta, was born, named in memory of her brother and of Wagner's oldest "daughter," as Bülow called the heroine of the *Flying Dutchman.* Cosima was extremely ill and in spite of the strict regime the doctors tried to impose on her, recovered her strength very slowly. The baby was "very nice," she wrote, "not more stupid than is indispensable for her future health, not more like a monkey than is necessary for her future beauty, and not more of a bawler than is necessary for the development of her lungs." [3] Cosima did not add here her concern over the fact that little Daniela had eyes of a different color—one blue and one brown. Cosima worried that this signified an unstable and changeable character.

By March the improvement in her health was still minimal, and Liszt finally wrote of his concern to Blandine. "I will no longer conceal from you, dear Blandine, that Cosima has given me great anxiety. I received news from Berlin six weeks ago that she showed symptoms of a serious illness of the lungs. Her mother-in-law and sister-in-law have done everything possible to persuade her to take care of her health—but without success." [4] He said that he had finally prevailed upon her to visit him in Weimar where he succeeded in persuading her to see a doctor in whom he had great confidence. The doctor stated that she must undertake a serious cure. Her extreme thinness, the dry, hacking cough which continued for hours at a time and which kept her from sleeping were horribly reminiscent of Daniel's condition and caused the greatest anxiety for her health. Blandine offered to go anywhere with Cosima, to the south of France or wherever her health required.

"One cannot depend on anybody else," Blandine wrote her father. "Bülow is ill himself and although he may worry for a moment, Cosima will answer him that she is fine and he will be reassured. As for Madame von Bülow, the mother, you know as well as I do that she is there *pour la phrase.* Cosima could die in six months if she has only those people about to persuade her to take care of herself. You are the only one who can save her." [5] It was finally decided that Reichenhall in the Bavarian Alps would be the best place, and the early summer of 1861 found Cosima established there.

Blandine and Liszt were not the only ones who recognized that the greatest problem lay in persuading Cosima to take care of herself. Wagner wrote to Bülow that "the worst enemy of Cosima's health is her own temperament. She is from entirely too extraordinary an origin and therefore difficult to care for! . . . It is understood that you must not leave Cosima . . . Greet Cosima affectionately and tell her how fond of her I am and how happy she would make me if I heard that she is being good and sensible." [6]

It is not surprising that Cosima's health came near to breaking at this point. The severe strains, both physical and emotional, of her brother's illness and death followed so quickly by her pregnancy and the birth of Daniela; the fact that she was the support in so many ways of her husband, whose moods of depression seemed only to increase with time; the need, the desire, to boost the spirits even of her father, who was going through troubles and disappointments of his own, all this represented a one-way drain that challenged the strength even of Cosima.

It was all these burdens which prompted the mood in which she wrote: "I do not know whether I am making myself old . . . But I am more and more afraid (for others) of that which is not daily bread, and I wish for my daughter not intellect, nor fervor, nor passion but a humble and tender heart, an upright and firm soul and a sober intelligence." [7]

Throughout these tribulations it was still from Liszt that Cosima received her greatest sustenance. "How right it is," she wrote, to use the word "grandiose for that personality which seems to have been made of love and of inspiration. Every time that I am here [Weimar] it seems to me that I am renewed, and that everything that life brings that is sad, burdensome, and especially all the mud that it deposits on our soul which it deprives of its purity, that all that vanishes and that I have come back to my homeland, to *the place* of my soul. I am consumed with incessant wishes for him; I wish I do not know what of vague, of great, of infinite. What can one wish for him that is positive? Earthly property? His great soul could only disdain it. The kingdom of heaven? But it is his." [8]

Bülow once described himself as a sort of Hamlet, someone who drowns in a sea of trifles, unequal to his task. Perhaps this scorn toward himself explains in part the extreme nervousness of his temperament, the violence of his outbursts of temper which he was unable to control, and the black moods which assailed him and left him exhausted both morally and physically. Bülow's outbursts were so violent that Cosima's doctor was surprised that she could stand them. Cosima, however, recognized that these were nervous manifestations and that they did not represent the truth of Bülow's nature, not that this really made him easier to live with. A friend once summed up Bülow's complexities: "Your great knowledge and lofty and generous nature which arrives at the surface, like gold, only after a great deal of work, the mass of carbonic acid which makes up the diamond in your character, sometimes as hard as a diamond although as polished; this terrible irascibility which is not absolutely necessary with a very nervous temperatment (as proved by Berlioz); the strangest mixture that one could imagine of aristocracy and democratic ideas, all this . . . makes me forgive many words!" [9]

Liszt did all he could to help Bülow, who often turned to him in his Hamlet moods, and to encourage and stimulate him.

"Allow me again, my dear, to beg you not to let yourself go in these moods of migraine. You are most decidedly someone and with something to do in this world. As hard and unbearable as life sometimes is, it is a question of using it well. Continue, therefore, simply to go on as before and to live with what you are. It is good and beautiful to do so—believe me." [10]

Throughout all this, the *Merlin* libretto lay on Bülow's desk. All he had done was to pencil in a few vague sketches. The *Tristan* piano arrangements continued to devour him, and the daily contact with that overpowering music made him more than ever aware of what he felt were his own deficiencies.

Tristan was finished, the full score of all three acts done. Wagner now had the first two operas of the *Ring* and two acts of the third, plus *Tristan* complete and ready for performances which seemed as far away as ever. With no prospects of having any of these works produced, Wagner was in a state of restless depression. He had spent seven months in Venice and then six in Lucerne but now he felt an overpowering drive to hear his works performed, to present them, to establish somehow, somewhere, the possibility of taking his giant scores from the shelves and bringing them to the light of day. Small towns and quiet were what he wanted when he was in the throes of composition, but now he looked again toward a big city where he would find stimulus and interest and, most of all, the chance for producing his works.

With the ban still on in Germany, he decided, with Liszt's advice and in spite of his reserve toward the French, to go once again to Paris where he had hopes of having *Tannhäuser* produced. Now that *Tristan* was finished, the magic that Wagner had found in Mathilde Wesendonck had dissipated. He found his meeting with her melancholy and "felt as though he were passing from one dream to another." [11] Amazingly, he urged his wife, Minna, to join him in Paris, which she did. Her health, however, far from having improved, had deteriorated and soon the old scenes and reproaches began again.

Wagner saw a good deal of Blandine and her husband in Paris, and Blandine was very understanding about what he was going through in regard to his work. "He is in great torment," she wrote to Liszt. "He has got it into his head that the year 1859 must not end without something definite being done for him . . . There is nothing more frightful than to see genius locked in combat with the common obstacles of life. It is the eternal and pathetic story of Gulliver enmeshed in the thousand-and-one little threads of the Lilliputians." [12]

Financially, Wagner was, not surprisingly, in a disastrous position, and the *Tannhäuser* production met with endless delays. Wagner, as always, turned to Liszt for money, and even Bülow, with his limited resources, helped him out. Liszt was slowly getting out of patience with Wagner's ineptitudes in the handling of his finances and, undoubtedly prodded by the Princess, whose dislike of Wagner and jealousy of his stature had reached enormous proportions, he was somewhat embarrassed by his friend's "peculiar talent for managing his affairs badly."

Wagner, on the other hand, pursued his dream with a singleness of purpose that excluded everything else. As far as he was concerned, nothing mattered except his art and the things that he needed in order to create and produce his masterpieces. There was no sacrifice on the part of his friends that he did not think was to be taken for granted. "Good Gracious!" he once wrote Liszt, "such sums as I might *earn* . . . people ought to *give* me, without asking anything in return beyond what I am actually doing, and which is the best that I can do. Besides this, I am much better adapted to spend sixty thousand francs in six months than to 'earn' it. The latter I cannot do at all, for it is not my business to 'earn money' but it is the business of my admirers to give me as much money as I want, to do my work in a cheerful mood." [13]

Liszt's cool counsel, the fact that he did not come to Paris while Wagner was there, added to the hurt and frustration that Wagner was experiencing. The misery reached a climax when *Tannhäuser* was finally produced, after some 163 assorted rehearsals. It was received with shocking displays of brutality. The three performances were so disrupted with hisses, shouts, whistles, fights, and catcalls that the music could scarcely be either heard or performed. Bülow, who had come to Paris to help Wagner in whatever way he could, was still hopeful after the first performance. In the end, even he was utterly despairing. Wagner kept up a brave front after the final performance, although he was mortally tired and discouraged. Only the slight trembling of his hands showed what he was going through. It is at this period of Wagner's life that his eminent biographer, Ernest Newman, describes Bülow's relationship to Wagner: "The only one who never misunderstood him, never complained, and never failed him was Bülow—who happened to be the only one of them all who was making what, for him, were serious sacrifices for Wagner's sake." [14] Bülow, as always, was at Wagner's side sharing his friend's struggles.

On his way back to Berlin, Bülow stopped in Karlsruhe, where he hoped that he could pave the way for a possible performance of *Tristan,* and perhaps even find a place where Wagner could live and work peacefully. The ban on Wagner's entry into Germany had been lifted, at least to the extent that he was no longer forbidden to set foot in the country, and he could come and go without hindrance if the trip concerned performances of his works.

Liszt had not gone to Paris for the *Tannhäuser* production. Indeed it seemed as though for some time he had almost been trying to avoid a meeting with Wagner. The letters flew back and forth between them—Wagner's full of impassioned descriptions of his sorry financial condition and requests for help. Mainly, however, they show a man desperate with the need to be understood, to be accepted and helped, without any attempt to change the unalterable, individual self that was Wagner. Liszt was still the person to whom he turned with the greatest need. "Your friendship is an absolute necessity to me," he wrote, "I cling to it with my last vital strength . . . Have you an idea of the position in which I am, of the miracles of faith and love which I require in order to gain new courage and patience?" [15]

Liszt's letters were more cool in tone, although at times he too bursts into a real effulgence over the genius of Wagner's music. He is full of advice and counsel as to how to proceed in establishing a firm footing. Here is where the two friends split: Wagner could never accept any need to importune or to move cautiously in a situation. He might have taken Descartes' dictum and turned it into "I compose, therefore I am." But Wagner would not have stopped there. Without question he would have added, "It is up to the world to do the rest."

Liszt, who had been brought up in a very different school, was torn between his admiration for the artist and vexation at how difficult Wagner made it to help him. Liszt had too long been pleased and flattered by his acceptance into the highest aristocratic circles not to have been more than shocked at Wagner's tactlessness and total disregard of the "right way" to go about things. Wagner felt increasingly that he could not talk with real openness to Liszt any longer, while Liszt grew more aware of Wagner's resemblance to those "high mountains, radiant at the summit but enveloped by mists below." [16]

Possibly Liszt did not go to Paris while Wagner was there because he was depressed and preoccupied with his own personal troubles. Shortly after Daniel's death, he had come under a scurrilous attack which was certainly not new and probably did not disturb him much, if at all, but was, nevertheless, disagreeable. Although Liszt was not specifically named, it was clear that the public denouncement of the "New German" school was directed as much against him personally as it was against the Music of the Future. This incredible document was signed by a group of musicians that included Brahms and Joachim. In addition, Liszt's position in Weimar had become increasingly burdensome to him. On one occasion, when the performance of a work by the contemporary Peter Cornelius had been hissed, Liszt tendered his resignation to the Grand Duke. This resignation was not accepted, but Liszt felt increasingly, and for many reasons, that the end of his tenure at the Weimar Court was at hand.

Although the Princess had received her divorce, her marriage to Liszt had still not been sanctioned. In May of 1860, she had finally gone herself to Rome to try at first hand to secure the permission necessary from the Church to permit her to remarry. Thus Liszt was left alone in the large Altenburg where he had spent twelve years under the indefatigable attentions of the Princess. Letters passed back and forth almost daily between them, but it was hardly the same as it had been. Princess Marie had also married, in 1859, into the Hohenlohe-Schillingsfürst family, and although Liszt remained in contact with her throughout his lifetime, the old, very close, charming rapport had come to an end.

Liszt was evidently in a state of deep depression. He was approaching his fiftieth birthday; the future was uncertain and confused. "I am mortally sad," he wrote at this time. "Only prayer can comfort me at moments . . . May God give me grace to pass through this moral crisis." [17]

Liszt finally did go to Paris, arriving there the day after Wagner's departure, whether by accident or design, and while he was there he visited Marie d'Agoult. Liszt's marriage to the Princess seemed now to be feasible and it was planned for his fiftieth birthday in October. Marie, who kept herself informed of every detail of his life, was well aware of this plan. Typically, Liszt wrote the Princess, but only one month later, a full description of his visit with Nelida, one which was, obviously, not very flattering to his former love. "If Nelida saw me again, it was not in the least that she might talk to me about anything which might have interested us, but merely because many people have talked to her about me and my poor success, and also, no doubt, about my kind words. My daughters' names were only mentioned in passing, and that at the end of my last visit, on the day of my departure from Paris. Then she asked me why I had prevented Cosima from following her true vocation, which should have been the career of an artist. According to Nelida, that would have been the best thing which could have happened to her. On this point, as on so many others, I have no choice; I cannot share her opinion." He went into details of the arrangements for a luncheon at his second visit, who was to be there, and so on, and then continued in what he called a more personal turn. "The question of Wagner and the Music of the Future, and of the interest which I take in the new musical movement, had already been touched upon at my first visit . . . She was astonished at the voluntary isolation which I continue to maintain, perhaps, too, at the straightforward consistency which is to be found in my artistic life, of which she herself never had much realization . . . As she heard me talking . . . of the absolute similarity between my efforts at that time and my ideas of today, and of the permanency of that she had found so 'hateful' in me, she suddenly felt an emotion which I could not understand, and her face was covered with tears. I kissed her forehead, for the first time in many long years, and said to her: 'Come, Marie, let me speak to you with the peasant saying: "God bless you and may you wish me no ill." ' She was unable to reply at the moment, but her tears flowed more copiously. Ollivier told me that during her travels in Italy he often saw her weeping in various places which particularly recalled our youth to her. I told her that I had been deeply touched by this reminiscence, and she replied, almost stammering: 'I shall always remain true to Italy—and Hungary.' And on this note I left her, calm and gentle. As I came downstairs, she showed me a picture of my poor Daniel. Nothing at all had been said about him during the three or four hours which I had spent chatting with his mother." [18]

Liszt, at fifty, was still handsome and vigorous and possessed that ineffable charm which lasted till the end of his days. Even twelve years after this interview with Marie d'Agoult, when Liszt was already sixty-one years old, a young American pianist wrote about him:

"Liszt is the most interesting and striking looking man imaginable. Tall and slight, with deep-set eyes, shaggy eyebrows, and long iron-gray hair, which he wears parted in the middle. His mouth turns up at the corners, which gives him a most crafty Mephistophelean expression when he smiles, and his whole appearance and manner have a sort of Jesuitical elegance and ease. His hands are very narrow with long slender fingers that look as if they had twice as many joints as other people's . . . Anything like the polish of his manner I never saw . . . But the most extraordinary thing about Liszt is his wonderful variety of expression and play of feature. One moment his face will look dreamy, shadowy, tragic. The next he will be insinuating amiable, ironical, sardonic; but always the same captivating grace of manner. He is a perfect study. I cannot imagine how he must look when he is playing. He is all spirit, but half the time, at least, a mocking spirit, I should say. I have heard the most remarkable stories about him already. All Weimar adores him and people say that women still go crazy over him. When he goes out he bows to everybody just like a King!" [19]

It was a painful scene for Marie with this father of her three children and the past must have come back to her with an unbearable poignancy.

In the meantime, the news from Cosima at Reichenhall was better. The climate, the long walks in the mountains, the peace and quiet were working wonders with her health. She had not been allowed to attend the music festival at Weimar, which took place in August 1861, a brilliant affair that celebrated in a sense Liszt's last appearance there and Wagner's return to Germany. Bülow was incredibly active and conducted, among other things, a remarkable performance of Liszt's *Faust Symphony*. Blandine was present with her husband, Émile Ollivier, and Wagner so enjoyed their company that he decided to prolong the pleasure after the festival ended and to accompany them on a visit to Cosima in Reichenhall. On the station platform, while saying good-bye to Liszt, Wagner was full of praises for Bülow and the remarkably distinguished role he had played at the Festival. But, Wagner added jocularly, there was no necessity for him to have married Cosima. "That was a luxury," Liszt answered enigmatically, with a slight bow.

After a trip of several days, during which Blandine and Wagner were in high spirits, joking and laughing at everything including Ollivier's difficulties with the German language, they arrived in Reichenhall. They were delighted at Cosima's health and vitality and all fears for her were forgotten. The two sisters were overjoyed at their reunion. They shut themselves away from the two men constantly and were filled with such merriment, and their laughter pealed out with such gaiety, that Wagner willingly put up with having to spend so much time with Ollivier.

Wagner was in an unusually gay mood during this visit. He

found Cosima and Blandine so amiable, unusual, gifted, and charming that he even suggested jokingly, on one occasion when he managed to gain admittance to the two sisters, that he adopt them, as their father paid no attention to them. He spoke once to Blandine about Cosima's "wild ways" which he deplored, but Blandine easily translated that to mean that her sister had a shy timidity. Wagner must have smiled at this sisterly loyalty but he was not put off his real opinion for he later wrote Bülow about his impressions of Cosima. "I was very happy with her in Reichenhall. If only the naughty child would take really good care of herself. I hear that she is again visiting her father. If only she does not allow herself to give way to those small, but to her harmful excesses again. She is a wild child—that I stick to! But she has great nobility. You must stress this in order to induce her to make every sacrifice, even to her small, harmful habits. She must, out of pride, become calm and serene. For the rest, her appearance set my mind very much at rest. Certainly things will go well and cheerfully for her." [20] Wagner did not add in his letter that when he said good-bye to Cosima at Reichenhall he "caught a glimpse of almost timid inquiry from Cosima." [21]

Cosima's cure complete, she returned to Berlin and visited her father once more, for the last time at the Altenburg, in Weimar. This house, which had been the scene of so much brilliance, over which the argumentative, cigar-smoking, religious, domineering woman had so long reigned was to be given up. Before his final departure, Liszt wrote to his Princess in Rome: "It is impossible for me to collect in a single focus the emotions of my last hours at the Altenburg. Each room, each piece of furniture, to the very steps of the staircase and the turf of the garden, everything is illumined with your love without which I should feel reduced to nothingness . . . I cannot contain my tears. But after a last station at your prie-dieu, where you always knelt with me before I set out on some journey, I experienced a sort of feeling of liberation that comforted me . . . On leaving this house, I remember that I am going to you and I draw a loftier breath." [22]

Liszt's fiftieth birthday, the day scheduled for the marriage, was October 22, 1861. He arrived in Rome on the twentieth. Everything was in order for this belated wedding, which had been postponed so long that the attachment which had sparked it had altered markedly, if not in degree, in kind. The bride and groom spent a quiet evening together on the twenty-first, in quiet contemplation of the final realization on the next day of so many of their hopes. Their tranquillity was shattered suddenly when a messenger arrived with the news that the marriage was off. The whole question of annulment was to be reviewed once more.

This last setback, arriving as it did at the very last moment, when fulfillment seemed achieved, produced a peculiar and unpredictable result. The Princess looked upon it as a decree from on high that this marriage was not to be. And she accepted the cancellation finally and completely, with a readiness that belied the tenacity with which she had fought so long for the union. She had grown, over the years, ever more immersed in religion and in a mystical approach to life. She had now only two desires left: to work at her voluminous writings on theology and to persuade Liszt to dedicate his talent to the composing of religious music.

Liszt, too, accepted the decree against the marriage without protest and settled down in Rome, that city which Cosima said had been described as the place where grief loses half its force. She was deeply and genuinely hurt for both her father and the Princess and looked forward to visiting him in Italy when she could.

It was a busy winter for Cosima and Hans, and they were

almost never out of the concert hall. Hans had the greatest respect for Cosima's musical knowledge and judgment, and she played the role to which she said women were condemned, half-participant, half-passive.

Wagner was as unsettled as ever, traveling from Vienna to Venice to Paris to Karlsruhe, seeking some sort of haven where he could work in peace and comfort and where his far from small demands would be satisfied. He decided upon Biebrich, a small town near Wiesbaden, sent for all his furniture from Paris, and determined to settle there. Minna shortly appeared on the scene again, but it was to be the brief and final convulsion in a relationship that had long since become unbearable. When she left, after ten days in which her sick, tortured mind drove Wagner to despair, they were never to meet again.

Inevitably, Wagner begged Hans to come to him, and just as inevitably, Bülow agreed. And so another two summer months were spent together. Hans was exhausted after the active winter season in Berlin, and Cosima was not in the least enchanted with Biebrich, but she put up with it cheerfully, and her good spirits helped make the situation bearable.

Wagner put Bülow to work as usual, in spite of his evident fatigue and tension, and he copied the *Meistersinger* libretto, 145 pages of it, in 5 days. He accompanied at the piano while Wagner rehearsed the *Tristan and Isolde* roles with the Schnorrs.* He read off the *Meistersinger* manuscript at sight at the piano while Wagner demonstrated what he had written of the new work by singing all the parts. Bülow was tremendously impressed by the new opera, which he considered a masterpiece. But in spite of the fascination that Bülow always felt in Wagner's presence, he was in a state of severe depression which grew worse day by day as did his mood of irritability which

* Ludwig Schnorr von Carolsfeld (Tristan); Malvina Schnorr von Carolsfeld (Isolde).

went along with it. His outbursts of temper were sharp and on one occasion, after an irritating day which he considered wasted, he let himself go in front of Wagner in a real fury. He was more than ever disgusted with himself, and in one of those same moods that he once described quite graphically: "I feel sometimes as though poisoned by opium, my head so heavy, the flesh disobedient to the instigations of the spirit. What makes me the saddest in all this is that I do not recognize either the right or the necessity to be in such a state. I am not yet wholly without initiative, but everything that I begin finishes only in inspiring me with the most profound disgust both of myself and of the thing I am doing." [23]

Wagner and Cosima, on the other hand, were unusually gay and laughed together all the time. On one occasion at the Casino in Wiesbaden, Wagner asked Cosima to risk half of a small sum he had received as royalty. Flinging down one gold piece after another, Cosima lost almost the whole amount at once. Wagner snatched the rest away from her and at another table was lucky enough to recoup his losses. "This soon put us in a very merry mood," Wagner relates.[24] On another occasion, at the end of the summer, Wagner suddenly suggested to Cosima that he wheel her across a square to their hotel in a wheelbarrow. Cosima agreed at once, which so disconcerted Wagner that he lost his courage to carry out the venture.

The sort of madcap gaiety to which Wagner and Cosima were prone could hardly have appealed to Bülow. Not only was he exhausted and nervous but he could not help once again comparing himself to Wagner, his own works to *Tristan* and the budding *Meistersinger*. With his penetrating mind, his taste, musical insight, and honesty, he did not spare himself in this judgment and saw clearly the difference between a composer of genius and what he termed his own "paltry efforts." No wonder that he was exhausted, irritable, and depressed.

Cosima had decided long ago that humor was one of the saving graces of life. "I like to laugh over all worries, over all sorrows. Laughter is not a cheat as hope is, blindly, and it sustains one just as much." [25] Cosima basically had a marvelous sense of fun and a wit that was sharp and penetrating.

Wagner was in a mood of gaiety partly because he was working on the *Meistersinger.* As always he was very much under the impress of the mood of the music he was composing. But his developing feeling for Cosima played an important role too. In his autobiography, Wagner described his sentiments as they parted at the end of the Biebrich summer: "This time we could take leave of one another cheerfully, although the increasing and often excessive ill-humor of poor Hans had drawn many an involuntary sigh from me. He seemed to be in perpetual torment. On the other hand, Cosima appeared to have lost the shyness she had evinced toward me when I visited Reichenhall in the previous year, and a very friendly manner had taken its place. While I was singing 'Wotan's Abschied' to my friends, I noticed the same expression in Cosima's face as I had seen on it, to my astonishment, in Zurich on a similar occasion, only the ecstasy of it was transfigured into something higher. Everything connected with this was shrouded in silence and mystery, but the belief that she belonged to me grew to such certainty in my mind, that when I was under the influence of more than ordinary excitement my conduct betrayed the most reckless gaiety." [26]

Cosima's cheerful mood did not last long. No sooner had the Bülows returned to Berlin than Cosima received a letter from Émile Ollivier in St. Tropez telling her that Blandine was desperately ill. Blandine had given birth to a son several weeks earlier. Before Cosima could go to her, on September 11, Blandine died. Cosima, with her little girl Daniela, left at once for Paris to be with her grandmother, and the two tried desperately to console each other in this latest loss. Cosima did not see how she could leave her grandmother now and formulated a plan whereby she and Hans would move permanently to Paris. It was Liszt who opposed this idea so forcefully that it was abandoned. He sympathized with Cosima's feelings toward her grandmother, but he pointed out that for Bülow to leave Germany at this moment in his career was impossible and would be extremely harmful for his future. Cosima was somewhat relieved in her anxiety for her grandmother when she saw that her brother-in-law's fondness for the old lady was as lively as ever. And so Anna Liszt remained comfortably in an apartment in Émile Ollivier's house with her tiny new great-grandson, another Daniel.

Cosima's heart was heavy with grief. "My sister was the most exquisite creature that I ever learnt to know or knew. She was beautiful, gentle, good, heroic . . . The extraordinary position created for us by our birth had forged a bond between us three, such as the majority of brothers and sisters can scarcely picture to themselves, and which I now drag about me like a heavy cumbersome chain. I shall never love again as I loved her, and I often feel as though I had been torn up by the roots, for my heart is always seeking these two beings, who were so young, so original, so truly saintly, so completely mine, and I feel nothing but emptiness." [27]

CHAPTER VIII

SHORTLY AFTER COSIMA'S RETURN to Berlin she accompanied Hans to Leipzig where he was to play Liszt's new 2nd Concerto on a program on which Wagner was to conduct his *Meistersinger* Prelude and *Tannhäuser* Overture. Leipzig was another hot bed of anti-Wagnerian feeling, and the actual concert was a total failure with the public staying away in droves. The spirits of the performers, however, were extraordinarily gay. Wagner described Hans' performance as "glorious" and he himself was very pleased with the effect of the *Meistersinger* in the nearly empty hall. Even Hans was in a happy mood and during the concert Wagner and Cosima, who sat together when Wagner was not conducting, laughed so incessantly that Wagner's niece and sister who were present were distinctly offended. They felt that everyone should be as depressed as they were over the poor attendance.

What prompted this inordinate good humor on the part of Wagner and Cosima? Wagner actually was in terrible straits. His position had not improved in any regard, and he was in despair as to where to go and to whom to turn. "My friends were well aware of the terrible and utterly forlorn condition in which I found myself," he wrote of that time.[1]

Cosima, too, was calling on all her reserves of physical and moral strength. She was expecting another child and her health was again precarious, especially after the grief and strain of Blandine's death. But being together, recognizing more and more clearly the growing bond that existed between them, the excitement of discovery lent an air of enchantment even in the somber circumstances.

Wagner had been miserable and lost in Leipzig until he saw Cosima at the rehearsal. "I felt myself suddenly transported when I discovered Cosima sitting in a corner of the hall, in deep mourning and very pale, but smiling cheerfully at me. She had returned shortly before from Paris—where her grandmother now lay hopelessly bedridden—filled with grief at the inexplicably sudden death of her sister, and she now seemed, even to my eyes, to be leaving another world to approach me. Our emotions were so genuinely deep and sincere that only an unconditional surrender to the enjoyment of meeting again could bridge the chasm." [2]

The time passed all too quickly, however, and soon Wagner started off on his restless wanderings again and Hans and Cosima returned to Berlin. Madame von Bülow had moved in with them, after the marriage of her daughter, and this critical, nervous, humorless woman hardly added to Cosima's peace of mind.

A few months later Wagner stopped off for a night's visit on his way to Russia, and the merriment and fun continued. Bülow was worried that Wagner would be upset at seeing Cosima in her advanced stage of pregnancy, as he had once voiced his aversion to such a sight. But nothing could put Wagner out of humor with Cosima, he assured Hans, and he took her for a long drive during the afternoon.

A baby daughter, named Blandine in memory of the recently lost sister, was born on March 20, 1863, shortly after Wagner's departure. Whether by chance or neglect, Cosima bore the child alone and only afterward was a midwife sent for. Certainly, Blandine had been right in her estimate that Madame von Bülow was there only *pour la phrase* as far as Cosima was concerned and that neither she nor Hans could be counted on to take proper care of Cosima. In later years, Cosima remembered that the only person who was concerned about her condition at that time was Wagner. And he was far away.

That Hans was hardly much of a family man is not surprising, perhaps, in view of his highly nervous temperament and the immense amount of work he drove himself to accomplish in spite of his ever-precarious health. Now that he had two daughters he spoke of needing only a third to make a King Lear out of him.

When Wagner returned from Russia in April, Bülow was delighted at the success of the tour and was sure that Wagner's troubles were at an end. Cosima was in good health and fine humor which did a great deal to dispel Wagner's gloom about his own future. He did not see things as optimistically as Bülow and certainly did not feel that the receipts from his Russian trip were what he had hoped for. He set out again, this time back to Vienna, where he rented the upper part of a large house in the suburb of Penzing. Again he sent for all his furniture, including his Erard piano, from Biebrich, engaged a couple, Franz and Anna Mrazek, who were to remain with him for many years, and even found a dog, Pohl, to whom he became very attached. He and his friends hoped that here he had found his real Asyl, his home where he could work and be happy and where his operas could be performed.

Cosima nursed little Blandine through a grave illness and by the summer her own strength was once more at a very low ebb.

Wagner did not call for them that summer, and so Cosima and Hans spent their holiday near Copenhagen where Cosima could bathe and profit from the sea air. By the time the return to Berlin came, she was once again her energetic, capable, and healthy self.

It was November before they saw Wagner again. On his way to a concert in Löwenberg, he had detoured by way of Berlin, planning to stop off only briefly between trains. Hans was giving a concert that night and persuaded Wagner to stay over for it. Wagner was in his usual financial distress and while they were all three dining at the hotel, he received the money, 270 marks, for a royal gift, a gold snuff box which he had put up for sale. The incident brought on many jokes and a great deal of laughter. Bülow had to leave early to complete the preparations for the concert and so once again Wagner and Cosima drove out in a fine carriage. Their laughter was silenced as soon as they were alone together. The moment of truth had finally arrived. "This time all jocularity died away into silence," Wagner wrote. "We gazed speechless into each other's eyes; an intense longing for an avowal of the truth mastered us and led to a confession—which needed no words—of the boundless unhappiness which oppressed us. The experience brought relief to us both, and the profound tranquillity which ensued enabled us to attend the concert in a cheerful, unembarrassed mood. I was actually able to fix my attention clearly on an exquisitely refined and elevated performance of Beethoven's smaller concerto (in C Major) and likewise on Hans' very clever arrangement of Gluck's overture to *Paris and Helen*." [3]

This is Wagner's own description of what happened between him and Cosima on that famous drive. One sentence from it was deleted in the published version, which added that with tears and sobs they sealed their confession to belong to each other.

There was a supper party after the concert which they had to attend, and which drove them almost to despair. They longed for peace after the emotional impact of their mutual avowal.

Wagner left early the next morning. His farewell reminded him "so vividly of that first exquisitely pathetic parting from Cosima at Zurich, that all the intervening years vanished like a dream of desolation separating two days of lifelong moment and decision. If on the first occasion our presentiment of something mysterious and inexplicable had compelled silence, it was now no less impossible to give words to that which we silently acknowledged." [4]

What turmoil and torment must have gone through Cosima's heart after the first marvelous excitement of loving and knowing she was loved had quieted. Her passionate nature, her heart which had sought since childhood for its place, had found its real home at last. She loved Hans, of course she loved him, but her feeling for him was more that of friendship, of affection, even of pity, than the kind of love of which she knew she was capable. Cosima had always dreamed of being absorbed into a relationship beside which nothing else in the world mattered. She had felt since childhood that she had a mission in life, that she would find a cause to which she could devote all her abilities, her heart and her talent. Here at last was the man. Here at last was the mission. But here too was Hans—the husband to whom she was devoted, to whom she had pledged her marriage vows. Hans who was her friend, who had been at her side and suffered as she did when Daniel died; Hans who was like a son to her father; Hans who was the most devoted and true friend to Wagner, the man she loved.

There was the past too—the loneliness and grief of her childhood where she had seen at first hand how love can turn into bitterness and how flaunted conventions can lead to misery for the innocent. She had suffered too much as a child, she had thought too much of the consequences of parents' behavior on their children and she had determined that never would she allow to happen to her children what had happened to her and her brother and sister. She might love Wagner, and probably she had done so unconsciously ever since that highly charged summer of 1858 at the Asyl. But she could not let it affect her marriage with Bülow or her home in any way. There was only one road, one goal for which to strive—the strength to sacrifice love to duty. And so Cosima's life continued as it had before with only the secret wonder hidden deep in her heart.

Bülow's career prospered. He was given a doctorate by the University of Jena and in February went to Russia for a highly successful concert tour. He was so impressed with the reception he received there and the advantageous offer of a post as conductor in St. Petersburg that he was sorely tempted to accept. He turned it down, however, primarily because he feared the move for his wife and children to such a severe climate. Cosima occupied herself with her children, her writing, and her difficult mother-in-law toward whom she remained courteous and correct at all times. She took care of Hans' correspondence and participated in all his musical activities. Cosima's course was charted and her life moved along gently within its prescribed circle. At least outwardly.

Wagner, after conducting in several cities, Prague, Karlsruhe, and Breslau, returned to Penzing in an odd mood, a strange mixture of optimism and blindness. He had let himself go without restraint in the furnishings and arrangements of his house. With his passion for luxury this had led him into enormous expense. Self-destructive, foolish, or just plain willful, he continued to borrow money to pay for his luxuries and even involved his friend Tausig, another great Liszt pupil, in signing a promissory note. Full of projects, as always, for raising the cash he needed, either from concerts or royalties or from friends, or princes, he continued recklessly along the same path. On

Christmas Eve he invited a group of friends to his house, where he gave each one what he called "an appropriate trifle." Peter Cornelius described these 'trifles' as elaborate presents that could be conceived only by the imagination of an Oriental: overcoats, silk scarves, gold shirt studs, dressing gowns, waistcoats, merschaum cigar holders, and a mass of other gifts hardly appropriate from a man who was on the brink of financial disaster. By February, Wagner was faced with complete financial ruin and disgrace. He had piled bill upon bill, had signed one note after another, trying to pay off the first with a second and so on until the structure reached such proportions it was on the point of collapse. A planned concert trip to Russia fell through; no one came forward with the necessary sums. In the end, there was only one recourse left—escape, for Vienna at that time still had an active debtor's prison. And so he said good-bye to Anna and Franz Mrazek, his dog Pohl, and his Vienna friends and took off hurriedly for Munich, where he spent two days recovering from the anxiety and disturbances through which he had gone.

Wagner by now had exhausted the patience, and the purses, of his friends. His incessant demands, his egotistical attitude wherein all that mattered were his own creative powers and what he needed for them to which everything and everyone must be sacrificed, the force of his personality which swept everyone into his maw—all this had made his friends extremely wary. The unquestionably shady and involved financial maneuverings that he had indulged in for so many years, coupled with his need for luxury and his inept financial capacities, had alienated most of those who had tried to help him in the past. Many of his friends now felt that he was a man who could not be helped.

Where was he to go after his forced flight from Vienna? The Wesendoncks had turned down his request to stay with them.

Hans and Cosima had a small apartment in Berlin and with the presence of Madame von Bülow and the two small children it was out of the question for him to stay there. Other friends had long since shown their reluctance to take Wagner in.

He found a temporary refuge at the home of Dr. Wille in Mariafeld. The good doctor was away on a trip, but his wife helped set Wagner up in two rooms of a house next door. When Dr. Wille returned, however, he was not at all pleased with the situation and made it clear, as Wagner tells it, on two counts: first, that he feared being touched for money but, more important, that he felt out of place in his own home in the presence of a man who, he considered, was enormously his superior.

Wagner even discussed, cynically, one evening with Frau Wille, the idea of recouping his fortunes through a rich marriage. His relationship with Minna was finished; there was no chance that the two could ever live together again. Minna was content in Dresden, and Wagner supplied her with what money he could.

With all the complex facets of his personality, Wagner, in a strange and touching way, was a family man. That was one of the ties that had kept him with Minna for so long, for he appreciated that she was a wonderful housekeeper who could create a home, and often did, on very limited funds. To live footloose and alone was not something that appealed to his nature at all.

As far as productions of his as yet unperformed operas were concerned, there had been no progress at all since the disastrous *Tannhäuser* performance in Paris. The hoped-for production of *Tristan* in Vienna had fallen through, and there seemed no chance for a first performance either of it or of the two complete *Ring* operas or the partly finished *Siegfried*.

It was the lowest ebb of Wagner's life. In financial ruin and disgrace, despaired of and rejected by most of his friends, without house or home or the prospect of one and with the only means of earning any income through the occupation he hated above all, concertizing, Wagner approached his fifty-first birthday.

Cosima's heart bled for the artist who seemed like a half-blinded, caged animal, destroying himself against the barriers that pressed more closely around him, penning him finally like a despairing wild creature.

And then the miracle happened. In early May a letter from Wagner arrived. "Once again! An unheard of wonder has entered my life!" he exulted. "The unbelievable is true. A young king is my most trusted disciple. He is undertaking the mission of bringing before the world all of my works in the way that I want and to protect me against every care." [5]

Wagner claimed later that even in his darkest moments he had the presentiment that something wonderful was in store for him. But perhaps only Wagner's fantastic imagination could have dreamed up the miracle that had so suddenly and almost mysteriously entered his life. The dramatic new change was as important for Cosima's future as it was for Wagner's and in the end it altered the whole purpose and direction of her life.

King Maximillian of Bavaria had died a few days before Wagner passed through Munich on his ignominious flight from his debts in Vienna, and the whole city was in mourning for the monarch who left as heir his eighteen-year-old son, Ludwig II. This young man had a sensitive, ardent nature. From the moment of his first contact with Wagner's work, at the age of thirteen, he felt an overpowering attraction for it, an almost mystical urge. At the age of sixteen he begged his father to order a production of *Lohengrin.* He read everything that Wagner wrote and sopped up Wagner's ideas. He learned by heart all the published texts of Wagner's operas. When he read the preface to the *Ring* poem, the ideas that Wagner expressed there, thrown out in the bitterness of his frustration at the difficulties he met in the production of his operas, found their true mark. Wagner had castigated the German theater in a violent attack against the Philistines. In his despair at ever finding the conditions for an acceptable performance of his work, he laid out his own plans and ideas for a special theater, with a special staff and special singers trained by himself that would be capable of realizing the *Ring*.

The youthful Ludwig caught fire with these ideas and concepts and within weeks after ascending the throne of Bavaria, he sent an emissary to find Wagner. This was more easily said than done, and the path led from Penzing to Mariafeld and finally to Stuttgart where Wagner had gone in hopes of arranging for a performance of *Lohengrin*. At the end of his tether and utterly despairing, he suspected a trick when the "Secretary to the King of Bavaria" asked to see him, and it was only with the greatest reluctance and even trepidation that he agreed to meet him the next day. Twenty-four hours later Wagner was on his way to Munich and to a new life.

His first meeting with the King confirmed this fairy-tale dream come true. The young monarch promised him everything that he wanted, for his life, for his creative work, and for the production of his operas. And in return all he asked was that Wagner be his friend.

It was a moving meeting that Wagner had with this handsome, visionary young king hardly more than a boy and utterly naïve. Ludwig wanted to make up to Wagner for everything that he had suffered in the past. He assured him that he would never need to worry about the cares of everyday life, that all burdens would be removed from him so that he could spread his wings and soar in the pure air of his art. He told Wagner that he had long dreamed of doing this since from his earliest youth his only real source of delight had been in Wagner. Ludwig offered him a more than generous salary, money to pay his debts, furnished him with free residences and did everything to indulge the artist to the full. Eager to see as much as possible of the man who meant so much to him, the King arranged for Wagner to move into a house for the summer, the Villa Pellet, on the Starnberg Lake, near the royal residence.

One of Wagner's first thoughts in all this was for Hans. Strangely enough not for Cosima at first, but for his old friend and musical ally. He begged Hans to come, not with Cosima, but alone. He was eager to show the King the music of the *Ring,* and *Tristan,* and he needed Hans' help and his marvelous ten fingers. A week later, however, he wrote Hans again urgently: "I invite you with wife, child and maid to take up your quarters with me this summer for as long as possible . . . For Heaven's sake, children! Children! No! 'No'! I could not bear it! Telegraph: Yes! I beg you. Awake! Come to your R.W." [6]

But Bülow vacillated, as he did so often, and Wagner grew frantic. He tried to persuade his friend, the composer Peter Cornelius, to come from Vienna and live with him. He wrote pleading letters to other friends. Here he was in a magnificent house, three whole floors with all sorts of extra bedrooms, a gorgeous view of the lake, and he was alone. The King had to leave for a month, and Wagner simply could not stand the solitude. Besides, even with the King in residence, he needed to come down occasionally from the rarified heights that he and the young man explored ecstatically in endless conversations. In spite of the miracle of good fortune that had befallen him, and with the prospect of everything happening as only his wildest dreams could have hoped for, Wagner was lonely.

By the end of June he even wrote to his old friend Mathilde Maier, simply begging her to come and take charge of his house —on any terms. He told her he could not go on living as he was doing, with no woman in the house to run things and to be a companion to him. Four days later, he recanted hastily on this proposition. Cosima was on her way and a few days later, on June 29, she arrived at Starnberg with her two little daughters. Wagner's frantic search for companionship was over.

Bülow had not found the decision to come an easy one. His health was poor and he was in one of his black moods. His nervous tension was more acute than ever. He was nearly thirty-five years old and he felt acutely the need for freedom and independence, the chance to develop his own gifts his own way. He was aware of the danger for him of Wagner's towering personality and genius, that he found irresistible and overpowering. Knowing Bülow, however, it was obvious that he could not resist Wagner's invitation for long. He had never refused Wagner's calls for help and he was not going to begin now. He sent Cosima on ahead and he himself arrived only eight days later.

Those eight days on the Starnberg Lake were the fateful ones. Together at last, strong in the knowledge that each loved and was loved, duty and good intentions were powerless. They found each other completely—and forever. A marvelous peace descended on them. Cosima felt that the world was distant and remote, unreal and forgotten. Nothing existed except the little village of Starnberg—and Wagner. The daughter who was born nine months later was called Isolde, that tragic heroine of death-in-love. She was Wagner's child, not Bülow's.

When Bülow arrived on July 7, he was in a frightful state both physically and nervously. The damp air at the lake did not agree with him, and neither his health nor his nerves improved at all. Nevertheless, he managed to fulfill Wagner's wish and played the *Ring* to the King, who was pleased not only with the superb talent he displayed as a musician but with him as a person. Ludwig invited him to dinner alone, a signal honor from the shy young monarch, and asked him to move permanently to Munich. Ludwig was ready to offer him the position of pianist to the King at an annual stipend of 2,000 florins. Like Wagner, Bülow was not to have any fixed duties and was to be free to pursue his concert tours as he wished. There were further plans in the air which Wagner and the young King had in view for the future: the establishment of a music school which Bülow was to head and which would carry out Wagner's theories on music and performance, especially of German works and most especially of German opera—meaning his own.

Bülow was again uncertain and indecisive. He had been dissatisfied in Berlin for some time past, but, nevertheless, the move to Munich, the constant proximity of Wagner and the natural resultant immersion in him, his music, and his problems, the feeling of a certain threat to his own individuality, all this combined to make him waver.

His health had deteriorated at Starnberg and finally in mid-August he moved to a hotel in Munich in a state that Wagner described as "ill and furious." He had to cancel his appearance at a music festival at Karlsruhe, where he was to have conducted.

Plans had been made long in advance for Liszt to come for this festival, even though he was reluctant to leave Rome, and it had taken a good deal of persuasion to bring him. The day that Bülow moved to Munich, Cosima went on alone to Karlsruhe to meet her father. Undoubtedly Bülow insisted that at least she go. It was Liszt's first visit to Germany since he had left Weimar three years earlier and everything was starting off wrong. Wagner had refused to attend the festival, several other friends had declined, and now Bülow had been forced to cancel.

The month at Starnberg with Wagner, two children, and Bülow ill and in one of his black moods had not been an easy one. Cosima had been pulled in three directions at once. Seeing her father again and being with him for several days was a source of strength and comfort to her. Liszt was also very happy with Cosima. His compositions met with great success, more or less the first time that such a reception had been accorded them, Liszt noted. There were concerts, suppers, dinners—the whole gamut to which Liszt had been accustomed and where he met many old friends and musicians. The only cloud was Hans' illness, and Cosima persuaded her father to return to Munich with her although he had not planned to do so. He found Hans "in such a sad condition both physical and moral that I have scarcely left him during the last two days . . . The principal character of his trouble is nervous, according to the Doctor . . . During the past week he has had a paralysis of his legs. It is located now in his left arm, and gives him great pain." [7]

Wagner came from Starnberg and took Liszt back with him for a night where they talked for five hours without stopping. Wagner played parts of *Meistersinger,* and Liszt, in turn, played excerpts from his oratorio *Christus.* Liszt found Wagner unchanged but hoped that the great good fortune that Wagner had struck would soften to some extent some of the harshness of his character.

On September third Liszt left for Stuttgart, and the same evening Cosima, Hans, and the two children returned to Berlin. Bülow was determined not to take a cure at some spa, as the doctor had recommended. He claimed that the Berlin air would be the best possible treatment for him.

Hans did improve in Berlin where he was under a strict regime of daily baths, massage, and sleep, and a special diet with plenty of meat and red wine to build up his strength. Although still not very social, by the end of September he was fully convalescent.

Just as Liszt had been actively opposed to the idea that Bülow should move to Paris, he was equally positive that he must accept the extraordinary offer made by the young King of Bavaria. He noted that Bülow had already met with the King four times during the summer and once dined with him tête-à-tête and he remarked, a little wryly, that Hans seemed to have made more progress in the King's favor in a few days than he himself had done at the Court of Weimar during ten years.

Cosima had remained outwardly calm and good-humored throughout this period. She kept her inner feelings to herself under rigid control. She had spoken truly when she told Bülow that first winter in Berlin that she never complained of that from which she suffered most. But the enormity of the emotional experience which she was going through; the sight of her husband, helpless and hopeless, and the consciousness of her tie to him; Wagner, who was discovering that he could not live without her; the child she was carrying which was not her husband's, all this was a source of profound conflict and took a great toll of her health and strength.

Wagner sent her an ecstatic love poem in which he described how the sinking sun of his life was renewed by her star. "I love and I am loved," he exulted. Now that he had found her, he could not bear to give her up. But Cosima's joy in finding her love at last was counterbalanced by her strong feelings of guilt and compassion toward the man she had married.

Wagner maintained a perfectly normal relationship with Hans during all this time, but at the end of September we find him writing: "Cosima's ailing condition distresses me also. Everything that concerns her is extraordinary and unusual: her due is freedom in the noblest sense. She is childlike and profound—the laws of her being will always lead her only to the highest. No one will ever help her except herself! She belongs to a special world order which we must learn to grasp through her. In the future you will have more favorable leisure and freedom to observe this and to find your noble place by her side. And that too is a comfort to me." [8] Wagner had written Bülow before about Cosima, after his visit to Reichenhall, and in much the same terms. In this letter, however, there is not only Wagner's understanding of Cosima, and what she was suffering, but the added exhortation to Hans, the effort to bring him to a greater insight into Cosima's nature. It was almost as though Wagner was trying to prepare him for the truth of what was the actual situation between them.

Bülow finally made the momentous decision which had been hanging over him for two months. He would accept the King's offer. But that was only the first step. He still had to make the actual move.

As a name-day present to Cosima he sent her on a trip to Paris with her father where they stayed at the house of Daniel Ollivier, where Cosima's grandmother lived too. For the first two days they went almost nowhere, spending all their time with that gentle old lady. Later they saw many of Liszt's old friends—Berlioz, Erard, Rossini, Belloni. They even visited Madame Saint-Mars, the formidable Madame Patersi's sister. No mention is made of the old governess, so perhaps she had left Paris or was no longer alive.

A few days after their arrival they had dinner with Marie d'Agoult. Cosima had not seen both her parents together since her earliest childhood but the time had long passed when such an occurrence had any real importance. Marie d'Agoult had been pleased and satisfied that Liszt's marriage to the Princess had not taken place, as she had predicted it would not. She was nearly sixty years old, with white hair, aging with her usual grace. Liszt, still tied to the Princess, was turning more and more to religion, though his attraction to and for women was still very much in evidence. Most of them were casual affairs, relatively speaking, though there were a few more serious attachments and, as always, some attempts to dominate him by the same type of strong, passionate woman with whom he so often found a mutual attraction. His health was hardly helped by his large daily intake of cognac, coffee, and strong cigars. Part of him longed for simplicity and quiet and solitary religious communion. Another part needed people, activity, and society.

How different Wagner seemed to Cosima. Less than two years younger than her father, at fifty-one he was as full of ardor as a young man. A whole new life was opening for him and he grasped it with sureness and confidence, with a truly youthful energy and determination.

As Cosima sat at dinner with her two parents, feeling already Wagner's child stirring to new life, many thoughts must have passed through her mind about these two who had loved each other with such intensity, who had broken all conventions and promised to belong to each other forever. "Not an angel's, not God's, only thine," Liszt used to tell Marie. And she would ask what could she desire either in heaven or on earth other than him. But other lives and other loves have little real meaning to someone in love. Cosima was sure that her love and Wagner's would not follow the same dreary path as that of her parents. She wanted to give him all she was capable of giving; she would ask nothing from him and make no demands. Never would she fall into the superficialities and the desire to enslave as her mother had done. Cosima knew that Wagner loved her, that he needed her, and that she could help him. Her spirit soared at the wonder of it. But Hans. There was always Hans.

Cosima accompanied Liszt as far as Marseilles and then returned to Munich. Hans was in Berlin still caught in a mood of "innate procrastination" that he had often recognized in himself. "Without allowing myself to advise you," Liszt wrote him, "I nevertheless insist on the opportuneness of your prompt establishment in Munich. There is nothing more to delay for. A complicated task and painful duties are awaiting you. You will succeed in them. In so doing your public career will be enlarged and your interior self will rise to its natural height." [9]

Cosima journeyed back to Berlin to close the apartment, pack their belongings, and effect the move. Bülow had finally set the date for their departure, which had not been easy for him to do. It was not that he knew or suspected that Cosima and Wagner were in love. Not yet, at any rate. Rather it was that he was now tying his life and career irrevocably to that of Wagner; that he would live and work under the shadow of the composer whose genius he admired above all others; that he was being pulled into the vortex of a man far greater than he. Liszt was well aware of Bülow's self-deprecatory feeling, the reasons for which he could not understand and which he deplored.

"Very dear and incomparable friend," he wrote Bülow a few days before the move to Munich. "For so many years you have given me so much for which to love you, to be grateful to you, and to be proud of you that I urgently beg you to do away with the only chagrin which is mixed occasionally in our unchanging affection. This sorrow concerns your injustice toward yourself and the inexplicable, strange lack of confidence in your own superiority that is so evident and, moreover, so well demonstrated. Fair and generous toward everyone to the point of heroism, you persist in bestowing on yourself only faults and imaginary mistakes. I would like to persuade you to abandon such a habit—which is no better for being very rare—and to find yourself completely in unison with me on the feeling of your true worth of heart, of character, of intelligence, and of talent. So try to leave your migraines and rheumatisms of all kinds with your old furnishings in Berlin—and start new in Munich." [10]

It was a fresh start for Bülow in Munich. But the road was to lead in a tragic direction.

CHAPTER IX

WHEN WAGNER MOVED TO MUNICH in October of 1864, he believed absolutely that he had at long last found his true home, that here his works would be performed as he wanted them to be, that he would have no more material cares and pressures and would be free to compose and develop a center for his music. In short, he looked upon the King's promises as complete assurance that he had come to the pot of gold at the end of the rainbow.

Wagner's enthusiasm, his boundless self-confidence was contagious, and he persuaded his friends that here at last was the Wagnerian Utopia. All of his past problems were forgotten in the jubilation of his dream come true, a dream which he had always been sure would come true, for Wagner, even in his worst days, never lost faith in his own destiny.

The young King, as we have seen, was an obsessed Wagnerite of the first order. The letters that passed between him and Wagner were high-blown, superromantic expressions of sentiment that were not as unusual for those times as they would be for ours. After listening to Wagner's music, Ludwig felt himself "Carried aloft into celestial spheres . . . I feel more and more clearly that I am not in a position to reward you as you deserve; whatever I do, whatever I am able to undertake for you can only be a stammered thanks. An earthly being cannot requite a godlike spirit. But to love, to honor, that he can do; my first, my only love is and will forever remain you." [1]

This strange, tormented, idealistic young monarch felt that through Wagner and through his music he was able to move into a transcendent area where he could lose himself far away from mundane and depressing reality. Wagner became for him a necessity, someone whose genius furnished the nourishment that his sensitive spirit feasted on. In Wagner's music, in his dramas, in all that he wrote and thought, Ludwig found the reality of his own vague dreams and longings.

Young as he was when he came to the throne, totally naïve, he nevertheless had a strong sense of the power and dignity of his position. He believed in autocracy and even spoke enviously of the rule of the Russian Czars. He was quick to suspect anyone who might take advantage of him, and he realized that his youth and inexperience would lay him open to all kinds of such attempts. There was a strange duality in his nature—part the visionary, the ecstatic dreamer who longed to live in an ideal world of art and imagination, and part the young monarch who was jealously aware of the reach of power.

It is not surprising in view of the degree of this young king's championship that Wagner felt secure and looked forward to spending the rest of his days in Munich in conditions of personal and artistic satisfaction. Not one ever to hold back, Wagner let himself go even more than usual when it came to his living arrangements. One of the provisions of Wagner's agreement with the King was a rent-free house, and the King provided him with one which suited Wagner's extravagant taste. It was an opulent house on the Briennerstrasse with a large and beautiful garden, and even a garden house suitable for a small family. Wagner suggested that Cosima and Hans might want to use the garden house in the summer. For their permanent home he suggested a small house on the Ludwigstrasse at a rent of six hundred florins, exactly five times less than the three thousand per annum rent that the King was paying for the Briennerstrasse house.

This handsome residence into which Wagner moved in early October would alone have been enough to arouse suspicion among the conservative Munich citizenry as to what this Richard Wagner was up to with their youthful monarch. Wagner's reputation was not unknown in Munich. Added to this was the extremely generous financial agreement he came to with the King for the *Ring* and the three years he anticipated that it would take him to complete it. There was talk too of a great new theater that would be built and plans for a new music school.

One can hardly imagine that the musical establishment of Munich was overjoyed at Wagner's sudden ascendancy. His strictures against the existing music in Germany, his calm and arrogant conviction that he and only he could lead Germany back onto the true path of music, that he and only he could create a cultural renaissance which would add to the glory of Germany and the German people met with a jaundiced reaction.

Politically, too, Wagner was viewed with suspicion. Not only had no one forgotten the cause and fact of his exile from Germany, but the politicians close to the King feared the influence that Wagner might have on the very young, very new monarch. Ludwig's fanatical devotion to Wagner was quickly apparent and aroused the greatest suspicions and doubts throughout the government establishment, which viewed Wagner's power as a direct threat.

When Cosima and Bülow, with bag and baggage, children and maids, arrived to settle permanently in Munich, Hans knew he was going to have a fight on his hands. He saw this more clearly than Wagner did, but Bülow was never one to shrink from a fight. Indeed he relished it, and his invective skill was highly developed. But he too was in no doubt that total victory for Wagner and his cause could be won with all the resources at their command and the powerful backing of the King.

The young King was impatient to start as soon as possible on the vast projects he had planned with Wagner, but most of all he was longing to hear a performance of one of the operas. *The Flying Dutchman* was chosen, in order to try out the whole operation with one of the less complicated works. Wagner himself conducted it on December fourth. On December twenty-fifth Hans gave his first concert, playing a conservative classical program of Bach, Mozart, and Beethoven in order to give the lie to the numerous "croakers," as he called them, who foresaw in the Wagner-Bülow incursion a destruction of all musical values of the past.

The influx of Wagnerians brought not only Bülow but several other of the Wagner adherents, not all of whom behaved with discretion. Bülow himself was never one to suffer fools gladly. With his impeccable artistic standards and his limited patience he would often burst out in uncontrollable scorn and irascibility, which was hardly suited to endear the Wagnerians to the Munich citizenry.

In the closing months of 1864, however, success for the cause seemed certain. Cosima divided her time between her family on the Ludwigstrasse and Wagner's house on the Briennerstrasse. There she acted as hostess, as confidante, and as secretary, taking over from Wagner every burden and duty that she could spare him. Wagner was busy with his plans for the development of the music school, with which Bülow helped him enormously, the new type of theater which he envisioned for the production of the *Ring*—in short the creation of reality from his dreams.

On the surface everything seemed serene, but underneath the apparent tranquillity, the simmering hostility began to come to a boil. All the grandiose schemes devised by Wagner and the King were not secret and as word about them began to spread, the politicians grew anxious as to the expenses that would be involved, expenses over and above the already large amounts that had been or would be turned over to Wagner personally. The musical and literary circles too were waiting to pounce the moment they could find an opening.

The first explosion occurred in February 1865, and as so often happens, it was a minor incident, about payment for a portrait of Wagner that the King had ordered, that provoked it. But the storm it aroused showed the extent to which the hostility to Wagner had already hardened in the few brief months since he had come to Munich, and the power of the opposition to him.

The King was irritated with Wagner possibly over the incident of payment for the portrait, possibly because he was told that Wagner had allowed himself on one occasion to refer to the King as *mein Junge,* but quite surely because of behind-the-scenes machinations by Wagner's enemies. At any rate, on February sixth, Wagner was refused an audience with the King. It was a brief tempest, and six days later the King published a denial that Wagner was in disgrace. Already on the fourteenth his letter to Wagner was full of the old adoration. "Miserable, shortsighted people who can talk about 'disgrace,' who can have no conception of our love! 'Forgive them, for they know not what they do!' They do not know that you are everything to me as you have been, and will be unto death, that I loved you before I ever saw you; but I know that my Friend knows me, that his faith in me will never fail. O write to me again! I hope to see you soon!" [2]

Brief, however, as the estrangement was, it was enough to unleash the fury against Wagner, and the newspapers quickly took up the hue and cry. Wagner's luxurious tastes were attacked, his financial affairs and the payment of his past debts were dragged out in the open, he was accused of ingratitude and prodigality.

Wagner, and Bülow too, were snared into answering these allegations. Wagner sought to justify himself and the situation in one of his lengthy, masterly protestations of innocence. Wagner was a past master, as Cosima became too, in the art of dialectic through which he managed with a show of openness and sincerity to achieve a truly marvelous obfuscation of the actual situation. As to the charges against his luxurious manner of living, Wagner merely dismissed them. They were his private affair, he said, and an artist was justified in having around him whatever surroundings he wanted that were conducive for his work.

The Press had a real frolic, and was to continue to have one for a long time to come. Caricatures, cartoons, and burlesqued articles appeared, which must have given many a solid Municher a hearty laugh. If Wagner's enemies hoped that any of this would estrange the King from Wagner, however, they were very much mistaken. The attacks only aroused Ludwig's desire to help and protect his "Friend" even more.

At the same time, the free and easy relationship had been broken to some extent and the two men no longer saw each other with their previous regularity. They did, however, correspond constantly, and this task devolved increasingly upon Cosima, who brought every ounce of her intelligence and her diplomacy to bear.

What Ludwig longed for above all else was to hear Wagner's operas performed. Before the composer began on plans for the production of *Tristan,* however, he wanted still further reassurance from the King that all was well again. In categorical terms he wrote and asked him if he should stay or if he should leave Munich. Ludwig answered with equal clarity: "Remain here," and he promised him that everything would once again be as glorious as before.

Encouraged by this, Wagner set to work on the proposed *Tristan* production. Bülow was to be the conductor and he was ready to begin rehearsals when he returned from a three-week concert tour at the beginning of April.

The leitmotiv of *Tristan* that ran through the marriage of Bülow and Cosima appeared again here. The first appearance had been on their honeymoon when Wagner was completing the libretto and read it aloud to the young pair. Then, during their first two years in Berlin, Hans was consumed with the head breaking task of reducing the score for piano. This time, in Munich, Bülow set the first orchestral rehearsal of the opera for ten o'clock on the morning of April 12. Two hours earlier, Cosima gave birth to her third daughter, and Wagner's first child. Most fittingly the baby was named Isolde. As for Bülow, he had not the slightest suspicion that this child was not his own.

After nearly a month of rehearsals, and endless postponements and delays, *Tristan* was finally performed. The unplayable was played, the unsingable sung—and the success was resounding. Eight years after he had begun to compose this masterpiece, and six years after its completion, Wagner heard it performed for the first time.

Cosima had scarcely recovered from her recent confinement, but she was more active than ever. Her double household duties, at her own home and that of Wagner, and her three children would have been enough to occupy her time to the full. But Wagner depended increasingly on her in every way, and even the King began to rely on her as an intermediary in his communications with Wagner. Cosima also was buffer in the endless petty altercations that were constantly arising between Wagner and the Ministry. Her abilities were put to full use in this precarious situation, and she was able to smooth over many sources of potential strife through her watchful tact.

As time went on, Cosima began to enter directly into the relationship with the King and Wagner. She worked on an embroidery as a present for the King in which were depicted symbols from the different Wagner operas. This gave Ludwig great pleasure, but he was even more delighted with her efforts in copying for him many of Wagner's writings with which he was not acquainted, and as a token of his gratitude to her, he presented her with a lovely sapphire. Another task which Cosima would later assume, and one which interested her enormously, was taking down by dictation Wagner's autobiography, for she herself, as well as the King, longed to know all the details of Wagner's early days, some of them so difficult, many of them fraught with despair and struggle.

In the whole of the Munich period Wagner was happiest during the *Tristan* preparations. It was a brief respite, however, for troubles were to develop with increasing momentum soon afterward. The first blow came only three weeks after the final *Tristan* performance. Ludwig Schnorr von Carolsfeld, Wagner's ideal tenor, the man of whom he thought as his Tristan, died very suddenly. Hastening to Dresden with Bülow for the funeral, Wagner arrived too late. His return to Munich was gloomy. The optimism and confidence of the previous year had disappeared under the constant attacks from the press and from his enemies. Wagner's already tense nerves made him vaccilate between unbearable depression and periods of almost hysterical gaiety. Cosima did all she could to cheer and comfort him, but Wagner's health and his nerves did not improve. Then, in early August, Cosima and Hans left to go to Pest, where they were to meet Liszt, who was to conduct the first performance of his *St. Elizabeth.*

Cosima was to see her father for the first time in the long cassock of an Abbé. In a letter of April 28, he had announced to Hans that he had received minor orders and was taking up residence in the apartment of Monsignor Hohenlohe at the Vatican. This was far from being a sudden decision on Liszt's part, nor was it the hypocritical act that some of his enemies claimed for it. Since his early youth, he had been drawn to the Church. "It was my instinct and aspiration between the age of 15 to 18 years," Liszt wrote. "The sorrow of my mother and the advice of my then Confessor, Abbé Bardun, decided me otherwise." [3]

Anna Liszt received the news of her son's action with deep emotion, and burst into tears when she first read his letter telling her of it. It was not a complete surprise, however, as she had sensed that Liszt had been getting ready for this step for some time. She fully realized its validity for him. "It is a great thing," she wrote him, "but you have prepared yourself for it for a long time—at Monte Mario. I have noticed it in your letters for some time. You sounded so beautiful, so religious, that I was often very moved and shed a few tears for you." [4]

Liszt is certainly not the only person to have possessed a duality of personality. It is perhaps the essential flamboyance of the Don Juan, the temperament of the *Zigeuner* that have been most apparent in Liszt. But the recognition of those aspects of his personality is no reason to deny the reality of his spiritual nature. Cosima herself, in later years, spoke of her father's deep and real and simple faith. This was innate with him from his earliest years and was in no way derived from the Princess, who was bound up in a mass of theological complexities about which Liszt once admitted that he did not understand a word.

Cosima and Hans remained away from Munich for five weeks. First of all, there was Liszt's *St. Elizabeth,* which received two highly acclaimed performances in Pest. His *Dante Symphony* was also performed with great success. Both Hans and Cosima wrote articles on the music, and Liszt was pleased that his compositions were received so enthusiastically in the country of his birth. On the way home they stopped for a visit in Gran, where a huge crowd gathered under the windows one evening in the hope of seeing Liszt. The piano was moved out onto the balcony. Liszt and Hans both played to a crowd so silent that every note could be heard.

These were the happy moments, the successful moments. While listening to Liszt's music or to his magical playing, Cosima could forget for a little while the anxious problems and questions which were tearing her to pieces. Wagner, she knew, was in misery without her. Pressed on all sides by the ever-increasing cabal against him in Munich, exhausted physically and nervously, he needed her more desperately than ever before. She had given him a leather diary, his Brown Book, in which he wrote down for her his innermost thoughts and feelings while she was away. "O Cosima! You are the soul of my life! Completely and wholly! . . . The thought of Munich without you. Everything is the grave. Nothing, nothing more without you! You are the soul of everything that still lives in me . . . Nothing, nothing more without you!" [5] The thought that they were apart was unbearable to him. "Stay, stay with me. Do not go away again. Tell poor Hans openly that without you I cannot go on. O Heaven, if only you could quietly be my wife before the world!" [6]

Wagner's misery, and her own, at their separation was only

a part of Cosima's torment. In spite of the many elisions and suppressions in the biographical source material, it is hard to believe that the trip of Cosima and Hans to Pest was no more than simply a pleasurable musical excursion. Wagner and Liszt, and Bülow too, were public figures who aroused tremendous interest in everything they did. There was as much interest in their private lives as there is in that of any high-priced movie or singing star today. Gossip and rumor flew in its age-old way. Everyone knew everything about everybody else's business and made a point of talking about it. Certainly, Liszt had heard of his daughter's growing involvement with Wagner. Besides, for a man with his experience, it was impossible for him not to have noticed the change in her that must have occurred when her love affair with Wagner commenced. On their trip to Paris, after he had met her at Karlsruhe for the music festival, he could not have helped but see the glow, the new glory within her. Hans was not a ladies' man, never had been and never could be. Nor did he want to be. It is perfectly understandable that he would not have noticed anything new in his wife's look or behavior. He was far too detached and imperceptive about such things. Most important of all was his respect for the ideals and character of his wife. He would simply not have believed that she could betray him with his best friend. But Liszt! That tremendously experienced man of the world who had captured so many feminine hearts was certainly a great deal more realistic and cynical as to what women are capable of when they fall in love, and he could spot the signs of a woman in love as few others could. It is hard to believe that Liszt did not see the danger signals in the summer of 1864. And it would not have taken him a moment to guess with whom Cosima was involved.

Liszt, with his amorous career, was hardly in a position to criticize his daughter even had he wanted to, which is dubious. It seems probable that he did not mention anything about what he suspected, or rather was sure of, and that she did not either. He could not really blame her, for he recognized as much as anyone, perhaps more than anyone, the force and power of Wagner's nature. He also knew intimately Cosima's emotionalism, her need to be loved and her innate powers which sought to find their own level. As long as she remained discreet, as long as she fulfilled her outward obligations to Hans, he was perhaps willing to close his eyes to what was going on, even though it was distasteful to him.

Discretion, however, could never be a part of Wagner's nature, nor did Cosima count the cost when she felt there was something worth fighting for. Certainly by now the rumors of Cosima's behavior had come to Liszt's ears, as they must have to those of Hans, some time during the year of 1865. She had gone too far and acted too recklessly for Liszt to ignore the situation any longer.

The trip to Pest was most probably undertaken in an effort to bring Cosima to her senses, to distract her and change her course of conduct. The hope was that her love for her father and the influence he had always wielded with her until now would have a stabilizing effect on her. It did not.

Cosima wrote constantly to Wagner during his absence, and her letters roused him to even greater fury. Hans had not allowed her to visit his former house in Penzing when they stopped off in Vienna on the way to Pest. "What insanity!" Wagner noted in his diary. "Can one believe it!" [7]

Wagner felt that Liszt and Bülow did not understand Cosima at all. "Oh! if only it were possible to find the magic word that would let your family see you as you are!" he complained in the Brown Book. "How does their knowledge of you remain partial and full of holes. Now they are dragging you around from place to place. It humiliates me deeply that they dare to do so! But that you allow yourself not really to be dragged but, instead, because of your unhappiness you drug your weaknesses and try to make yourself believe that it could be good, and that this and that are also right—and the difference between what I know and what other people say to you:—then absolutely could I and can I not stand by and look at it: then nothing has any more sense for me and my love itself seems to me a weakness! Then you appear wholly lost to me, completely untrue." [8]

This was the first time that Wagner's jealousy of Cosima's love for her father became apparent. It is not surprising that the trip to Pest, and the hoped-for effect that it would have on Cosima, was a failure. When she returned to Munich and read in the Brown Book all that Wagner had written while she was away, all that he had suffered from her absence, she saw more clearly than before his desperate need for her and was more than ever determined not to disappoint him or to let him down.

Another factor contributed very much to Cosima's actions and attitudes on her return to Munich. The cabal against Wagner had grown in vituperativeness and in strength. Wagner had never been one to economize, even when he was absolutely without funds. It would be hard to imagine, with the royal purse dispensing such largesse, with all the assurances from the young King that everything that he needed would be given to him, that Wagner would not spend and spend wildly. He never looked upon his expenditures as extravagances. When he ordered masses of luxurious draperies for the large rooms of his Brienner Street house; when he fitted out whole walls with satin hanging from floor to ceiling, he did not find anything remarkable in these indulgences. To Wagner, these trappings seemed a necessity, without which he felt he could not live and work. From Vienna he ordered endless yards of varicolored satins—yellow, pink, blue, white, brown, red, and violet. Wagner felt that in no other way could he draw on the realm of his imagination except through this exclusion of the outer world of coarse reality. His clothes were equally luxurious often made with satins and velvets in colors matching the heavy hangings of his rooms.

No wonder, then, that by August he was already again in financial distress. He had settled only some of his myriad past debts and had incurred plenty of new ones. Once more, he had a plan, an invincible, perfect plan, dependent, of course, on further largesse from the King. Ludwig had by now bought for him the Brienner Street house which Wagner asked to be assured to him rent free for as long as he lived. Next, he requested a lump capital sum of two hundred thousand gulden from which he could have at once forty thousand for his own personal use, with the rest of it being put out at interest which, he reckoned, would bring him eight thousand gulden a year.

By now even the generous young King was more than a little wary of Wagner's financial wheelings and dealings, and his ministers were thoroughly aroused. Although Ludwig finally acceded to the request for the forty thousand in cash, the delay was humiliating to Wagner. The capital sum was not granted, but an income of eight thousand was agreed to.

The whole subject of the forty thousand gulden had become so distasteful by the time Wagner was notified that it had been granted, so many harsh words had been written by the Cabinet ministers, who more often than not addressed their letters directly to Cosima, that Cosima wanted to efface the unpleasant impression and to bring the gift directly, so to speak, to Wagner from the King. Thus, she decided to go herself and pick up the money. With Daniela and the governess, she took a cab to the Treasury, expecting to be given the money in banknotes. The officials, however, determined to make things as difficult and unpleasant as possible, declared that she would have to take the money for the most part in silver. Nothing daunted, Cosima hired a second cab to which she transported many of the heavy sacks herself. Needless to say, she did not miss the occasion of informing the King of the way she had been treated.

By now, Cosima had moved even closer to the center of Wagner's life, in every way. She and the King wrote each other endless letters, filled with dedication to Wagner. "Let us two," Ludwig wrote her, "take a solemn vow to do all it is in human power to do to preserve the peace he has won, to banish care from him, to take upon ourselves, whenever possible, every grief of his, to love him, love him with all the strength that God has put into the human soul!" [9]

At the end of October, Wagner went for two weeks to Vienna, where he undoubtedly ordered many more exquisite things from the "little dressmaker" who furnished so many of the luxuries for the Briennerstrasse house. By the time he returned to Munich, the die was cast, the fight to the death had begun in earnest.

When Wagner first moved to Munich, he had no interest in political affairs nor any intention of becoming interested in them. As the cabal against him grew in strength and hostility, however, he gradually became convinced that his artistic aims could never be realized unless the political climate were altered. Never one to hide his light behind a bushel, or to have any doubts as to the importance and validity of his ideas on any subject, Wagner decided that it was up to him to educate the young and inexperienced monarch and to guide him onto the paths of true enlightenment. In September of 1865 he started a journal for the King's edification, dealing with the ideal of a German state and the role of a German prince as Wagner saw it. He argued that Germany's future depended on the leadership of a truly German prince who would guide the state along the path of its true development, dependent on nothing outside itself to enable it to reach its lofty goal. And he went into details of this concept in specific terms. Wagner sincerely felt that it was his duty to guide the young King and that in some mystical way he would bring about the salvation and regeneration of Germany through his works.

Wagner sent his journal to the King, who wrote Cosima that he had read it with the greatest enthusiasm and thanked her in terms that convinced both her and Wagner that they had nothing to fear and were in complete control of the situation.

In November Wagner spent a week with Ludwig at the Hohenschwangau Palace and never had the King seemed more elated and inspired by the composer's presence. Wagner returned to Munich absolutely sure that his influence with the King was stronger than that of any other. Needless to say, during his absence from Munich the cabal against him was not idle. Charges and countercharges appeared in the newspapers. Rumor, gossip, lies, and exaggerations were rife. Finally an article appeared in which an exaggerated picture of Wagner's financial dealings with the King were set out, and the calls that his luxurious way of living made on the national treasury and his methods of extracting money were spelled out in insulting terms.

Wagner and Cosima decided that the moment to act and to act forcefully had come. Strong in their conviction that they had the King's complete confidence, they had no qualms about taking the offensive against Wagner's enemies. On November 29 an anonymous article appeared in a Munich newspaper. It had been delivered by Cosima herself to the office of the newspaper and was in her handwriting. Professing to set out the entire background and relationship of Wagner and the King and all their plans, it was a powerful defense of Wagner and the purity of his motives and ideals. Free and overfamiliar use of the King's name ran throughout the argument, which ended by suggesting that if two or three persons were removed from their positions, everything would run smoothly and there would be no further troubles of any kind.

Wagner and Cosima were supremely confident in the whole situation, although Wagner was careful to hide behind the veil of anonymity. Cosima had moved wholly into the orbit of Wagner's egocentrism. Anyone who attacked or even criticized Wagner not only became an enemy, but was clearly mistaken. Wagner's truth was the only truth. It was from this base that they delivered this public blast. And in their narrow range of vision, they did not foresee the result it would bring.

Sure of triumph, Wagner continued to press the King directly to replace the Cabinet Ministers who, he felt, stood in the way of the realization of all their plans together. But Wagner's enemies were far too strong, and Wagner had blindly blundered and misinterpreted too often for there to be any question of the final issue. Ludwig, after all, was King, not Wagner.

On December 6 Wagner was informed, and the news was brought to him by one of his most active opponents, that the King requested him to leave Bavaria for six months. A letter from the King the next day did little to ameliorate Wagner's feeling of shock and bitterness in spite of Ludwig's assurances that their ideals would continue to be faithfully fostered. He begged Wagner not to misjudge him and assured him that his love would never die. He explained that he had been forced to act as he did in asking Wagner to leave Bavaria, but that it would certainly not be forever.

The dream was over. Wagner's Asyl was lost again. But this time it was not just a pleasant house in agreeable surroundings, as had been the case so many times before. This had truly been a sanctuary, a home for the spirit as well as the man, a last great glorious hope. And it was gone—shattered to smithereens.

It was a cold early morning four days after he was told of the King's decision that Wagner left Munich, accompanied only by his servant and his old dog, Pohl. Only three friends in addition to Cosima, saw him off. Peter Cornelius described the scene. "He has left . . . Wagner looked so ghostly; pale, with a confused expression and his long, loose hair quite grey . . . Cosima was completely broken." [10]

CHAPTER X

COSIMA WAS LEFT ALONE in the city of the enemy. Hans had been away on a concert tour since the first of November and was not due to return until just before Christmas. Cosima had only one remaining hope—to further Wagner's cause in every way she could, especially through maintaining a close and continuing relationship with the King on whom so much depended.

The fact that not all of Wagner's friends were friendly toward Cosima isolated her more than ever. Peter Cornelius was one who came to view her relationship with and influence upon Wagner in a not very favorable light. He felt that Wagner was completely under her thumb. Before his departure no one had been able to see Wagner alone for some time, and even letters to him could not reach him directly but were opened by Cosima and read aloud to him. Cornelius was extremely fond of Bülow and he obviously resented intensely Cosima's closeness to Wagner and was perfectly aware of the actual relationship between them. "The main thing," he wrote in a letter to his fiancée, "is the love affair between Wagner and Cosima von Bülow. This has developed since my arrival in January of this year and must have entered into full bloom sometime or other in the spring or summer of this year. Since then Cosima has also, as the third member of the alliance, entered into correspondence with the King. Since then Wagner has been completely and unqualifiedly under her influence." [1]

Cornelius was not at all blind to the depth of feeling between Cosima and Wagner and quite clearly saw all the implications in the affair. On the day of Wagner's departure he wrote: "There is a complete affair between Wagner and Cosima. One might even conjecture that she will follow him with the children . . . But what about Bülow? Has he given over his wife to Wagner completely in a high-romantic understanding? Was Wagner's embrace at the railroad station his thanks for this? The actual marriage between Hans and Cosima has for a long time been only an apparent one. Otherwise Hans' behavior would be inexplicable." [2]

If Peter Cornelius noticed Wagner's pallor and pathetic appearance on the station platform that morning when he departed from Munich, how much more did Cosima see and feel. Only a year and a half earlier everything had seemed perfect. And now? A cold, early morning farewell on a windy station platform, and once again the start of restless wandering.

The official decision had been that Wagner was to leave Bavaria for six months. Cosima was determined to do all in her power to insure that at the end of this period he would be able to return to Munich.

After a few days in Vevey, Wagner moved on to Geneva where he found a house that suited him. Situated with a marvelous view of Mont Blanc, *Les Artichauts,* although another elegant dwelling as always according to Wagner's taste, was hardly a model of efficiency, and the cold and drafts made the highly reactive artist miserable. In addition to this, he was even more depressed by the death of his dog, Pohl, friend and companion since his Vienna days. And so it was not long before he took off again, this time to the south of France, by way of Lyon. It was in Marseilles that he received word that his wife Minna had died suddenly and unexpectedly, and Wagner returned in a few days to Geneva.

In the meantime, the young King was distraught at the absence of his "Friend." He missed Wagner and longed for the day when he might return to Munich and they could continue with their plans. In spite of her emotional involvement, Cosima saw everything with a cold, clear eye. She kept in constant touch with the King both in large things and in small. The matter of Wagner's salary was settled, and it was to continue. Although the King seemed eager from the start to plan for Wagner's return to Munich, Wagner was pessimistic and negative about it. Cosima hoped that Wagner would not jump to any hasty conclusions and the King begged him not to lose faith. "The storm will abate, the sun will shine again . . . I will do as you desire, will govern firmly like a King in the fullest sense of the word." [3] But nothing that the King wrote, or that he transmitted through Cosima, raised Wagner's hopes at all. He was totally disillusioned and discouraged and wanted only peace and quiet away from the turmoil created by his enemies. Most of all he wanted Cosima. "Enough of words, deeds and sorrows," he wrote her . . . "For God's sake, dear one, no more half measures! We have suffered enough, not to want new torments. In a month, God willing, we will be peacefully reunited, no more talking, through with Munich: final escape! . . . Let me look out for the nest of our peace." [4]

Although Wagner's heart and mind were longing for Cosima, he worried about Bülow, too, whose position in Munich, as Wagner's right hand, was also becoming unpleasant. But Bülow did not flinch from the fight. Wagner was pleased and he wrote to his old friend: "Your letter was good, clever, and manly. You are the only fellow whom Fate has brought to me who truly has fire and self-reliance. Greetings and praises from all my heart. Adieu, best most beloved Hans." [5]

In March Cosima, with her oldest daughter Daniela, went to spend a month with Wagner in Geneva. Distraught and bitter, he had been unable to work or to concentrate on anything. But as always, Cosima brought him peace, and under the warmth and understanding that flowed from her, he shortly began work on the *Meistersinger,* to her great delight. He took up again, too, his dictation to her of his autobiography.

It was toward the end of her visit that they made an excursion for a few days which took them to Lucerne. There, on the shore of the lake, they saw a house. It stood on a small promontory of land, surrounded by a lovely park with tall poplar trees. The view across the lake and to the great mountains of Pilatus and Righi was magnificent. The house was called Triebschen, and Wagner at once set about renting it. The King, in a generous gesture, instead of sending Wagner, as he had asked, a lump sum for the rest of his salary for the year, made him a gift of the five thousand francs for the first year's rental. Wagner was jubilant. "Welcome Fate!" he wrote Cosima. "Triebschen be my refuge!" [6] For once Wagner was right. This time he had found his Asyl and never again was he to be buffeted about by fate like a poor thing. There were to be agonizing moments and heartrending decisions ahead, but with Cosima at his side everything was changed for good.

Wagner did not think of separating her completely from Bülow, his "best, most beloved Hans," and even before he moved in, he wrote Hans suggesting that he and the whole family come and stay at Triebschen for as long as possible.

Just when Bülow became aware of the extent and the degree of the relationship between Cosima and Wagner is a question that the various elisions and suppressions in the biographical material do not allow to be answered clearly. The often repeated story is that when Cosima had left for Triebschen in May of 1866, going ahead with the children in response to Wagner's invitation to Hans for them all to come and stay there, that same day Bülow saw a letter from Wagner to Cosima which opened his eyes to the true situation between them; that until he read this letter, which he opened only because he thought there might be something in it that he should telegraph to his wife, he had not had the slightest inkling of what was going on.

In the light of the letters of Peter Cornelius, who had recognized for well over a year the existence of a full-blown love affair between Wagner and Cosima, and the increasing public gossip on the subject, it is impossible to believe that Bülow alone remained in total ignorance of the true state of affairs. Bülow was not a man who talked much about his private life, even with his closest friends, especially when the circumstances were as humiliating to his pride and as damaging to his wife as these. Only once, Cornelius stated, did he let drop anything on the subject of Wagner and Cosima at this period, and that was merely that Liszt had been furious with Cosima for going to Wagner in Geneva. That remark, however, is enough to show that he was not the blind innocent whose eyes were rudely opened by the chance reading of a letter. His own later letters state clearly that he had been aware of what was going on for well over a year, since early 1865.

Wagner's love affairs were well known. He was not a Don Juan by any means, but neither was he impervious to the attractions of romance. And many of his love affairs were primarily that—high-blown, overromanticized emotions which gripped him for a while and transported him into distant realms of dreams, as in his affair with Mathilde Wesendonck. There was sometimes as much fantasy as actuality in Wagner's love affairs, and Bülow had seen him go through at least two which seemed desperately important for a while and then subsided quietly into nothing. Would Bülow have been too far off the mark in imagining that Wagner's feeling for Cosima might be still another of those "ideal" dreams and that time and patience would soon see the end of it?

Cosima had not the slightest plan to leave Hans permanently or to break up their marriage. She saw her love for Wagner to some extent in terms of renunciation, a glorious, world-shaking feeling but one that would have to be limited by certain compromises because of her relationship to Hans.

In April she and Bülow had gone to Amsterdam, ostensibly to be with Liszt on the occasion of the performance of his *Gran Mass.* It was extremely well received, and Liszt was presented with a silver laurel wreath. Bülow appeared, too, playing the Schubert Wanderer Fantasy in Liszt's orchestral version. According to Cornelius, however, the actual reason that Cosima made the trip was for the purpose of making her peace with her father, who was very much annoyed with her for having gone to Geneva to Wagner.

Exactly how much Liszt knew about the events at this time is also a question, although, as already mentioned, he was certainly aware of the affair between Cosima and Wagner. Liszt, however, was tired and burdened enough in his demanding relationship with the Princess not to look for involvement when he did not need to. It had been many years earlier that he had written to his young daughters how much he longed to be free of the need for paternal discipline and strictures. With his own history, past and also present, he was hardly in a position to object to Cosima's behavior as long as she behaved discreetly. But when she overstepped the limits, as he felt she had done when she openly visited Wagner in Geneva at a time when gossip mongers were at their most avid, he was irate.

What grieved Liszt the most was what was being done to Bülow. Hans had always been his favorite, as pupil, as musician, as man. Liszt honored and respected his son-in-law, but more than that, he loved him deeply. The wounds that Hans received from Cosima hurt Liszt almost as deeply. It was at about this period in the Wagner-Cosima affair that Liszt's letters to Hans became even more than usually affectionate. He addresses him as "Very dear friend and well-loved son," and signs himself "from heart and soul yours." Liszt's affection for Hans had always been evident, but now an extra tenderness, an extra warmth made itself felt in his letters.

Liszt's sensibilities seemed not to have been offended by the plan that the whole Bülow family would spend the summer with Wagner at Triebschen, and he wrote about it quite calmly to the Princess. "Wagner has rented a country house near Lucerne for a year. Cosette and Hans, with the little ones, will spend the months of July and August there." [7]

Liszt, after all, knew better than anyone that there was nothing to be done to sway Wagner once he had made up his mind, and the father certainly saw in Cosima an equally inflexible will and determination. The most he could ask for was that an effort be made to keep up appearances and, like Bülow, he hoped that the whole affair would gradually pass. But any pretense in regard to the true situation of the triangle was to grow increasingly difficult to maintain.

The King was truly heartbroken at Wagner's absence from Munich and at the interruption of the projects that meant so much to him. He corresponded ardently with Cosima, seeking news of Wagner and hoping to be able to arrange soon for his return to Bavaria, at least, if not to Munich. Nothing that had happened had in any way decreased his attachment to Wagner or his dependency on him. "Forgive my impatience," he wrote Cosima in April, "but the longing of my soul is too intense. I should be so glad to know whether you have had any news from our beloved Friend today." [8]

When Cosima returned from her visit to Wagner in Geneva he implored her "to tell me in the meantime all you have heard from our beloved Friend. How is the dear fellow's health? Oh what glorious days you must have spent with him!" [9]

During this whole period Cosima grew to be almost indispensable to Ludwig, who turned constantly to her not only for news of Wagner but for the comfort and understanding which only she knew how to give him.

Ludwig's letters to Cosima were full of optimism for the future and determination to carry out their dreams. But his personal torment at being separated from the source of his joy grew unbearable, especially after Cosima and the children left Munich to go to Triebschen in May and he no longer was buoyed by the proximity of the one person to whom he could pour out all his feelings. He even suggested to Wagner that he would abdicate the throne so that he could be near the one man who "can save me from despair and death." [10]

Wagner and Cosima counseled caution and restraint. Their hopes lay not in the abdication of the King but in the defeat of their enemies. However, an event transpired which was to deliver still another weapon into the hands of their foes.

The young King could bear the separation no longer. Eager to celebrate Wagner's birthday with him, he went secretly to Triebschen with only an aide-de-camp and a groom. He took the most elaborate precautions to keep his visit secret, but needless to say, almost before he reached Triebschen on the twenty-second of May, the news had leaked out. And by the time of his return two days later, the situation was disastrous.

Politically, for some time Bavaria had been caught between the growing power of Prussia and its hostility toward Austria. Mobilization had been ordered ten days before Ludwig made his clandestine visit to Triebschen, and the Cabinet was outraged at the young King's detachment from the important political events and his refusal to involve himself closely with the people. The visit gave the newspapers exactly the fuel for which they were looking. Abuse poured from the presses directed not at the monarch but against Wagner and, increasingly, against Cosima. "It is not a year," wrote the *Volksbote* on May 31, "since the well-known 'Madame Hans de Bülow' got away in the famous two cabs with forty thousand gulden from the Treasury for her 'friend' (or what?). But what are forty thousand gulden? 'Madame Hans' ought again to be looking around for more cabs; for the day before yesterday an action was entered against Richard Wagner in connection with bills for no less than twenty-six thousand gulden—a fact absolutely vouched for to the *Volksbote*. Meanwhile the same 'Madame Hans,' who has been known to the public since last December by the descriptive title of 'the carrier pigeon,' is with her 'friend' (or what?) in Lucerne, where she was also during the visit of an exalted person." [11]

In the face of this public attack on his wife, Bülow could no longer maintain his brooding attitude. He had to act. He demanded an immediate retraction and challenged the editor of the *Volksbote* to a duel. Both demands were ignored. He then published an answer of his own in a rival paper couched in his most vitriolic and unreasonable style, which did little if anything to ameliorate the situation and may have done more to inflame it still further. A week after the first article appeared, Bülow left for Triebschen. Peter Cornelius, in the running commentary on the whole affair that he sent to his fiancée, saw Bülow's trip to Triebschen in highly dramatic terms. We must remember, however, that Cornelius was not very sympathetic to Cosima, and certainly he looked at Wagner with clear open eyes that were in no way affected by his admiration for Wagner's art. "Bülow is a noble, important nature and I deplore with real pain, that he is the martyr to his situation," he wrote. "His marriage with Cosima was a sacrifice to friendship that he made for his Master, Liszt; to give to the illegitimate child a brilliant, honorable name and through it deep satisfaction and peace of mind to the father. This was his motive, it was an act of gratitude. This devotion was poorly rewarded by Cosima. After ten years of marriage, which was scarcely a bed of roses, he finds himself now needing to travel to Lucerne to pose to her the decisive question: Do you want to belong to me or to Wagner? That was the basis of why his confidences to me were constrained and checked, for through them questions might come into the conversation that he scarcely dared ask himself. Now he must see discussed in the newspapers in the most insulting way that which he did not dare to talk about with his friends, that which only once, you know, did he let drop from his lips —that Liszt was very angry with his daughter that she journeyed to Wagner. Well, today is the anxious, decisive day in Lucerne. I know how it will come out. Cosima will stay with Wagner." [12]

Dramatic as this sounds, it seems more likely, in view of what transpired, that Bülow went in order to consult with Cosima and Wagner about the latest development and what action should now be taken in regard to the open attack on Cosima's honor, and his own, and the consequent threat to his position in Munich on which they all depended.

Cosima met Hans in Zurich on the sixth of June. On the same day, Wagner sent a letter to the King referring to the attacks on Bülow and Cosima and begging him to take action to protect them. He enclosed the draft of a letter which he hoped the King would send to Bülow, a letter which Bülow could publish and which would vindicate his honor and Cosima's. The letter was couched in highly laudatory terms toward Bülow and spoke of the King's outrage at the attacks against him. It affirmed that

Ludwig "had been able to acquire the most exact knowledge of the noble and high-souled character of your honored wife," and closes with a promise to investigate "those criminal public calumnies" so that justice might be done.[13]

The question was, would the King send the letter? Incredibly, the naïve youthful Ludwig had not the slightest suspicion of what was going on between Cosima and Wagner. His own ethereal attachment to Wagner was so complete that he saw only the same sort of devotion in Cosima.

On the seventh, Cosima added her plea in an emotional, highly charged letter. "For the first and last time I implore you on our behalf. I fall on my knees and beg for the letter to my husband, that we may not leave in shame and disgrace the country in which we have desired nothing but what is good—and, I may say, done nothing but what is good. My dear and exalted Friend, if you make this public statement, then all is well; then we can stay here; then we shall be ready to build once more upon the ruins, full of courage and consolation, as though nothing had happened—otherwise we must go away, insulted and abandoned, depriving our distant Friend of the only Friends who could give him no more than their own existence, with their fame and reputation, and who must now build all this up again somewhere else, in order to be able to offer him an abode. My august friend, who entered into our lives like a divine apparition, oh, do not consent that we, the innocent, should be driven out. Your royal word can restore our honor, which has been impugned; it can do so completely, everything will go down before it . . . To-morrow I return to my husband in Zurich. From there we journey on, we know not where. Perhaps we shall leave Germany for good. If there is a possibility of your gracious letter, then I will persuade my husband that we should return home—otherwise—how could we stay in a city in which we might be treated as criminals? How could my husband manage to carry on his work in a city where the honor of his wife has been called in question? My royal lord, I have three children, towards whom it is my duty that I should preserve their father's honorable name unstained; for the sake of these children, that they may never cast aspersions on my love for our Friend, I beg you, my most exalted friend, write the letter. If the letter is possible, I will gladly bear all earthly trials in return for this happiness. If it is not possible, then I herewith take my leave of our kind friend, I kiss his royal hand in humility and gratitude, I call down the blessing of God on his exalted head and withdraw with my noble husband, who has perhaps received his deathblow, to a place where peace and respect await him, the weary and innocent one." [14]

Cynics say that every man has his price. Certainly Cosima sacrificed every code of honesty on this occasion in a complete surrender to the concept that the end justifies the means. The letter is a masterpiece of diplomacy. Cosima knew Ludwig and understood him through and through. She appealed to his chivalry and to his sentiments of fair play towards Bülow and herself, who had come to Munich especially at the King's wish. She appealed to him as a fine and noble monarch, one who had a sense of justice and right and also one who was all-powerful. In her constant reference to going away, she is in effect saying, "write this—or else." In view of the dependency on her that the King had developed, especially after Wagner had left Munich, since she knew that he looked to her for the inner sustenance he could not do without, this was a not too delicate threat of an action which would leave the King in total despair.

Most of all, however, the letter was a masterpiece of deceit. What it must have cost Cosima to write it is hard to imagine. She was deeply honest by nature and had been imbued with the strictest code of ethical behavior since childhood. She was an idealist—perhaps that was how she was able to sense so clearly the young King's personality. Wagner, of course, was an old hand at dissimulation, though he never thought of it as that. He was accustomed to it through many years of experience in putting debtors off with empty promises, in disposing of rights to his operas that had long since been turned over to someone else. For Wagner there was only one reality—the product of his genius. Everything else was of no importance in relation to that. Everything served only the purpose of furthering his art, of creating the conditions in which he could produce this art. Probably he had not the slightest concept of what he did in his financial wheelings and dealings, in the incessant and almost superhuman demands that he made on his friends. It was not, actually, that he sought fame and glory, or even success in the usual sense. More it was that he believed that his creations were the work of genius and that they were destined to illuminate into the vast reaches. Any sacrifice, from anyone, any gift was right and to be expected. Anyone who held back was a back-slider to the cause. And the cause was Wagner.

Cosima recognized and suffered from the deceit that she and Wagner perpetrated on the innocent young King. And yet she did it wholeheartedly. She had already been deceiving Hans, and her father; she had given birth to a child that was not her husband's and yet who went under the name of Bülow. This action toward the King was no worse in her eyes than all the rest that she had done, all the dishonesty with which she had been living.

How could such an upright soul as Cosima's be a part of such shabby deceit? It was her love of Wagner, her penetration into his heart and mind that made it possible. Cosima saw far below the awkward ugliness of Wagner's nature—his selfishness, his egotism, his extravagance, his chicanery—to the deep reality of the man. She recognized how bitterly alone and helpless he really was. She saw his need and she knew she could fill it and that only she could do so. His life became hers, his mission her own. But added to that was her own mission to love and protect and sacrifice everything for him, to dedicate herself wholly to him. She was ready to face public scandal, humiliation, and deceit. She was ready to assume any burden, pay and price. And she did.

It is not surprising that Cosima was ready to go to any extreme through her love for Wagner. She had a strong and passionate nature that had been denied much of its normal expression through a difficult and deprived childhood. She had suffered humiliations of rejection by her parents. She had been made to feel the anomaly of her position as an illegitimate child by many people, not excluding the ever-present Madame Patersi. She had lost the two life companions whom she treasured most deeply, Daniel and Blandine. And from the first, her marriage to Hans had been difficult and unsatisfying, although she would never have thought of breaking it if she had not known Wagner. Nor did she complain about it either. In Wagner she met a man who would test every fibre of her being—her emotional strength, her intellect, her passion. When a woman of strong will and superior intelligence coupled with a powerful emotional endowment falls in love, she is very apt to go to extremes of devotion especially if she feels that the man with whom she is in love is superior to her in every sense, that he is someone to whom she can look up and who will challenge and engage every facet of her personality. In such a case, and with such a woman, she becomes an instrument of the man's destiny; the world exists only for and through him; everything becomes relative only to him; right and wrong, morality and immorality, honor and dishonor are real only in so far as they affect him. A whole new code of behavior and judgment comes into being wherein the first duty is that toward the beloved and any means are allowed to this end. It is a selfless emotion in one way—total dedication to another—but the identification eventually becomes strong.

In spite of her devotion to Wagner, however, Cosima could not and did not forget Bülow and in so far as it was possible, she wanted to try to spare him. The letter she wrote to the King was written in an effort to vindicate Bülow's honor as well as her own and Wagner's. Wagner wrote more letters to the King, in one of them going into detail that quite sordidly distorted the truth. By now Ludwig was convinced that his friends had been the subject of a gross calumny and were as innocent as the driven snow. The result was that he signed the letter that Wagner had dictated for him with no changes at all, and sent it to Bülow, who had it published in two of the Munich newspapers.

The King's letter did little to quiet the hostility, but other events briefly deflected the limelight from the Wagner turmoil. Bavaria declared war on Prussia, a near-suicidal act which resulted in total defeat within a month. Prussia, however, was not too harsh in victory, leaving Bavaria its independence, although requiring heavy reparations in the form of money and the ceding of some territory. The fact that Bülow was a Prussian did not help his position at all.

In June 1866 there is not the slightest question but that Bülow was aware in every detail of Cosima's relationship with Wagner. In a cryptic letter to Raff at about this time, he said that "since February 1865 I was not in the least doubt of the rottenness of things. To be sure I never dreamed to what extent this would develop." The letter is not specific as to exactly what 'rottenness' he is referring, but the conclusion is inescapable—that it is to the Wagner-Cosima situation. "Just as the correct formulation of a problem can be regarded as half the solution of it," Bülow continues, "so the clear exposition of a scandalous situation is already a halfway point to relief from it. Truly the most shameful part of the case in question was the frightful confusion, the difficulty of bringing the fellow sufferers to a just perception, i.e. to a pessimistically calm desperation. Forgive me if I talk in oracles again," he goes on, "and cannot now consign to the devil those 'considerations' which all along I have wished at the devil! And so—later." [15]

This letter, although it indicates that it was only recently that the whole subject had been brought out into the open between the three, clearly indicates that it was with his eyes wide open that Bülow went to Triebschen that June to stay until September in Wagner's house, just as he had done many previous summers. What could possibly be the explanation for such an extraordinary situation?

Obviously he felt the vital importance, as did Liszt too, of trying to quiet the rumors and open attacks against his own and Cosima's honor. Only by removing this powerful weapon from their enemies could they hope in any way to resurrect the plans for the future—the new theater, the productions, the music school—the whole panoply of Wagner's schemes. So much was on their side, most especially the eager young King who remained as devoted, as staunch, and as wildly enthusiastic as ever. Bülow's position in Munich was, at the moment, untenable. There was even more than a suspicion that both he and Cosima might be subject to actual violence if they returned there at that time. Bülow's Prussian background did nothing to help in this regard, and he was even accused of being a Prussian spy. But the first essential at the moment was to maintain a solid front of deceit about the true facts of the Wagner-Cosima-Bülow triangle.

It seems almost incredible that a man of Bülow's character could agree to this ignominy. He was an aristocrat who from childhood had been impressed by his proud mother with the importance of the position and dignity of a Baron. His temper and thin-skinned irritability were famous. He was quick to take affront; he was immensely scornful of stupidty and baseness. And he was a profoundly honorable man. That Cosima would go to the stake for Wagner is predictable. But that Bülow would live in the same house with his wife and her lover, and Cosima was again pregnant, is almost incredible.

What motivated him was a complex of factors which made him disregard his personal feelings in favor of those "considerations" that he mentioned in his letter to Raff, just as he had been doing since he first began to suspect the truth of what was going on. He had great admiration and respect for Cosima and as her husband of nearly ten years he felt it incumbent upon himself to protect her honor and her reputation. She was the mother of his children, whom he also felt the need to protect. His love for Liszt, which was returned in such full measure, made Bülow want to spare him in any way that he could. Although what Cornelius wrote about Bülow's marriage to Cosima, that it had been an act of sacrifice on Hans' part for Liszt, was not true, what Bülow was doing now was most certainly motivated in great part by his feelings of affection for and gratitude to Liszt. And Wagner. One cannot exclude Bülow's feelings toward Wagner. His life had revolved for so long around that of Wagner, he had lived through so much with him, had been so much a part of his struggles—how could he abandon him now, when his need for loyalty was greater than it had ever been? Bülow had for too long drawn sustenance from Wagner to cut himself off suddenly. Even during that ghastly summer of 1866, living under the agonizing conditions that he did; lonely, mortally tired, and depressed, with the future bleak and empty, without plans or hope, Wagner could still make him cry out: "My God! All that is still ideal and worth preserving in the German spirit lives in this one head." [16]

As the summer passed, Wagner was hard at work on the

Meistersinger, and Cosima felt that all the sacrifices were worth while. The King still talked from time to time of abdication, and the situation in Munich did not improve at all. By September, although his contract still had two more years to run, Bülow felt that he should not go back to Munich for the present. He toyed with several ideas for other arrangements but finally decided upon a plan to move to Basel, establish himself there as a teacher, and make it his center for concert tours, at least until he could return to Munich. Basel was chosen, actually, because it was near enough to Wagner so that Cosima could easily go back and forth to Triebschen without seeming too obvious. Clearly Cosima, Wagner, and Bülow had decided on a course of action, the main premise of which was to maintain in so far as it was possible a solid front of "respectability" before the world and to work to maintain their position in Munich.

Although the attacks in the Munich press had died down, more scandal soon appeared in the form of the widow of Wagner's Tristan, Malvina Schnorr. This strange woman, deranged possibly as a result of her husband's sudden death, developed a passion for Wagner which soon included a hatred of Cosima. She tried again and again to open the King's eyes to the true situation, in the hope that by destroying Cosima she would get what she wanted. But in the end she failed completely. At that point, no one was a match for the artful diplomacy of Cosima.

On February 17, 1867, Cosima gave birth to another daughter, Eva, Wagner's second child and her fourth. Bülow had written his friend Bechstein the day before from Basel: "I leave early to-morrow morning . . . to go to my wife. I am rather anxious about her; she is on the eve of her confinement and is lying in bed with a fever." [17] It must have been a grim visit. Having fulfilled his task of keeping up appearances, Hans returned to Basel a week after Eva's birth.

Many of Wagner's demands in his letters to the King centered now on Bülow and what his actual position in Munich should be. He stipulated that Bülow was to be appointed director of the proposed music school with full powers; he was to be in complete charge of the opera with the choice of orchestral musicians and singers entirely in his hands. In short, he was to be given dictatorial powers. In addition, Bülow himself demanded a Bavarian decoration due him, he felt, as a Prussian nobleman. This last request almost broke Wagner's patience, and he wrote the King of his exasperation, and Cosima's, at this nonsensical behavior.

After many letters and interviews, the appointment was finally arranged to Wagner's and Bülow's satisfaction and Bülow was ready to return to Munich. To the amazement of Peter Cornelius and others who knew the whole situation, Bülow rented a large apartment in which two rooms were set aside for Wagner's use with his own furniture, and on the eighteenth of April, Hans and Cosima moved in. The two older girls, Daniela and Blandine, who had been staying with their grandmother in Berlin, joined them there. To the outward prying, hostile eyes it looked as though the Wagner love affair was finished and that Bülow's marriage had settled back into its old course. Even the astute Peter Cornelius was deceived into thinking that everything was over between Cosima and Wagner.

Outwardly things may have looked calmer than in several years, but the peace was only apparent. Underneath, the same storms raged with as much violence as before. Hans was in torment and was later to describe these months in heartrending terms. Cosima was miserable. On the day she left Triebschen to meet Hans and go back with him to Munich, she had telegraphed a brief verse to Wagner: "It is determined in God's counsel that man must separate from what he loves best." [18] Once again Wagner poured out his feelings in his Brown Book. "I have never been as sad as now in all my life!! . . . I foresee severe illness and death. I can stand nothing more, desire nothing more . . . Today she departed . . . What help are meetings? The separation remains. It is misery." [19]

Nevertheless, in spite of their distress they kept to their decision and to their plans directed toward the furtherance of Wagner's work and ideas. No sacrifice was too great; no demand too heavy.

Plans for the new theater were moving along rapidly. Although Wagner and the King disagreed, a few times even violently, as to singers for the proposed *Lohengrin* and *Tannhäuser* productions, they did take place. If a visit by Wagner to the King at Starnberg was not the success it had been three years earlier, nevertheless it was possible at least for it to have occurred. Things seemed well under control. Cosima continued to write enormously long and detailed letters to the King, couched in the exaggerated style that, in later years, she claimed was necessary for her dealing with this strange young idealist. The *ménage à trois* limped along somehow with Wagner making occasional visits to Munich and Cosima flitting back and forth to Triebschen.

Liszt came to Munich for two of the performances. He found Hans in very poor health, with a heavy cough and loss of voice which a cure at St. Moritz had done nothing to help. Liszt noted, however, that in spite of the fact that he had to spend half the day in bed, he continued with his conducting and kept busy all day long with preparations for the proposed music school. In spite of Bülow's illness, diagnosed finally as a tumor of the neck, the *Tannhäuser* and *Lohengrin* performances took place as planned. The doctor forbade Bülow to speak, yet he directed a six-hour rehearsal of *Lohengrin* and then the performance, which was a great success, according to Liszt—"Full hall, emotion, general enthusiasm."

Liszt lunched and dined each day with the Bülows and found

Hans, in spite of his illness, not looking badly nor in too bad a humor. He and Cosima spoke of his mother, Cosima's affectionate grandmother, who had died the year before, and he told her of his sad task of having to go through the few simple things she had left.

While he was in Munich, Liszt took the occasion for a brief visit to Triebschen with his old friend, whom he had not seen since their meeting in the summer of 1864. He found Wagner quite changed in appearance, thin and lined. Liszt felt, however, "his genius not weakened at all. I marveled at the incomparable vigor, boldness, abundance, verve and *maestria* of the *Meistersinger*. No one but Wagner could have produced such a masterpiece." [20]

Had Liszt gone to Triebschen to have it out with Wagner about Cosima? Perhaps. But knowing his aversion to interfering in other people's lives, it is doubtful that anything of import took place. Liszt knew Wagner too well to hope to alter anything in his plans or his thinking. And, too, he knew Cosima's stubbornness. The old friends, only two years apart in age, probably settled for that area where there was no conflict, nor would there ever be—music. Liszt had an incredible ability for reading full manuscript scores at sight. Wagner, as usual, sang all the vocal parts. The result was an unforgettable performance of the *Meistersinger*. In the face of such a work of art, Liszt could not help but melt.

He prolonged his visit in Munich, on his return there, for more than a week beyond his original plan. He thought that Hans was recovering slowly and that his own presence might be helpful to him. Cosima was more relaxed now too, having heard from Wagner that the visit to Triebschen had been a peaceful one.

A few days after Liszt left, Wagner completed the full score of the *Meistersinger*. All the hopes were now set on a worthy production of this revolutionary new work. The King was in ecstasies over the thought. Bülow, of course, was to conduct. Many of the stage rehearsals were directed by Wagner and the performance promised to be one that would meet his high demands both as to music and drama.

The first *Meistersinger* performance took place on June 21, 1868. Wagner sat with the King in the royal box from which he took his bows. For a man who had been exiled as a revolutionary, who had been asked to leave Bavaria less than three years earlier, such behavior represented the height of presumption. Although Wagner was in the box at the express invitation of the King, the feeling that he was trespassing on royal prerogatives aroused a new wave of hostility. The hounds which had been checked briefly were in full cry again.

CHAPTER XI

From a purely artistic point of view, the *Meistersinger* performance was the high point of Wagner's Munich period. Although he was tired, tense, and often ill, Wagner was filled with energy and good humor throughout the month-long, difficult rehearsals. Everyone worked well, and the performance was the finest that any of his works had ever received.

Cosima felt that all the trials and tribulations through which she had been, the time and energy she had spent in her careful diplomatic juggling between the King, the Ministers, the various theater intendants, and Wagner had been more than recompensed in this magnificent new work.

During the long *Meistersinger* preparations, Wagner had come to the belief that basically it was impossible for him to realize his plans for the production of his works unless he was in complete control of his own theater. To deal with and through other directors, even with Cosima there to help him, to have to argue and explain every inch of the way simply was not possible. It was impossible to expect the average theater directors to give over their powers completely to the occasional production even of a Wagner. And Wagner was not one who was ready to flatter or cajole or to be tactful in artistic matters. He was blunt, harsh and to the point. Cosima had her work cut out for her.

Wagner returned to Triebschen on June 24, three days after the first *Meistersinger* performance. Whatever mood of optimism he and Cosima might have had was soon dispelled by the events that were to follow quickly. On July 12 the King wrote to Cosima that once again the stories about her and Wagner were being circulated. "You will understand that it was difficult for me to tell you of this; but I have always had such good wishes for you that I should always have reproached myself if I had not disclosed it to you." [1]

Cosima and Wagner ought to have realized that there was really no longer any hope of succeeding in the dissimulation of the truth about their relationship. Nevertheless, Wagner wrote a letter of high indignation to the King. Cosima, he said, could no longer bear these calumnies. On orders of the doctor she was leaving Munich, perhaps forever. Bülow too would hardly be able to continue his work under these circumstances and would be forced to resign. It was the same pattern as before: complete distortion of the actual facts, an attack on the "enemies" who spread such slander about them, various appeals to the King's idealism, and flattering phrases of homage to his benefactor. This time, however, Cosima was not able to bring herself to write the King in this vein, as she had done two years before when the scandal first broke. Wagner wrote that Cosima "begs me to lay her humble farewell greetings at the King's feet and to entreat you to grant her your kind permission to be allowed not to answer." [2] He explained that she was simply too distressed to be able to do so.

The web of deceit that they had woven for the King about

their relationship was so extensive by now that they were helplessly caught up in it themselves. Later in the summer they made a few tentative hints that might have indicated a desire to throw away deceit and unburden themselves at last. But they had done too much and gone too far to be able to alter their course now.

Cosima joined Wagner at Triebschen less than two weeks after the King's letter. A month later Bülow went for a short visit to his friend Raff in Weisbaden, returning on September 9 to Munich. During the whole summer Bülow was at great pains to conceal Cosima's whereabouts. By now the relationship between the three was very tense. Wagner had felt strongly Bülow's "profound hostility and alienation" at the time of the *Meistersinger* rehearsals and, typically, had not been able to understand the reason for his antagonism and had been very depressed by it. Now that gossip was once more flying about Munich and ugly rumors increased, Bülow's position was endangered again. When Cosima left for Triebschen in July, it must have been clear to Hans that the hope of maintaining a front of marriage before the world was shattered. Nevertheless he tried to keep up the pretense before his friends that Cosima was away visiting her half sister Claire Charnacé in Versailles, or her father in Italy, anything but the bitter truth that she was again with Wagner.

Cosima and Wagner, too, continued in the deception and tried to keep the truth of her whereabouts concealed. In September, they went together to Italy where they hoped to find some peace and a solution to the terrible problems that faced them. On their way home, in the Tessin, they met with storms that equaled the ferocity of their own inner struggle. On one occasion they were caught in a thunderstorm through which they had to walk for six hours. With flood waters already high, they did not think that they would be able to survive. "Illusion could no longer prevail!" Wagner wrote afterward. "To look death in the face is to know the whole truth; to save what is eternal in one means turning one's back on all false appearances." [3]

It was from Faido, just after this experience, that Cosima wrote Hans that she and Wagner had resolved never to be separated again. They had gone to Italy looking for peace and a solution to their problem. It was through their brush with death that they faced the reality of what they must do and what they could no longer hide.

By this time, Bülow too had come to accept the fact that there was no possibility that things could ever return to what they had been or that the fiction could be maintained any longer. Perhaps by now he did not even desire it. His friend Cornelius found how much more agreeable it was to be with Bülow when Cosima was not there—that he was a completely different man. Certainly the life *à trois* had been an intolerable strain on all three of them. For Cosima and Wagner a separation or divorce would mean an end to lies and dissimulation. Cosima could take her place openly by Wagner's side. The attacks on her could not be worse or more painful than they had already been. Most important of all, they would not have to part again.

For Bülow, however, it meant not only the loss of his wife, but of everything that he had worked so hard to build up in Munich. To remain there would become totally impossible. Bülow had given up his Berlin career to go to Munich where he was Court conductor, director of the Music School and an extremely influential musical figure. All this would have to be abandoned. Finally, of course, the blow to his honor, the open admission that all the ugly gossip had been true, would represent humiliation and disgrace to anyone, especially to a proud nature such as Bülow's. All that he had done, all that he had put up with, all the ignominy he had suffered would have been for nothing.

A week after her return from Italy, on October 14, Cosima, with all four of her daughters, went to Munich. Her purpose was to try to settle the whole situation once and for all, to ask Hans for a divorce and to affirm categorically that she would not agree to be separated from Wagner again.

By now all of them were in such a state of nervous tension that it is not surprising that the visit accomplished little except to exacerbate everyone's nerves still further. Wagner was filled with anguish and self-pity. Bülow was beside himself, and Cosima was under such extremes of tension that she could hardly control herself. Liszt was shocked. Cosima, a Catholic, even thought of changing her religion and at one moment during the tense October weeks she considered going to Rome to discuss this with her father and to explain to him herself what she wanted to do and why. Wagner, at this moment seeing more clearly than she, realized that this would serve only to antagonize Liszt still further. In an effort to control Cosima, whom he described as beside herself, he sent for her half sister, Claire Charnacé, to go to Cosima in Munich.

Cosima must have remembered when her mother had sent Claire to Berlin at the time of her engagement to Hans. Her reaction now was even more violent than it had been on that occasion, and she lashed out at Wagner in no uncertain terms for having written Claire. "Arbitrary interference makes existence unbearable," she wired him. Less than an hour later another telegram followed: "Through Claire's arrival the unpleasantest situation created for me, through objections to Rome the saddest." [4] She did, at least, give in about the trip to see Liszt.

Free and easy as Liszt had been all his life in amatory adventures, he was profoundly opposed to divorce and as an Abbé, he could not countenance it. He was horrified at what Cosima was planning to do and he advised Bülow not to give her a divorce. He wrote Cosima in the strongest terms.

"Where are you going? What are you telling me? What, is everything dead for you except for one single being to whom you believe yourself necessary because he says he cannot do without you? . . . May God keep me from misjudging you. I know that 'nothing ignominious, nothing base or frivolous has influenced you,' but a vertigo has taken hold of you and you are dissipating the ardent and sacred forces of your soul to seal a bad action. This turning aside, this adulteration of the gifts of God breaks my heart . . .

"Yes, my daughter, what you are planning to do is wrong in the eyes of God and of man. My faith, my convictions, my experience protest it and I conjure you by your maternal love to renounce this melancholy intention . . .

"It is to Hans that you are *necessary;* it is he whom you should not fail. You married him of your own free will, with love—and his conduct toward you has always been of such nobility that it calls on your part for a different 'mutual reciprocity' than that which is pleaded in court. What delirium to ask him now to subscribe legally to your dishonor.

"You are *necessary* also to your four children and to merit their respect ought to be of prime necessity to you . . .

"You should not abandon the most noble of husbands, you should not lead your children astray, you should not bear witness against me and plunge yourself madly into a whirlpool of moral and material misery; finally you should not renounce your God. Passion destroys itself when it is not animated by the sense of higher duties . . .

"Not only do I justly condemn that which you propose, but I tell you this in begging you to come back to yourself and not to let yourself fly from my benediction. May God forgive me and may the memory of your father make you become again the child of God, our Father and our all in eternity." [5]

Claire Charnacé counseled caution and delay. Although she was extremely affectionate toward Cosima, she had great sympathy for Bülow, whose conduct in the face of cruel betrayal she felt had consistently been of the highest order.

Things reached such a pass that Cosima moved out of Bülow's apartment to the house of Wagner's former servants, the Mrazeks. Bülow threw himself into frenetic work. Finally, on November 16, after a month of torment and frustration, still with nothing definitely settled, Cosima, with Wagner's two daughters, Isolde and Eva, left Munich—and Hans. She wrote to Claire from Triebschen saying that she had left Munich peacefully and had asked for a year in which to think things over. The plan was to be that Hans would say that her health was not good and that she was staying with her family in Paris. All letters would be addressed to her care of Claire, although Bülow, of course would know where she really was.

Although there is here an intimation that Cosima had agreed to think things over again before taking any final action, her heart and mind were perfectly clear. She had left Hans never to return. It was to be eleven years before she saw him again. The day after her departure, the grim and difficult Madame von Bülow arrived in Munich to take over the care of the two daughters Cosima had left behind, Daniela and Blandine. Liszt must have shuddered at this vision of the ghost of his own and Marie d'Agoult's past.

The day that Cosima left Bülow finally, she began a diary which she was to keep faithfully until Wagner's death. It was to be for her children, she wrote, so that they might know and understand her. The year 1868 was the outward turning point in her life, she tells them. "In this year it was granted to me to carry into action what had inspired me for the past five years. I did not seek this action, nor try to bring it about, it was destiny that imposed it on me . . . When it was so ordered by the stars . . . that I saw my only friend, the guardian spirit of my soul, the revealer of all that was noble and true, driven out into solitude alone, abandoned, joyless, and friendless, I cried to him: 'I am coming to you and I will find my highest and most sacred happiness in helping you to bear your life.' "[6]

Wagner, too, noted his thoughts for this fateful day. "To this refuge too, the woman fled who was to establish it as a fact that I could indeed be helped and that the axiom of so many of my friends, that it was impossible to help me, was wrong. She knew that I could be helped and help me she did."[7]

The stipulation to which Cosima had agreed, that her presence at Triebschen be kept secret, was an obvious impossibility. Not only were there neighbors and servants and plenty of prying eyes, there was also her correspondence, especially with the King. Here Cosima's and Wagner's efforts to pretend that Cosima was not at Triebschen reached almost ludricrous proportions with all sorts of ridiculous subterfuges being employed.

It was not that Bülow had any hope left that the marriage could ever be salvaged. If only it could appear that Cosima had left him, but not on Wagner's account. If only there could be a separation for a year or so, but not with Cosima known to be with Wagner. If only the two headstrong lovers would hold back for a little, would check the course of events long enough for Bülow's honor to be salvaged, at least in part.

These were pipe dreams on Bülow's part, hopeless, unrealistic imaginings. Nothing could be done to salvage anything now, for Cosima was again pregnant by Wagner and on June 6, 1869, she gave birth to her fifth child. She recorded her feelings on that day. "When the woman said to me: 'I congratulate you, it is a boy,' I could only weep and laugh and pray. May God who gave him to me preserve him for me, may he be the support of his sisters, the heir of his adored father." [8] They named him Siegfried.

Bülow read of the event in the newspapers and now he understood bitterly why Cosima had refused to stay on in Munich until Liszt's promised arrival in January. Ten days later he received a lengthy letter from Cosima which she had decided to write after the birth of her son.

She has learned, she says, that Hans has resigned his position in Munich and that he would like to know from her the destiny of their children and what is to happen to their belongings. This gives her the courage to write to him. "I do it with great timidity," she states, "and beg you not to be irritated if I come at an inopportune moment. I have always had little luck in my conversations with you; when I tried to reinstate an honorable peace between us, you answered me with irony; when I asked you for a definite rupture, you did not want to listen to me. Today I beg you to listen to me with kindness, in communion with yourself without external preoccupations, and in remembering what for years we have suffered in common."

She goes on to discuss at length his position in Munich. If he is leaving because he cannot put up with the intrigues and villanies he has found there, that is one thing. But if he is leaving because of her and the necessity for lies and dissimulation, she does not agree with his decision. No blame or shame could ever fall on him for what has happened. His character is too well known and respected for that. It is she who will be blamed: it is expected that a woman will maintain the moral order; that a mother will be ready to sarcrifice herself for her children. Also it is known that he is a man of honor whom she married by her own wish. She hopes that he will decide to remain in Munich for several reasons, in part that with his salary he would be able to put aside something for the children and also that he is not made for a vagabond life. She believes that nowhere in Germany or anywhere else could he find a better place. "In the solitude and silence of my present life," she continues, "I have often gone over my previous existence and questioned my conscience; I have never dissembled the burden of my guilt toward you for you have none except that you married me. I can say that during the seven months of our separation I have had no other preoccupation and sorrow than you (and I hope that you will listen to me with enough tranquillity and kindness to believe what I am telling you); a hundred times I have asked myself what I could, what I should do and I swear to you that it is not a selfish judgment which has prevented me from hastening to you. The memory of our inner life from the second year of our engagement has always appeared before me to prove to me that, no matter how much good will I put in, I did not make you happy at all. Nothing that I did succeeded. How many times when you were ill did you send me away from your bedside without my knowing the reason why. And you remember when I was pregnant with Loulou I did not dare to tell you, as though my pregnancy was an illegitimate one, and that I told it to you as a dream. Nevertheless, I admit that I would never have left you had I not met the life on which mine is so dependent that I no longer know how to detach myself from it. You will never know how I have struggled and all I have suffered. It would be impossible to describe to you the consternation that took possession of me when I realized that the project of a life *à trois* revealed itself to be unrealizable. It was not the humiliations that you inflicted on me that distressed me then; believe me, I have arrived at the point where I stand grief almost more easily than happiness, and that all expiation of my wrongs as of my joy is welcome; it was the presentiment that it could not last that way, and that you yourself would hasten the catastrophe. But if I had to separate from you and if you had to contribute fatally to this separation, that which could not and never will change is the concern that I have for you and for your destiny. You are the only being in the world of whom I think, the only one whose heavy griefs I share in from afar. I do not believe that you can disdain this affection which has always been the same and which survives all the elements of our situation. It is in the name of this affection that I ask, if you have the strength to separate publicly from me, to allow me to bring up our children, and to remain in contact with me." She will bring them up for him, she assures him, so that they will be able to console him some day. There is no one else who can care for them; his mother, whom she never permitted herself to judge as long as she had obligations to fulfill toward her, is in no way fitted to bring them up. As for their possessions, she begs that he will keep everything of hers for the children including the six thousand francs income she receives from her father and mother. "I do not know what else to say to you," she closes, "nevertheless my heart is heavy and swollen. It always seems to me that my suggestions are unfortunate ones and that I will have to suffer one of those bitter answers which you can feel you have the right to give me, but which my soul and my conscience know not to have merited." [9]

Hans received this letter just at the time of the rehearsals of *Tristan*—that fateful opera which had run like a thin red line throughout his marriage to Cosima. He himself saw a kind of fatality in that he had begun his duties in Munich with *Tristan* and he would end them with it too.

He answered Cosima's letter at once. And here we see at last much of the real inner man, shorn of all the superficial and petty complaints and nervous irritabilities. We see the man whom Liszt loved like a son and whom Cosima left only because of her irresistible passion for Wagner and her sense of mission toward him.

"Dear Cosima," he wrote. "I thank you for taking the initiative and I will give you no reason to regret it. I am too unhappy —through my own fault—not to want to avoid hurting you by any unjust reproach. In the very cruel separation in which you feel yourself obligated, I recognize all the faults from my side and will continue to emphasize them in the most energetic way in my inevitable discussions on the subject with my mother and your father. I have very badly, very meanly recompensed you for all the devotion which you have lavished on me during our past life—I have poisoned yours and I can only thank the providence that offered you an ineffective counterbalance at the next to the last moment when the courage to continue your burden must have left you. But, alas—since you have left me—my only support in life, in the struggle is lost to me. Your mind, your heart, your friendship, your patience, your indulgence, your sympathy, your encouragement, your advice—finally and above all your presence, your glance, your words—all that formed and constituted the support of my life. The loss of this supreme good, the total value of which I recognized only after its loss has made me fail, morally and artistically. I am bankrupt. Do not believe that this complaint—I suffer so much that I can permit myself to complain because I refrain from accusing another author than myself—implies an irony, or a sharpness toward you.

"You have preferred to devote your life and the treasures of your mind and heart to a being decidedly superior—far from blaming you—I approve from all points of view, I agree that you are completely right. I assure you that the only consoling thought that has been occasionally a beneficent ray in my gloomy inner and outer torments has been this, at least Cosima is happy there."

After this "expression of faith," as he calls it, Hans goes on to talk of more practical matters. He explains that the reason he has given for resigning his position is his health but actually he no longer thinks the effort worth while—Munich has become a hell with her gone and with his very real exhaustion and bad health. He goes on to say, without any reproach to its author, that the fact that he was forced to occupy himself with the gigantic but fatal *Tristan* has really given him the *coup de grâce.* If someone had offered him a few drops of Prussic acid, he would perhaps not have resisted the temptation of taking them! He is convinced now that he must separate himself completely from everything that concerns both her and Wagner and to break all the bonds that tied him to the past. As for a divorce, if Liszt is not against it, he will not oppose it. On the other hand, he will not ask for it on his own account. The children, he agrees, should be left entirely in her charge. "If your excellent heart consents to bring up our children in spite of all the antipathy and all the just bitterness which you carry toward their father, I do not know why I should not also leave you my name." Whatever money or income is hers, she should have and use for the children. He will take only those things which are his alone—his books, his clothes, his music. He wants to leave Munich with as little baggage from the past as possible. He has been asked to reconsider his resignation but he plans to stay in Munich only until August, when the music school closes for vacation, and then leave quietly, supposedly for reasons of health on a leave of absence which he will later make final. He begs her to forgive his badly written letter, a poor answer to hers. "It is a kind of testament written by a brain and heart that is very ill, half deranged." [10]

If Cosima had shed tears over Bülow before, how many must she have shed over this letter which turns and turns again the knife in the wound. In spite of all his fine phrases, however, Bülow was profoundly bitter.

Claire Charnacé had remained in close touch not only with

Cosima throughout all this but with Hans too. She had hoped that the marriage could be held together somehow and her admiration for Bülow's conduct never wavered. It is to her that Bülow pours out the concentrated essence of three years of betrayal.

"You have had the kindness, Madame, to accord me until now flattering praises on the spirit of equity and unselfish accommodation that I have shown in a very difficult situation. I must fear that you will be disposed to withdraw your very precious approval from me in view of the latest step which I have had to take, a step which could well appear to you as gravely illogical. It is almost as painful for me to explain my action as it would be to leave that explanation to the passage of time. Believe me, Madame, I have done all that was humanly possible to do to avoid a public scandal. For more than three years I took it upon myself to live a life of ceaseless torture. You cannot form an idea of the corroding agitations to which I was incessantly a prey. In the end, I even sacrificed my artistic and my material position to this end. There was only one more thing that I could sacrifice—my life, and I confess that that would have been the simplest way to settle things, to cut the inextricable knot. But from that sacrifice I did recoil—can that be attributed to me as a crime? Perhaps I should not have shrunk even from that if only I had felt in him, in that man who is as sublime in his works as he is abject in his actions, the least indication of loyalty, the most transient sign of a desire to act in an upright and honorable manner. Alas, I should not bring any accusation lest I tarnish the one thing that remains to me, the consciousness that I have been less guilty toward him than he has been toward me. But this accusation that I have just formulated and of which twenty years of close relationship has given me more than sufficient proofs, was it not necessary in order to acquit another person who, formerly, as much in the superiority of her intelligence as in her loyalty, her openness and the nobility of her character bore such a close and sisterly resemblance to you, Madame? When your sister is free (perhaps we shall have to wait for a year from now for the judgment), when she has legalized her association with her lover before the world—she will come to herself—she will not have to lie from morning till night . . . Now what is the explanation of my inconsistency about a separation which I had at first rejected to make legal? In the month of November when I asked her a question that was almost indelicate as to the motives for her sudden departure (I had begged her in vain to wait until Liszt arrived in the month of January) Cosima thought it proper to answer me by swearing to a lie. It was this lie that I learned about *from the newspapers* which announced, without any beating about the bush, the happiness of the *maestro* whose mistress (as they openly referred to her) had finally presented him with a son, baptized in the name of Siegfried, a happy omen for the approaching completion of his opera. The edifice of my cuckoldum was thus crowned in the most resplendent fashion. I could not escape from Munich, but the hell that I have endured during the last part of my activity there is unimaginable. Always in contact with a crowd of musicians, professors, students, and with the publicity which did not spare me (after my last performance of *Tristan* the largest of the newspapers lauded the devotion which I put into the study of the work of my wife's 'friend') I had two choices, either to be considered with the most injurious kind of pity as an ignoramus, or to be taxed with the infamy of having accepted the most disgraceful bargain as favorite of a favorite of the King. At the same time, the newspapers announced, before I had taken the first step, that my divorce was imminent. There is no sacrifice that I would not have made to obtain the divorce with the least possible scandal, and the least friction. But I cannot change the law of

Prussia. By mutual consent? Impossible. There is nothing else except the complaint of desertion.

"I feel I have been too wordy in my explanations. May they serve, Madame, to prevent you from judging me unfairly, which would be the only thing that could grieve me now. They say that time heals many wounds; but this power has its limits. I am too covered with shame to be able to expect any benefit from that direction. I feel that I am exiled from my musical fatherland, exiled from all civilized countries. I will try to drag out the remainder of my poor life in an obscure position giving piano lessons. The only thing that upholds me now is the satisfaction of having compensated fully here below for my sins. I do not expect an answer from you, Madame, but encouraged by your offer of sympathy and friendship, I beg that you will do me the service of not bringing too severe a judgment to bear on your most humble servant." [11]

That Bülow should be so bitter and that his violence should have been directed primarily against Wagner is understandable. Like a malignant growth, Wagner had penetrated throughout the cells of Bülow's existence so completely that to try to cut it out was at the risk of his very life.

To lose Cosima and his children was a great grief to Bülow, for although he had not, perhaps, the obvious trappings of a brilliant husband and father, he was nevertheless devoted to his family and fiercely loyal to them. Even if he was a difficult family man, and Cosima had reason to complain of his many defects in this regard, he was nevertheless deeply attached to them in his own way. Cosima, of course, had represented to him from the first a superior being, someone whom he admired and whose gifts he recognized and felt in many ways were greater than his own. Her strength of character had supported him, her courage had inspired him, her mind had stimulated him. But, actually, it was more to Wagner that he had dedicated his life than to his family. Even the honeymoon was shared with Wagner and Wagner's music dominated the early marriage years when the piano score of *Tristan* drove him so often to despair.

The greatest irony of all was that it was Bülow who started it. It was he who was determined that Cosima should share his feelings for the "Master." It was he who tried to bring them together hoping that each would see in the other what he himself did. And now he had lost them both. Wagner's overwhelming personality, his cause in which Bülow believed totally, his monstrous egotism which had kept Bülow perpetually occupied was gone and Bülow was in danger of collapse.

Bülow was a man of outstanding talent and achievement in his generation. It is only before a Wagner that his stature, and even then not in every aspect, seems to diminish. In all other connections there were not many musicians of his time who were his equal. And yet, we have seen the self-doubts and self-questionings that wracked him from time to time when he was in one of his black moods. Gifted and fiercely independent as he was, Bülow seemed to need the sustenance of someone greater than himself; he seemed to draw strength and purpose from his connection with a genius and a personality that could nourish him. Perhaps at the root of this was a feeling of self-deprecation, almost of hostility to self which made him function in the cause of someone else far better and more easily than in his own. Whatever the explanation was, Bülow suffered a triple betrayal —his wife, his friend, and his life's work.

Liszt, by the time of the final rupture in June of 1869, had withdrawn from the situation as much as he could. He was no longer in any contact with Cosima or Wagner. He had opposed the divorce as strongly as he could and he could do no more. His feelings for Hans were filled with compassion and affection but he knew that at this moment at least, he could not help him.

Wagner was always unchangeably Wagner who saw everything only from the aspect of Wagner. He had his Cosima now all to himself and his fine family with five children. At no time did he make any differentiation between his children and those of Bülow. Triebschen was a charming place, a wholly private little peninsula on the lake. Wagner, as usual, did the interior over to suit him and, according to Cornelius, spent a fortune on everything inside and out. The setting was perfect.

Wagner seemed to derive great pleasure from the children, although he did sometimes complain that Cosima devoted too much of her attention to them. But that was normal for Wagner, as he demanded a totality of love and attention that was practically superhuman. And that is exactly what Cosima gave him. At last he had discovered the person who could lavish on him the intensity of feeling that he had always looked for and been so amazingly surprised not to find. "Have you an idea . . . of the miracle of faith and love which I require in order to gain new courage and patience," he had once written to Liszt.[12]

What was marvelous to him in Cosima was not only the totality of her emotion but the quality of it. To be loved, and loved to distraction, by a being of such superior qualities as Cosima —that was what made the magic for him. And he flowered under it now that the tensions and doubts about the future were more or less resolved. He worked, he laughed, he played and sang to her; evenings they read aloud, played duets together, and talked endlessly.

Most of all they explored and discussed and wondered at the miracle of their love for each other. Even allowing for the very different mode of expression in that romantic period, their feelings are expressed in terms considerably larger than life. Cosima confided to her diary: "Richard lavished his heavenly love upon me. He maintained that I grow more beautiful every day. He is ready to die of happiness. Little that is divine exists, he said

—only Cosima." [13] When he told her how well and happy he felt, she wanted to "fall on my knees in gratitude to God."

They agreed on everything, and Cosima shared completely all of Wagner's thoughts and ideas which he expressed with indefatigable energy and eloquence. "For twenty-four hours Wagner did not stop talking," Marie von Mouchanoff wrote, "and with what eloquence, what learning, what fireworks of aphorisms, observations, profound and original ideas. I understand that beside him the whole world seems to Cosima a pale solitude." [14]

Marie von Mouchanoff was an old friend of all of them—Liszt, Wagner, Cosima, and Hans. During the scandal she refused to take sides and did her best to bring about a *rapprochement* between Liszt and his daughter. She loved Cosima as much as ever, she wrote her daughter, but with an extra tenderness now for all she had been through, and she described the pair at Triebschen when she visited them there. "Their retirement is profound . . . He speaks with a noble independence of the possibility of a rupture with the King, preferring to save his work and lose his fortune. Wagner in a coat of black velvet with his *bonnet de magister,* glasses on his nose; she, with her young-womanly appearance, looks like his daughter. She reads his thoughts in his eyes and completes it as though their soul was one in two people. She cries a great deal, brings up her children marvelously, and works day and night for the glory of him who in her eyes is the sum of all perfections." [15]

Cosima did weep, but she hid her tears from Wagner. She could not forget the injustice that she had done to Hans and the pain she had inflicted on him. "Hans' sufferings rob me of all joy," she wrote in her diary.[16] She had made her decision in grief and torment and she had resolved upon her mission to serve Wagner. "Gladly will I suffer all if only I stand at his side," she wrote. "Let them heap insults upon me from generation to generation, so long as I have helped him, so long as I have been permitted to reach out my hand to him and say, 'I will follow you till death.' My only prayer is that I may die at the same hour as Richard. My highest pride is that I have given up everything in order to live for him, his joy is my loveliest happiness. Without him, as Cleopatra said, the world is a mere sty." [17]

Cosima had truly left everything for Wagner as her own mother had done to follow Liszt. Had Bülow opposed her having the two older children, she had been ready to sacrifice even them, just as Marie had done with little Claire. Devout as she was, she eventually abandoned her religion and became a Protestant, a step which cost her a great deal. She once asked Wagner whether he would have become a Catholic for her sake and was rather shaken when he replied that it was a "deuce of a question, he simply could not imagine it. At first I was dashed, and for one moment I felt that, after all, I was giving up religion and everything else in order to be united with him. But then I understood. The woman needs and ought to sacrifice everything for the man whom she loves." [18] There was unquestionably still a great deal in the thirty-one-year-old Cosima of the little girl of the rue Casimir-Périer who believed that her life should be one of obedience and of self-sacrifice.

Wagner's health rebounded as soon as he had Cosima beside him and knew that she would not leave him again. There were few visitors, but that is how he liked it, especially as the visitors who did come were devotees of his who came to worship at the grail. Cosima carefully screened everything from him, letters, of course, and also any people who might bring a breath of conflict into the house. Wagner rose early every day and worked productively, which was Cosima's primary delight.

Among the visitors that summer was the beautiful Judith

Gautier with her husband and a friend. She was just nineteen and an ardent Wagnerian, having written articles on him for the French newspapers. Wagner enjoyed the little group very much, especially Judith, whose admiration for him was strikingly evident. As always, when inspired by a pretty woman, he was full of mischief. He sent Cosima flying in a swing so high that she nearly fainted, and it was only at Judith's insistence that Wagner realized what he had been doing. Then, in order to distract Cosima, he merrily sprinted up the side of the house, by means of the shutters, moldings, stones and finally reached the balcony, all of this, quite naturally, causing Cosima even more fright than her own adventure in the swing. She begged Judith to pay no attention to him for otherwise you never knew what he might do next!

Cosima swam every day in the lake with her four little girls; picnics and excursions to neighboring villages and to the mountains were arranged; every day Cosima found new wonder and delight in Wagner's mind and ideas. It was only the ever-present shadow of Hans that darkened the idyl.

Bülow left Munich finally in August and went straight to Italy. Almost at the breaking point before he left, his spirits and his health began to improve as soon as he was on Italian soil. By now he may have felt a relief at being free of both Cosima and of Wagner. The state that he had so long hoped for —to be completely musically independent and free—had occurred. There were even rumors that he might have fallen in love, and he undoubtedly enjoyed a mild flirtation in Italy. He set about procuring the divorce, which had to be done in Berlin, but just as there had been delays in their marriage, there were now delays in its dissolution and it was not until the following year that the decree was finally granted.

A month later, on August 25, 1870, Cosima von Bülow and Richard Wagner were married. "Our marriage took place at eight o'clock," Cosima wrote. "May I be worthy to bear Richard's name. My prayers have been concentrated upon two points: Richard's well-being and my hope that I may always be able to promote it, and Hans' happiness and my hope that he may live a cheerful life far from me." [19]

CHAPTER XII

"ARIADNE, I LOVE THEE!—Dionysus." [1] This cry was wrung from the heart of a man in his last tragic, dimming days. He had kept his secret well. "Who besides me knows who Ariadne is," he wrote. "No one up till now has the solution for such secrets; I doubt whether anyone has even seen a secret here." [2] Friedrich Nietzsche's Ariadne was Cosima.

It was in the summer of 1869 that Nietzsche saw Cosima for the first time. Wagner had met the young man when he visited his sister in Leipzig in November of 1868. Nietzsche was already then an enthusiast of Wagner, and mutual friends arranged the meeting.

Nietzsche was in a turmoil of excitement beforehand and although he felt the whole encounter was a dream, he did worry considerably about more mundane matters such as what he should wear to meet his idol. A new suit that he had ordered was promised for the great day, but as the afternoon wore on and the suit did not come Nietzsche grew more and more anxious. Finally, at almost the last moment, the tailor arrived.

Enormous relief until a new crisis developed. The tailor demanded immediate payment in cash. Nietzsche was frantic, the tailor was adamant, a tussle for the trousers ensued in which the tailor emerged victorious, after which he scornfully packed up the box and departed with it, leaving Nietzsche with only his old, shiny, everyday suit.

Wagner, however, succeeded at once in making the young doctoral student forget such trivial matters. He was at his best, holding forth in his ever-changing moods—humorously, sarcastically, seriously, always with tremendous energy and exuberance, fascinating all those present with the wealth and originality of his ideas. Not only did Wagner and Nietzsche agree about Wagner's music, but they found further agreement in their admiration for Schopenhauer. At the end of the evening, Wagner invited the young man to visit him at Triebschen and to continue their talks on music and philosophy.

Six months later, Nietzsche was installed as Professor of Philology at the University of Basel. Soon after his arrival in Switzerland, in company with some friends, he found himself in Lucerne, hardly by chance we can imagine, and summoned up courage to present himself at Wagner's door. He arrived while Wagner was composing and from the doorstep he could hear the strains of music that he later identified as from the last act of *Siegfried*. Wagner sent out word that he always worked until two o'clock, but he invited Nietzsche to come back for luncheon. Nietzsche was unable to accept because of his waiting friends, but a few days later he did return. This was his first meeting with Cosima. Two weeks later he was invited to spend the night. It turned out to be quite an introduction to the Triebschen menage, for it was the night of June fifth, and the occasion of Siegfried's birth. Nietzsche fled the next morning and two days later received his first note from Cosima. "Since you wanted to 'vanish' I send, instead of giving you, the two articles you wished for and the book you were so kind as to lend me. But only do not be angry with Triebschen because of 'Neophyte confusion!' "[3] From then on Nietzsche became a regular visitor at Triebschen.

Wagner was fifty-six years old that summer of 1869, Cosima was thirty-one, and Nietzsche twenty-four. In some ways Cosima felt herself to be the oldest of the three. The events of the past few years had not only made her wise in the ways of the world, but had taken away something of her youthful verve and humor and eagerness for life. She had the feeling that she would live to be a hundred for the very reason that she no longer held to life, having once sounded its depths. Although Wagner had suffered much too, he had kept intact his overpowering confidence in himself and his mission. He had always felt set apart from the rest of the world, possessed of a higher destiny, and this feeling spurred him with a restless, driving energy.

Nietzsche was a shy, sensitive, inhibited young man, whose powerful brain and intellectual drive were in contrast to the strong emotions held in check beneath the surface. This turbulence was encased in an extremely neurasthenic organism, one that was susceptible to constant attacks of headaches, rheumatic pains, and various physical and nervous breakdowns. Brought up, after his father's death when he was only five, in a household of women—his mother and sister and aunts—Nietzsche spent a lonely childhood. During his six years at boarding school he was desperately homesick and miserable, plagued by severe headaches and bad eyesight. He suffered from the constant routine of school life that left him not one minute for the reflection and meditation which already at that early age he needed. His first groping years at the University were efforts at finding himself and freeing himself from the strong bonds that held him to his mother. The momentous event of his early days was his discovery of Schopenhauer. The great pessimist philosopher became for the young beginner more than the purveyor of a system of ideas. He became almost like a living presence, a friend and mentor, someone to replace the father Nietzsche could not even remember. Nietzsche began to feel free from his mother, although he remained unusually close to his sister; free from the inner doubts and confusion that had hampered him; free from the weaknesses and fears that had made him doubt his own powers. The horrors of a tour of service in the army during the Prussian-Austrian war of 1865 served to drive him further into his studies of Schopenhauer. When illness forced his discharge, he saw his path clear. He would teach and think and write and carry his ideas even beyond those of Schopenhauer. The professor who recommended him for the position at Basel wrote that he had never yet "known a young man . . . who was so mature as early and as young as this Nietzsche . . . You will say, I describe a phenomenon. Well, that is just what he is—and at the same time pleasant and modest. Also a gifted musician, which is irrelevant here." [4]

In Wagner, Nietzsche found a man not only whose music fascinated him but whose ideas, whose whole way of thinking had a profound appeal for him. Wagner represented to him an ideal, a cause that seemed in perfect harmony with his own. The long days at Triebschen were magical to the young philosopher. Wagner played him his music, and read aloud his prose works and they discussed everything under the sun—religion, politics, philosophy, Greek tragedy, and ever back again to Wagner's ideas on art and its supreme role in the creation of values in the life of the individual and the state. And always there was Cosima, listening, watching, delighting in Wagner's interest and response to the new friend.

Friedrich Nietzsche must have seemed like a gift from heaven to the two isolated from the world at Triebschen. What a wonderful addition to the ranks of Wagnerians this brilliant young man must have seemed. His delight in the "Master" was as complete as anyone could have wanted, even the demanding great man himself. "Wagner is really everything that one could wish," Nietzsche wrote shortly after his June fifth visit to Triebschen. "He has an extravagantly rich and noble nature, energetic character, fascinating personality and strong will power." [5] And he referred to Wagner as "my Jupiter."

It was more than a year before Cosima's marriage to Wagner took place that Nietzsche first came to Triebschen, and the only real constraint that he felt was in the irregularity of their relationship. Brought up as he had been by his widowed mother, Nietzsche was shy and inexperienced with women, extremely naïve and innocent. Wagner may have felt that Nietzsche was attracted to Cosima, or a spirit of contradiction toward Nietzsche's evident chastity may have goaded him, but he seemed to enjoy embarrassing him. Wagner was always something of a show-off and toward this much younger man he may have taken a malicious delight in crowing over his own virility. In any event he often referred to his relationship with Cosima in such coarse and suggestive language that it was extremely offensive to Nietzsche's fastidious taste. This, however, was the only small and occasional cloud on an otherwise idyllic situation and Cosima, with her ever-watchful tact, did what she could to dissipate it.

For Cosima, the young professor came like a breath of fresh air after the tensions of the last years. He was someone from another world with no connection at all to the past. He was only five years younger than her brother Daniel would have been had he lived, and bereft as she was of both brother and sister, she may have felt in Nietzsche someone with whom she might have a close "sisterly" relationship. Certainly it was not long before she was writing to him in a simple and affectionate way. There is a directness and a lack of affectation in her letters to

Nietzsche at this period, which is not always the case in her other letters or even in her diary where one often has the feeling, based on the published excerpts, that she is writing with one eye fixed on "history." In her letters to Nietzsche, the tone is one of complete ease and warmth. She keeps him informed of everything that is happening at Triebschen, what they are doing and thinking, and what the children are up to. And she makes him feel an integral part of their life. "Well, now you know about everything, dear Professor," she ends one of her letters, "and you also know how much we think of you in our quiet life. For us you are a Triebschener and in the material as well as the moral seclusion of our home, that says a great deal." [6] Although she addressed him formally as 'Dear Professor,' the tone of her letters is that of one companion to another.

Nietzsche was invited to spend the Christmas holidays with them, and Cosima flooded him with commissions, things she was unable to buy in Lucerne: tulle with gold stars for the Christ Child's dress; a Dürer engraving for Wagner; toys and games for the children. "I have to forget that you are a Professor of Philology," Cosima wrote him in one of her many letters about these commissions, "and simply remember that you are twenty-five years old and good to us Triebscheners." [7] She made clear how deeply he could count on their friendship. "Wherever we are or will be, whether in snowy or sunny surroundings, everywhere your room with us will be ready. And if you welcome our meeting in life as a friendly stroke of Fate then can you understand that we look upon it in the same way and how much we have come to value you." [8]

Christmas passed in happy animation. Cosima once described life at Triebschen in terms of "a pell-mell of Genius-work, children-confusion, people uproar, animal delight, etc." As far as Christmas was concerned, Cosima felt that Hans had never really enjoyed it, but with Wagner she was challenged to outdo herself, as she did for his birthdays also. She planned and arranged elaborate pageants and musical offerings by the children, carried out intricate and fanciful decorations throughout the house and garden, which she often stayed up whole nights preparing, and Wagner adored it all. On this occasion, the masses of commissions which had been sent to Nietzsche in Basel had all been satisfactorily executed and everything went off to everyone's delight.

The children took a great fancy to Nietzsche, looking upon him as a member of the family, and Cosima wrote him often of their remarks about him. "Eva, aged about three, told her sister that Nietzsche was called 'Fressor,' which can be translated roughly as 'devourer.' 'No, Professor, not Fressor,' Loldi replied. 'He does not devour anyone.' So you see," added Cosima, "you had better not neglect Triebschen!" [9]

She seemed to enjoy sharing anecdotes about the children with Nietzsche, and sometimes there were flashes of her former humor. "Lessons at Triebschen become more difficult all the time. After I spent the whole winter explaining to Isolde that a Poodle is a dog, and what a person, a tree, an animal, etc., is, I recently asked her: 'What is the difference between a tree and a bird?' Answer very vigorous and firm: 'a dog.' 'What is a peasant woman?' Answer somewhat hesitant: 'An animal.' 'How many legs has Mr. am Rhyn?' (who had just passed by). Answer: '6, no 1.' 'What is Pussy?' Answer: 'A person.' I am alarmed over the results and comfort myself with the thought that here, at least, there is no danger that dialectic would supplant music." [10]

Nietzsche's first lectures at the University were to take place in early January. Cosima was very concerned that perhaps not many people would attend this first venture of his and wrote him a long encouraging letter telling him not to worry if the hall was empty and exhorting him to do a really good job.

Afterward, Nietzsche sent her a copy of the lectures, which were on Greek Music Drama, and Socrates, and Greek Tragedy. They struck Cosima like a bolt from the blue. "The Master will have told you in what a state of agitation they put me in," she wrote him, "and that he had to spend the whole evening enlarging on the theme with me. I was in harmony with your basic point of view which from the first I found sympathetic, even familiar, and the boldness and simplicity with which you carried it out at first completely surprised me. The Master had to prove to me in certain passages how right you were. What agitated me, however, was not what you said and how you said it, but the brevity with which you felt it necessary to present the deepest and most far-flung problems so that the listener is challenged to a powerful collaboration which is always an exciting position to be in. As I now have gone through almost every sentence with the Master . . . yesterday I read through your work again for myself and let it quietly work on me. And this time the impression was far greater and more beautiful. Although your assurance really alarmed me at first, it now seems extraordinarily satisfying and I recognize in it the powerful mark of pregnant greatness." [11]

Nietzsche's thesis was that Socrates represented the turning point in Greek tragedy and was responsible for its ensuing decadence. The attack was not against the rational achievements of Socrates, but rather against his position toward artistic values, which he considered illusory and unnecessary, with the only truth lying in rational knowledge. With Wagner's belief in the universal role and power of art Nietzsche's lectures were gratifying in so far as they strengthened Wagner's position. Cosima clearly was surprised by the force and confidence with which this young man expressed himself. It was not the content of the lectures so much as it was the incisive independence with which they were expressed that amazed her. There was one other aspect of this first fine flash of Nietzsche's power that was not lost on Wagner and Cosima: that Nietzsche might not always remain docilely harnessed to the Wagner chariot.

Nietzsche personally seemed in total contrast to the boldness of his ideas. Shy, fastidious, extremely correct and precise in manner, he gave the impression at the same time of retiring modesty and of a reserve that was sometimes interpreted as arrogance. When engaged in stimulating discussion, his black eyes behind the thick lenses of his glasses burned with fervor. There was about him an air of secrecy, with his passionate inner self hidden below layers of defenses. It is not surprising that Cosima's first view into the depths of his nature was disturbing and surprising to her. Nietzsche himself admitted in later years that it was always hard for him to maintain his philosophy after an hour's pleasant conversation, "when it seemed foolish to insist on being right at the price of love, and to be unable to communicate the best in me without destroying the feeling of fellowship." [12] At this Triebschen period, Nietzsche was very strongly under the impress of Wagner's forceful personality and highly developed ideas and Nietzsche undoubtedly did far more listening than talking in his presence. These first daring, independent lectures shocked Cosima out of her "older sister" attitude toward the young scholar and gave her a considerably clearer idea of the caliber of man he was.

Wagner enjoyed this relationship with Nietzsche, who was by far the most brilliant man who had attached himself to the circle of Wagnerians. Cosima found in him not only a source of interest and stimulus, but someone in whom she could confide, someone with whom she could share some of the burdens she was carrying.

"I have the belief that you bring me luck," [13] she wrote him, and often she must have felt that luck was what she needed. The mission that she felt so strongly was hers, the task which she had sacrificed so much to try to achieve, was to create the possibility for Wagner to compose. Above everything, it was Wagner's music that moved and stirred her, and she bitterly resented any worries from the outside world that might interfere with his work. "Then how should he at last win for himself the peaceful spirit for continuing his work?" she asked Nietzsche. "What I build up with effort and love, the world tears down again." [14]

It was not only about Wagner and her concern for him that Cosima confided in Nietzsche, but she talked to him about her own inner troubles and suffering. In her desire to spare Wagner any distress, she tried not to let him see how often and how deeply troubled she was and how strong her feelings of guilt toward Bülow continued to be.

Cosima did not always agree completely with Nietzche's ideas, and sometimes she rather laughs at herself when she discusses them with him and finds it charming that she tries to teach him about philosophy! [15] But some of her remarks were not at all in a joking vein. Hope was a necessity for Cosima, hope and faith. The gloomy and morbid aspects of Schopenhauer's thoughts did not really sit well with her, although she tried to accept them intellectually. She found the philosophy of pessimism disturbing and although she leaned over backwards to be tactful about it, knowing Nietzsche's admiration for Schopenhauer, and referred to it as "this correct form of thought," her distress about it is quite clear. "Your letter this time was doubly welcome," she wrote Nietzsche. "I do not know why a melancholy impression remained with me after your last visit . . . Whether it was our conversation on Sunday morning, with the many veiled memories it conjured up, or whether my own mood that has been with me for years was in part the reason, I do not know and can only say that you seemed to me troubled and gloomy. When I thought about pessimism, and Schopenhauer's philosophy (as far as I am acquainted with it) and hopelessness it seemed to me that if this correct form of thought and this sure way of looking at things is brought into contact with life even in the slightest way, it represents a great danger." And then she goes on to make a plea for positive feelings: "But even you yourself speak of 'our hopes and dreams' . . . you speak of courage and belief, the defeat of the indifferent world and the final coming of the day of nobility which Goethe (certainly no optimist) awaited." [16]

These theoretical differences of viewpoint and belief, however, did nothing to alter the closeness and reality of Nietzsche's relationship to Cosima. Life at Triebschen continued its quiet way. Cosima had moments of tremendous happiness, but the undercurrents of guilt about Bülow were ever present. In July 1870 came the sudden shock of the Franco-German War.

Wagner was thrown into a state of near frenzy. He saw in the war the possibility of a renaissance of the true German spirit. He was obsessed with what he regarded as the corruption and decadence of the French, venting, perhaps, some of his spleen in memory of past affronts suffered at their hands. Although Cosima was in no way a weak or pliant nature, she showed how completely she had taken over all that was Wagner's, how her love for him made her see everything through his eyes. Her entire upbringing had been French; her mother was French; Liszt regarded France as his adopted country and spoke French always by preference. Cosima had not only inherited much of her mother's uniquely French grace and charm, but she had acquired fully the arts and graces of a Frenchwoman. Fluent as her German was, she nevertheless spoke it with a slight French accent throughout her long life. Among many Germans, envious or hostile or both, she was known as the "Frenchwoman," a title that was to remain with her for many years. Yet, like many converts, Cosima was more German than the Germans in her sympathies, especially during the frenzied period of the Franco-German War. "I am absolutely beside myself at the insolence of the French," she fulminated about the French ultimatum. "That nation deserves to be punished without mercy." [17] Wagner went even further and described Paris as the "kept woman" of the world and declared that it would and should be destroyed.

Basel was in a state of uproar with French and German nationals trying to get home. Nietzsche, who had had to become a Swiss citizen in order to accept the position at the University, was caught up in the general fervor and felt that he must do his German duty.

Cosima strongly opposed his desire to enlist and considered it a useless gesture. Only if Germany were to be invaded would it be necessary for everyone to enter the fray and protect each city and each house, she told him. The work of peace was just as important as ever and should not be left untended. She felt it her duty to tell him how she felt about it but added, "if you know me and my life well enough you would be sure that concern about life or property has never had a hand in or prompted either my actions or my advice. I know that you will follow your own feelings and that is right for it is perhaps better to act incorrectly in agreement with your own feelings than to do better in following the feelings of others." [18]

Nietzsche did make his own decision. Although he could not enlist as a soldier, because of his Swiss citizenship, he succeeded in entering the German ambulance corps. Cosima accepted his decision reluctantly, for she felt it was unnecessary, but at least she was relieved that he would not be fighting. In the end it might have been better for Nietzsche had he followed Cosima's advice, for he found the experiences on the battle field agonizing. Yet his very reactivity and sensitivity increased his dreams of strength and *sang froid*. On one occasion when he was entering a small town on foot he heard a distant thundering of hoofs. As he flattened himself against a high stone wall his old cavalry regiment hurtled past. Swept up in a surge of excitement he described the experience to his sister. "I felt for the first time in my life that the strongest and noblest Will to Life does not reside in our puny struggle to exist, but in the Will to War, the Will to Power, the Will to Superpower!" [19]

It was not long, however, before the strain and conflict proved too much for Nietzsche's precarious nervous and physical organism. He contracted diphtheria and severe dysentery, and it soon became clear that he could not continue in any kind of active service. Once he was definitely out of the war, Cosima felt free to express her feelings of anxiety about him more freely. "I was especially afraid for your inner spiritual condition which you described to me just as I had feared it would be. I know that there are experiences that stamp our inner being forever, just as the brand of a prisoner is stamped with a red hot iron." And here again she makes her plea for hope and belief. "In this deluge of suffering, let us think as deeply and nobly as possible; let us think that it will make men greater than they are and that we ought to be serene in losing those to whom Fate has decreed a noble death instead of a certainly troubled, and probably insignificant, life." She goes on to say that life at Triebschen continues as before, "the children merry, the Master active." Her own existence there she finds "as a heavenly liberation from life; only past griefs always clang behind as though, as it were, man dare not ever be completely free and must always drag the chains of former sorrows as a reminder." [20]

Nietzsche saw active service during only a little over a month, but that month was to have a long-term effect on him. Not only were his battlefield dreams of triumph the precoursers of his Will to Power, in spite of the wracking pity he felt for the sick and wounded, but the sacrifices that he saw on the battlefield put him violently out of sympathy with the complacent attitudes that he felt on the home front. Little by little he came to the conclusion that modern Prussia was one of the greatest threats to German culture. This concept was hardly one with which Wagner could agree. Wagner had too much confidence in man's need for intellectual liberty to envision that anything, even the militarization and materialization of German life that Nietzsche dreaded, could endanger it.

The month that had passed, however, had brought not only the experiences of war, but it had seen the marriage of Wagner and Cosima. A strange diffidence began to appear in the tone of Cosima's letters now. They are a great deal shorter and rarer than they had been. Nietzsche was invited, as the year before, to spend Christmas at Triebschen. The many requests for small commissions, however, are missing from her letters this year. A significant phrase in one of her letters in early December, exhorts him "not to lose his feeling for Triebschen completely." [21]

Certainly there were growing signs that Nietzsche was moving further away from the center of Wagner's orbit, that he was not wholly in agreement with all of the older man's ideas and thoughts, especially as far as the war and the German victory were concerned. Cosima did not hide her agreement with Wagner, but she seemed singularly unconcerned at that time about any possible difference of opinion. These were only very small cracks, however, in the façade of a singular relationship between the two men.

It is more than regrettable that we do not have Nietzsche's letters to Cosima, which are said to have been destroyed by Cosima herself. From them we might have learned the origin of the slight constraint in Nietzsche's relationship with Cosima at this time. The imagination cannot help but wonder if it was in any way connected with the fact of her marriage.

In spite of any moderation in the friendship at that time,

Christmas did see Nietzsche once again at Triebschen. For Cosima it was perhaps the unforgettable Christmas of her life. Cosima's birthday was always celebrated on Christmas day, and this year Wagner had been unusually secretive and busy before the event. On Christmas morning she was awakened by the sound of music, coming from the staircase outside the bedroom. "I can tell you nothing, my children, about this day, nothing about my feelings, nothing about my state of mind—nothing, nothing," she noted in her diary. "I will only tell you quite drily and barely what happened: As I awoke, my ear caught a sound which swelled fuller and fuller; no longer could I imagine myself to be dreaming, music was sounding, and what music! As it died away, Richard came into my room with the five children and offered me the score of the symphonic birthday poem—I was in tears, but so was the whole house. Richard had placed his orchestra on the staircase, and thus was our Triebschen consecrated forever. . . . I have spent the whole day as though in a dream, my spirit is still listening to the vanished sounds, and as it recalls them, my heart, oppressed by emotion, seeks release in music." [22] This was the *Siegfried Idyl,* as it was later to be called.

Nietzsche's gift to Cosima was his newly printed essay on the *Dionysian Outlook on the World.* He had read it to them both before he left for the war, yet it is interesting that it was not to Wagner but to Cosima that he presented it, for the Dionysus image was one of vital importance for Nietzsche in relation to his feelings about Cosima. He could not help but notice how Wagner's gift overwhelmed his own.

In spite of the Christmas visit, the old warmth and closeness is not apparent in Cosima's letters until Nietzsche falls ill again —this time with symptoms of a nervous breakdown plus severe physical indications of jaundice and eye trouble. "You poor man!" she wrote him as soon as she learned about it. "It is a real song of lamentation that you send to Triebschen! How would it be if you hung pedagogy on a nail and came here not to think, but to live a 'social' life, to drink Carlsbad water and to let yourself be looked after? You would be 'sung and played to' and in the end you would be healthy again." And she goes on to admonish him very much in the role of "older sister" here: "Above all I beg you that for once you should not think, especially do not think about your illness; do everything to overcome it, but do not be absorbed with thinking about it; that makes one jaundiced and hypochondriac." [23] There is no detachment or constraint here. Cosima showed at once that she was ready to respond with the same affection and interest as she had always shown as soon as Nietzsche sent her his "song of lamentation." Nietzsche, however, did not accept this warm invitation to Triebschen. He had always, even from the very earliest days, refused to move too closely into the Wagner orbit and he kept, not at arm's length, but nevertheless a certain distance between them, much as he revered and looked up to Wagner. In spite of his outward reserve and shyness, Nietzsche was as conscious of his own power as was Wagner, and felt that he too was an exceptional man. He was not another Bülow, who was ready to give up all for the "Master." He did not accept all the invitations, he did not spend entire summers at Triebschen, as they had urged him to do more than once. On this occasion, he sent for his sister, and the two of them traveled over the Gotthard to Lugano. In no time, Nietzsche's condition improved dramatically, and brother and sister had a grand time together. Nietzsche entered into one of his states of amazing creativity, and every day he worked at his first major book: *The Birth of Tragedy*. By the time he returned to Basel in April he had only a few more pages of it to complete.

The Birth of Tragedy was Nietzsche's Christmas offering to Triebschen that next year. He had been invited as usual but had declined in favor of visiting his mother. His book, which arrived shortly after the New Year, produced a sensation. "How beautiful your book is!" Cosima wrote him. "How beautiful and profound! How profound and daring! . . . In this book you have evoked demons whom I believed obedient to the Master only," she went on in what was for her a startling and unheard of comparison of Nietzsche with Wagner. ". . . I cannot tell you how much your book, in which you define with such truthful simplicity the tragedy of our existence, has seemed capable to me of elevating our thoughts . . . I have read this book as though it were a poem, though it opens for us the most profound of all problems; and I cannot lay it aside any more than the Master can, for it offers a reply to all the unconscious questions of my soul." [24]

The Preface was a dedication of the book to Wagner. In it Nietzsche speaks of his conviction that art is the highest task and the proper metaphysical activity of this life, art "as it is understood by the man to whom, as my noble champion on this same path, I now dedicate this essay." [25]

In this work, Nietzsche was to expand his earlier theories of Apollonian and Dionysian art taking some of the theories of Wagner and Schopenhauer as points of departure for a loosely joined structure that was, in effect, an ode of gratitude to all that Wagner had given him.

There was another Christmas present for Cosima from Nietzsche, however, nothing less than a musical composition entitled, imposingly, "Echoes of a New Year's Eve with Processional, Peasant Dance and Midnight Chimes."

Nietzsche had always been musical. He played the piano, improvised and composed with a good deal of freedom and seeming lack of self-consciousness. How seriously Cosima took his composition we do not know. However, she was definitely sympathetic to his musical gifts and wrote him on one occasion that she had again recognized "how deeply musical you are," and considered that this had perhaps helped him to grasp the kernel of Greek tragedy.

Hans von Bülow viewed the matter quite differently. Bülow had been very impressed with Nietzsche's *Birth of Tragedy,* and Nietzsche took the occasion to send him a copy of one of his own compositions, entitled *Manfred.* Bülow's reply is in his usual refreshingly uncompromising vein. "Your *Manfred Meditation* is the most fantastically extravagant, the most unedifying, the most anti-musical thing I have ever come across for a long time in the way of notes put on paper. Several times I had to ask myself whether it is all a joke, whether, perhaps, your object was to produce a parody of the so-called music of the future. Is it by intent that you persistently defy every rule of tonal connection from the higher syntax down to the merest spelling? . . . Of the Apollonian element I have not been able to discover the smallest trace; and as for the Dionysian, I must say frankly that I have been reminded less of this than of the 'day after' a bacchanal. If you really feel a passionate urge to express yourself in music, you should master the rudiments of the musical language: a frenzied imagination, revelling in reminiscences of Wagnerian harmonies, is no sort of foundation to build upon . . . You yourself, not without reason, describe your music as 'terrible.' It is indeed more terrible than you think." [26] There was never the slightest doubt as to what Bülow thought on any subject.

Cosima hastened to the rescue, performing a rather neat balancing act of tact in saying that, "I recognize in the articulate words the justified and always well-founded bluntness of Herr von Bülow," [27] but adds that she is sure that had he heard Nietzsche play it himself he would not have found it so unmusical. Besides, Nietzsche has no pretenses about his compositions, which give him pleasure and do not harm anyone, and she ends by comparing him to Goethe who distracted himself by drawing.

Nietzsche's musical gifts aside, it began slowly to look as though the Triebschen Idyl was beginning to lose a little of its luster as far as Nietzsche and Wagner were concerned. In spite of the many points of fervid agreement, the seeds of rupture were evident from the start in the egocentric natures of the two men. And between them was Cosima, wholly within Wagner's sphere but equally within the secret circle of Nietzsche's dreams.

Not long afterward came the final move away from Triebschen to Bayreuth. Wagner's plan to establish his ideal music center in Bayreuth had long been fermenting in his mind. Munich, in spite of the King's continuing hope to re-establish the composer there, was clearly a lost cause. Wagner went on ahead to Bayreuth while Cosima stayed behind to do the final packing and closing. On the last day Nietzsche came to be with her in the place that had meant so much to him. "We walked as if we were walking among ruins," he wrote. "The air and the clouds were heavy with tears. The dog refused to eat. The servants burst into sobs when we spoke to them . . . Oh! it was desperate! The three years I have passed so close to Triebschen, in which I have visited there twenty-three times—how much they have meant to me! Had I never possessed them, what should I be now?" [28] In moments of deep emotion, Nietzsche always turned to music and he did so on this occasion too, going finally to the piano and pouring his heart out in a sweeping improvisation that Cosima never forgot.

During the Triebschen years, Cosima had drawn Nietzsche very closely into the family circle on a footing of unusual intimacy. Aside from the young philosopher's admiration and excitement over Wagner's musical and philosophical ideas, the strong personal ties that existed between him and the Wagner family were very real. Not only had the private printing of Wagner's autobiography been entrusted to him, but he was designated as Siegfried's guardian should anything happen to Wagner. The Triebschen period represented the high point in his relationship, which began slowly to change after the move away from Triebschen. Only Nietzsche's secret Ariadne did not change.

It was inevitable that Wagner's and Nietzsche's mutual admiration could not last forever. Indeed, that it lasted as long as it did speaks for the profound feeling the two men had for each other. With the move to Bayreuth, with Wagner actively on the road to the realization of his plans and dreams, the tension between them was bound to increase. *The Birth of Tragedy* had a very poor reception—indeed it was practically ignored. In the meantime, Wagner became more and more of a celebrity. Wagner societies were springing up all over Europe and America, all dedicated to the realization of Bayreuth.

Wagner's almost pathological sensitivity where any suggestion of neglect by his friends was concerned was equaled only by a similar reaction in Nietzsche. Soon, understandably, each began to feel slighted by the other from time to time. A gift of Nietzsche's was not acknowledged for several weeks; Nietzsche turned down an invitation to spend Christmas, preferring to go to his mother's home for the holiday. These might be construed as trivial events to other natures than Wagner's and Nietzsche's. However, Wagner had long since proved that he could not stand a friendship wherein someone else or something else was ever given priority over himself. During the increasing coldness, which even all of Cosima's diplomacy could only delay but not check, Nietzsche began to look at Wagner with a more detached and analytical eye.

Cosima tried to maintain the old warmth and closeness, but it became increasingly hard to do. At the end of a two months' silence we find her writing Nietzsche that, "In time, it seems to be as it is in space, where one no longer calls out to far-distant persons knowing that they no longer hear us; thus in a lengthy separation in time, one has almost the feeling of no longer really being heard. That, dear friend, is the explanation for the long silence." [29] Her letters become increasingly rare. Instead of twice a month, or even more often, sometimes several months pass without a letter.

It was not lack of communication, however, that brought about the rift. Much later, Nietzsche divided the plan of his life into three periods which fit completely the pattern of his relationship with Wagner. The first path of the Way to Wisdom, as he called it, included "Worshipping (and obeying and learning) better than anyone else. Assimilating all things that are venerable and letting them struggle with one another. Putting up with every difficulty . . . time of fellowship . . . One cannot conquer without love." [30] Here are the Triebschen years, and Nietzsche's intense relationship with Wagner and Cosima, those years about which he wrote, "at no price would I have my life deprived of those days at Triebschen—days of confidence, of cheerfulness, of sublime flashes, and of profound moments." [31]

Sometime after the move to Bayreuth, when Wagner's ideas were put into vessels of bricks and mortar and fallible human flesh, Nietzsche began to be disillusioned at the actuality of the dream-made-real and to have shied away from the preoccupation with materialistic and mundane matters that was necessary for Cosima and Wagner in order to turn plans into reality. Certainly he also began to feel a criticism toward some of Wagner's ideas and attitudes in spite of the fact that he wrote a rhapsody of praise to him in his *Richard Wagner in Bayreuth.* It is clear that as early as 1874 Nietzsche started making censorious notes about Wagner and that he also felt a critical attitude toward himself on the part of both Wagner and Cosima. In spite of all this, however, the bonds were still very strong between them. This was when Nietzsche entered onto the second path: "Breaking the heart of the worshipper when he is most strongly committed. The free spirit. Independence . . . Critique of all that is venerated . . . The attempted reversal of evaluations." [32]

To follow the second path was not easy and it was an agonizing process for Nietzsche. The break touched Wagner far less, although he was somewhat distressed and confused by it. Nietzsche's sister writes that Wagner once asked her to tell her brother that, "I am quite alone since he went away and left me." [33]

For Nietzsche the break represented a traumatic experience and, in a sense, an unsuccessful one, for he was never really able to tear Wagner completely out of his heart. "I shuddered as I went on my way alone," he described the process of freeing himself from Wagner. "I was ill, or rather more than ill . . . I was doomed . . . to be more deeply *alone* than ever before. For I had never had anyone but Richard Wagner." [34]

Nietzsche knew that his defection from Wagner meant equally the end of his relationship with Cosima. He was aware of her complete identification with Wagner in every sense and he knew that personal as their own relationship had been, it could not survive in the face of his break away from Wagner. He knew too that to the deeply religious Cosima, who had often talked and written to him movingly of her faith, his anti-religious position, his concept that "God is dead" would be abhorrent.

In her selfless devotion to Wagner, Cosima epitomized Nietzsche's ideal of a woman. "The happiness of man is, 'I will,' " he wrote. "The happiness of woman is, 'He will.' " [35] Nietzsche declared that he had always looked upon Cosima "although from a distance" as the "most honored" woman he had ever known. But in his secret heart she was not so distant. She was his Ariadne.

Nietzsche realized the dangers that his Way to Wisdom represented and felt that "most people will perish, even on the second path." But he risked everything and sacrificed everything for it now and he had to drive on to the third path in which there would be "no longer any God or man above me!" He himself becomes "Fate. He . . . holds the lot of mankind in his hand." [36]

This period was the most creative of Nietzsche's life, producing his most famous works: *Thus Spake Zarathustra* and *Beyond Good and Evil.* It ended in a series of slanderous, frenzied attacks against Wagner. It is strange that after so many years had passed, after his independence from Wagner had long since been achieved, at a time five years after Wagner's death, Nietzsche should have catapulted himself into such violent aggression against Wagner and everything for which he stood. "What a wise old rattlesnake," he writes of Wagner. "All his life he has rattled before us . . . And we have believed him." He claims Wagner is "bad for youths . . . fatal to women . . . Ah, this old robber! He plunders us of our youths, he takes even our women as plunder and drags them into his cavern . . . Ah, this old Minotaur! What he has already cost us! Every year trains of the finest maidens and youths are led into his labyrinth, that he may devour them—every year all Europe strikes up the cry: 'Off to Crete! Off to Crete!' " [37]

Nietzsche's third path, "no longer any God or man above me," saw the fuller development of his Dionysian concept, expressed scorchingly in *Zarathustra.* It also saw Nietzsche's mystical self-identification with Dionysus, the philosopher-god, symbol of "the raging lust of the creator . . . the fury of the destroyer." [38] We see Ariadne appearing again and again, hinted at, suggested, no longer totally concealed. The long-suppressed feelings for his ideal woman were demanding deliverance, and sought release in mystical expression. "Whatever he may tell us, a labyrinthe man never seeks the truth but always only his Ariadne." [39] With Cosima as Ariadne, himself as Dionysus, Wagner became Theseus. " 'Ariadne,' says Dionysus, 'you are a labyrinth. Theseus has become lost in you, he has no more thread. What does it profit him not to be devoured by the Minotaur? What now consumes him is worse than the Minotaur.' " And Ariadne answers: "That is my last act of love to Theseus: I destroy him." [40] Nietzsche knew that to love a woman like Cosima was not simple and he was supremely aware of the danger that such a passion represented. But Nietzsche was a god now, and Ariadne could not spell danger to a god. "Be wise, Ariadne," he could say to her now, "I am your labyrinth." [41]

But Ariadne did not come to him, even though she was free to do so. And Nietzsche in blind fury lashed out at the man who had taken her not only in life but in death. If he could destroy the soul of Wagner, could he not then possess Cosima?

Two weeks after Nietzsche finished his last diatribe against Wagner, his mind exploded into another world. With all his preoccupation with themes of transendancy and power and pride, his last lucid moments were of a simple touching gentleness. He was walking along a street in Turin when he saw a horse being cruelly mistreated. Overcome by pity, Nietzsche ran to the animal and flung his arms about its neck protectively. In a little while, and with great difficulty, he was led back, sobbing, to his room where he eventually fell into a deep sleep. When he awakened it was to a world from which reality had vanished.

At the asylum, he told the doctors, "My wife, Cosima Wagner, brought me here." [42] Perhaps in a strange way he was right.

CHAPTER XIII

NIETZSCHE HAD NOT BEEN the only one to be sad when the Triebschen Idyl drew to a close. Cosima had loved it there. It had been a true Asyl for her away from the world from which she found her heart more and more withdrawn. She liked the long, quiet days, the total dedication to husband and children with only relatively minor distractions. Above all things that made her life valuable for her was Wagner's music. Much as she adored him, much as she admired his intellect, it was his music which held her most in thrall. Her diary is filled with references to her rapturous feelings in hearing his compositions. Nothing terrified her more than the thought that he might grow weary of the *Ring* after the many years that this gigantic task had occupied him. When he finally completed the orchestral sketch of the *Götterdämmerung* she wrote in her diary: "Strength fails me to describe the emotion which overcame me when Richard called me to tell me that the sketch was finished. He played me the conclusion, and I do not know whether it was the sublime music or the sublime achievement that affected me more deeply. I feel as though my goal has been attained and now I am free to close my eyes." [1]

At Triebschen, Cosima had built her life outside the world and she was content. Wagner, however, with his restless driving, with his frustrated artistic need to see his works performed as he envisioned them, to carry his "message" to the world, Wagner needed the realization that became Bayreuth. Although he was mortally tired, both in body and in spirit, he was driven on by his inner demon to take on the back-breaking, soul-destroying task of grappling with hostility, indifference, and passivity and wring from it by the strength of his will the fulfillment of his mission.

Wagner had long before given up Munich as hopeless. The cabals, the hostility of the musical and political establishments, the impossibility of achieving his unswerving artistic ideal had convinced Wagner long since against having anything more to do with that city. The performances there of his operas were a source of irritation and disgust and he had no part in them at all.

Wagner's relationship with the King passed through extremely heavy weather, not only in regard to the performances, which he strongly opposed and which the King desperately wanted, but also after the young monarch realized to what extent he had been duped and lied to by both Wagner and Cosima in regard to their relationship. However, the pull, the fascination, that Wagner exerted over Ludwig was too strong for anything to destroy. Nothing could keep him away for long from the man who gave him what he felt was his "true, his God-given vocation," [2] to cherish his friend, to be at the side of the man who was everything to him.

Although the move to Bayreuth meant, in effect, the end of Ludwig's dreams of closeness and identification with Wagner's work, he nevertheless maintained a generous attitude about what must have caused him great personal grief and disappointment. "In spite of the storms that appear to divide us, and the cloud-racks that pile up between us, our stars will find each other; even when the profane eye cannot pierce through the thick veil to the radiant brightness we two will recognize each other, and when we have at last reached the holy goal we had set ourselves from the beginning . . . we will render an account of our doings, the meaning and the aim of which were to spread that light over the earth, to purify and perfect humanity through its sacred flames, making it the sharer in eternal joys." [3]

It was with considerable sadness and even apprehension that Cosima prepared to re-enter the world again. She had not dreamt, when she left everything for Wagner, that she would live otherwise than in seclusion, devoting herself wholly to Wagner and her children. Her task remained the same, but it called now for a different path for its achievement. "The giving up of our idyllic existence is harder to endure than some may suppose, and I am bearing these fleeting days with a feeling that words cannot express," she wrote a friend just before leaving Triebschen. "Heaven forbid that it should be a presentiment. In the end it is not good to have staked all on a single thing, to live only in one's heart, for the outer world, which gives one nothing, steps in and takes its share." [4]

The share that the world was to step in and take included a toll of Wagner's health and strength, a cruel expenditure of vital force which unquestionably cut his life short. It was already in 1872 that Wagner told Cosima he thought he had heart trouble and that he noticed the first twinges of the heart spasms that were later to develop so cruelly. This cast a veil of mourning over Cosima's spirits and a cloud of worry that was never to leave her. Her early-learned habit of not showing what she suffered most stood her in good stead again and she moved through the active life she now had to lead, under the curious and not always friendly eyes of the world, with an outer composure which hid her inner concern.

Cosima did all she could to take as much as possible of the burden from Wagner's shoulders. She traveled throughout Germany with him to help organize and promote the funds for Bayreuth. She took over as much of the correspondence as she could. She met people and entertained, and continued to manage her household and the children. Most of all, she tried to encourage Wagner, to find things to distract him, to keep his spirits up.

The world was curious about this pair. Wagner was the most talked about man in Europe. Not only was his star on the rise throughout the world and especially in Germany, but the romance and the scandal were known and chattered about in every circle. But Cosima was not Marie d'Agoult's daughter for nothing. As Marie had done under very different circumstances, Cosima drew on all her pride "of a woman, of a great lady" and swept through the aristocratic salons like a queen. Extremely slender, with her wealth of golden hair beginning to show a little silver here and there, she wore with true French elegance the elaborate dresses that Wagner delighted in ordering for her. Her walk and her bearing were reminiscent of the immortal Sarah Bernhardt, according to Nietzsche, who was struck by the resemblance when he first saw the great actress. Cosima was described as a woman of "indescribable seduction," and a friend of Liszt's wrote to him of Cosima's success in glowing terms. "Your daughter is so irresistible and so adorable in everything that, in spite of my prejudice against universally admired phoenixes, I acknowledge that I myself am also under the charm which she inspires." [5]

As always, however, Cosima was followed by a double image, the duality which so long ago Marie d'Agoult had noticed in her, and there were some people who found her austere and hard on occasion. She was ready to do anything for Wagner's sake, but the sight of him wasting his strength and effort on an indifferent world incensed her.

Although Liszt followed all the reports about the progress of Bayreuth, and he even subscribed to three of the Patron Certificates with which the project was being financed, in spite of the fact that he was hardly in a position for such munificence, the estrangement between him and Cosima had not yet been bridged and it cost both of them much grief. They did not see each other nor did they correspond in spite of the efforts of several intimates to bring them together. Cosima had been deeply hurt by many of her father's acts: his persuasion of Bülow against the divorce, which had delayed it and confused things very much; his action after the war of 1870 when her income from France recommenced and he continued to have it sent in the name of Cosima von Bülow, although she was already married to Wagner; what she considered was his general lack of effort to understand her actions and beliefs. Liszt, on the other hand, had learned of her marriage to Wagner from the newspapers a week after the event, for Cosima had stopped writing to him a year earlier.

Cosima felt that she understood why her father had acted toward her as he did, even though she could not alter her conviction that he had made no attempt to understand her. She had accepted his censure, painful though it had been for her with her strong affection for him, and she hoped for a reconciliation. Nevertheless, she was no longer the timid little girl for whom everything depended on her father's approval. She had a cause far bigger than herself now, one to which she was wholly committed. Wagner took precedence over everything, and Cosima was not ready to bow the knee before anyone, even Liszt. She had once told Hans that it was not a question of forgiveness but of understanding and it was on that basis only that she was ready to make up with her father. After everything that had passed between them, it was no longer a question of father and daughter, she felt, but of two individuals, two souls. If he wanted to meet her on that level, she was ready to respond ardently.

Wagner too, hoped to draw his oldest and closest friend to him once again. The occasion of the laying of the foundation stone for the Festival Theater at Bayreuth seemed a time that might inspire them all to let bygones be bygones and to take up again the relationship that had bound them together for so long.

On May 18, four days before the celebration, Wagner wrote one of his masterly effulgences to Liszt. "My great and dear Friend! Cosima asserts that you would not come, even if I were to invite you. So that must we also endure, as we have had to endure so many things. But I cannot fail to invite you. And what do I cry to you when I say to you: Come? You came into my life as the greatest man to whom I ever addressed words of friendship; you gradually separated yourself from me, perhaps because I was not as close to you as you were to me. In your place there came to me your most inner being reincarnated who fulfilled my longing to have you completely close. So you live in full beauty before me and in me, as though we were joined beyond the grave. You were the first who ennobled me by his love; to a second, higher life am I now wedded through her, and can accomplish that which I could never have accomplished alone. Thus you were able to become everything to me, while I remain only so little to you: how enormous is my profit in comparison with yours! So if I say to you now: Come! so I say to you at the same time: Come to yourself! For here it is yourself that you will find. Blessings and love to you however you decide. Your old friend, Richard." [6]

Wagner, however, in spite of his assurances to the contrary, was not at all pleased when Liszt did not arrive. Why Liszt did not accept Wagner's warm invitation is a moot question. It would seem logical if he felt that such a public occasion was not the ideal moment to heal the long-standing breach; possibly he wanted first to consult with the Princess, whose hostility to Wagner, which now included Cosima, had only increased with the years. Most probably, it was for a much simpler reason: that the letter inviting him arrived so late. The preparations for the foundation-stone ceremony on Wagner's birthday had been going on for months. Liszt, who had for so many years been Wagner's chief ally and standard bearer, may have felt that the question of assuring his participation was a last minute afterthought. His answer, however, rose above any such petty considerations.

"Dear, noble friend—Deeply moved by your letter, I cannot find words with which to thank you. But I profoundly hope that all shadows and considerations that keep me at a distance will disappear and that we shall soon meet again. Then will you see clearly how inseparable my soul remains from both of you, how I live innerly in your 'second,' higher life where you are able to accomplish what you alone could not have accomplished. Therein rests my heavenly grace. May God's blessing be with you both, as is all my love." [7]

Liszt arranged that a friend deliver this letter to Wagner on the day of the celebration. Unfortunately, the friend was not one for whom Cosima or Wagner had any sympathy.

In a strange way, Liszt seemed to attract domineering women who wanted to rule his life. Although his relationship with the Princess remained the prime and closest one, Liszt was certainly in no way faithful to her and he did nothing to avoid the women who flung themselves at him as long as he lived. After a wild adventure which was publicized all over Europe with a Russian Countess Janina, Liszt found another Russian lady who was ready to devote herself to him. Baroness Meyendorff, a still youthful widow, played a role in Liszt's later years, acting to some extent as the Princess' spy, which is how Cosima regarded her, but establishing herself too on a footing of intimacy with Liszt. It was to her that Liszt had confided his answer to Wagner's letter. Although Cosima's hostility toward her eventually diminished, at the time of the Bayreuth celebration it was still very strong.

The Princess, needless to say, had to be informed of developments, but for once Liszt held his ground with her. A month after Wagner's letter to him, he finally wrote her about it and sent a copy of his own answer. "God will forgive me for taking the side of compassion," he wrote her, and he begged her to be compassionate too.[8]

These first essays at healing the breach led soon to another attempt, this time a successful one. Three months later, in August, Wagner wrote Liszt that he and Cosima wondered if a visit from them to Weimar would be welcome, and asked whether they could expect a friendly reception from him. Liszt's answer eradicated all doubts.

Many years later Liszt described to one of his students this meeting at Weimar with his daughter and Wagner. When he entered their room at the *Englischer Hof,* "Wagner met me with a speech which lasted twenty minutes. There was no one to hear it but his wife and myself. It was a speech I shall never forget." [9] Their supper party lasted until six in the morning. The quarrels and estrangement of the past were swept away.

The Princess did not like the new turn of affairs and she did her best to obstruct it. Liszt was adamant, however, and wrote her in no uncertain terms that he did not agree with her about his relationship with the pair at Bayreuth. He defended Cosima unequivocally, although with the ever-present tact he always maintained toward the Princess. "On the subject of my daughter, I especially remember your admirable solicitude for my three children—and I bless you for all you did during the long years of your frustrations and sorrows. Cosima is truly *ma terrible fille,* as I used to call her, an extraordinary woman of great merit, completely above ordinary judgements, and perfectly worthy of the admiring sentiments that she inspires in those who know her," and he adds a slight dig here, "starting with her first husband Bülow! She is devoted to Wagner with a total enthusiasm, like Senta in the *Flying Dutchman*—and will be his salvation, for he listens to her and follows her clairvoyantly." [10]

If Liszt was impressed and pleased with Cosima, seeing her again after the troubled years and in the altered circumstances of her life, Cosima's feelings contained much distress as she looked at her father again. She was struck with a certain languor of spirit, a fatigue which shocked and upset her. Although even as a child she had not been deceived by the apparent splendor of her father's life and position, and felt that he was unhappy and suffered with him for it, on this visit her heart was heavy, for in spite of the high spirits that reigned on several occasions she saw beneath the surface the loneliness and dangers that lurked there for her father.

In a strange parallelism, both Cosima and Liszt had to pay heavily for their brief meeting. The Princess was not the only one who was hostile to Cosima. Madame von Meyendorff was possessively jealous of Liszt and, according to Cosima, her father "had to suffer for showing me his great affection yesterday." [11] On the trip back to Bayreuth, it was Cosima's turn, and she was greatly distressed when Wagner burst forth in a jealous attack against Liszt even though she soon succeeded in appeasing him.

Wagner's jealousy of anyone who took Cosima's attention away from him was uncontrollable. Liszt made a short visit to Bayreuth not long after the Weimar meeting. He saw everything—the Festival Theater construction, the old opera house, and the start of the beautiful house, Wahnfried, into which the

Wagner family would soon move. He saw his grandson for the first time and his four granddaughters. And he confided in Cosima about the Princess, her moods and tempers, her unreasonable hostility toward his resumption of relations with herself and Wagner. Although Wagner read aloud the libretto of *Parsifal,* to which Liszt listened with overpowering emotion; although they made music together, and Liszt played incomparably; although Wagner felt that Liszt had really "come to himself" with them and was a part of them, he could not, after Liszt left, help once again bursting forth in fury at Cosima for her attentions to her father. "Formerly I had paid attention only to him," she wrote in her diary that he told her, "I had hung on him and his words alone, and this had sustained him and made him happy. But now, he said, everything was changed. He is profoundly mistaken"; she added, "only I cannot prove it to him and must keep silence." [12]

Among the things that Cosima had discussed with Liszt was a very important step that she was planning to take—she was going to become a Protestant at last. Her reasons for this hinged on her devotion to Wagner and her resolution not to be separated from him in time or eternity. Even at this age of thirty-four, she had a strange preoccupation with death and she had resolved that her ashes should be placed in Wagner's tomb.

Her entry into the Protestant church and her first Communion was an extremely moving experience for Cosima, as deep and real as her confirmation many years ago. She felt that only now, when they took Communion together, was her union with Wagner truly sealed and blessed. Profoundly religious as she was, she felt a deep need to be a part of a Christian community, and to share in it her most profound experiences and relationship.

Perhaps it was that her pious feelings were reminiscent of Liszt's, or perhaps he was irritated that she could find such joy and solace through something other than himself, at any rate, once again Wagner began to lash out at Liszt. Cosima was silent under the tirades, but they distressed her deeply and caused one of the rare critical flashes toward Wagner that she ever showed. "I must indeed have been guilty of some neglect during that time," she writes, "that Richard can continue to be so jealous. Nevertheless, it seems to me that it is not right of him to strike out at me so violently time after time. Still, it is not the wrong that is done us that touches the depth of one's heart. It is only the wrong that we do to others. And even if Richard is still suffering, I cannot see that I have done him any wrong except perhaps on that one morning when the sad revelations about Hans so upset me that in such a mood I could not venture near him. And now I could almost wish, for the sake of peace, that my father might never come here again. I do not do so, for I hope to be more fortunate and more adroit in the future." [13]

Cosima and her father had talked a good deal about Hans, for Liszt never failed in his affectionate and solicitous interest toward his ex-son-in-law. At this time, Bülow was enjoying an increasing success as a virtuoso, his concerts were sold out long in advance and he had plenty of engagements everywhere. Liszt was proud of his accomplishments, which he felt were a just tribute to the quality of his musicianship. The Princess, however, claimed that Cosima and Wagner were "guilty of the moral murder of Hans, etc." Cosima wrote, and she went on, "I was very troubled that my father should be so tormented in this way. He is so tired and they are always nagging at him. That wretched woman in Rome has never known anything better to do than to stir him up, but he will never abandon me, nor us either. This conversation detained me for a long time with my father and unfortunately I hurt Richard by leaving him alone for so long. It was difficult for me to find excuses and there was a slight tension all day." [14]

In the meantime, the Bayreuth project was continuing, though not smoothly, and work on the Festival Theater was progressing. Liszt said that "the extraordinariness of the enterprise would probably make it succeed—in spite of the faultfinding, criticisms, difficulties and gossip." [15] Wagner hoped to be able to hold the first performances in 1874, and he felt that it was time to look for the singers who could meet his exigent standards. So he and Cosima started out once again, on a grand tour of opera houses. Wagner undertook all these strains and efforts with a heavy heart. He grew increasingly disillusioned with the condition of music, of Germany, and of life in general. Cosima was concerned about his mood and his fatigue and her inability to help him. "Richard is weary of life," she wrote, "and I can only follow him and suffer with him, not help him! Only faith do I have, but no hope! The world is not ours, it belongs to other powers. But I will gladly suffer till the end of my life, and would rather be sad than glad—could it only be for myself alone. But I have no choice, and I ought to desire nothing but just accept what comes . . . God grant me the grace to do what is good." [16]

It was this spirit that carried Cosima through all the obstacles of the next years. The constant traveling about and being on show continued. The opening of the Festival was put off again and again in the face of delays of all kinds. The year 1874 passed and things were still a long way from completion.

That year saw another achievement, however, and one even closer to Cosima's heart than the Festival. Wagner completed the full score of *Götterdämmerung*. The tremendous task that had consumed him for so many years was over. The *Ring* was complete. The day that Cosima had hoped and sacrificed for had come, but it brought her sorrow as well as joy. On November 21 Cosima wrote in her diary: "Thrice holy, memorable day! Toward midday, Richard called me to bring him the newspapers. As he had complained to me yesterday how overstrained he was and assured me that he would not have finished before Sunday, I presumed that he was too tired to go on working. Timidly, I avoided the subject. In order to distract him, I tossed him the letter that I had just received from my father, thinking that it spoke in a friendly way about our journey to Pest. The bell rang for dinner; I met him reading the letter; he asked for an explanation, I told him what I thought of answering and purposely avoided looking at the manuscript of the score in order not to vex him. He was hurt and told me that it was finished, and said bitterly: when a letter of Father's comes, all sympathy for him disappears. I hid my suffering during the meal, but when Richard repeated his harsh complaints later, I could not help bursting into bitter tears, and I am still weeping as I write this. And so I have been robbed of this supreme joy but not through the stirring of any bad motives in me. That I have dedicated my life to this work in suffering has not won for me the right to celebrate its completion with joy. And so I celebrate it with pain . . . If Genius consummates its flight so high, what can a poor woman do? She can suffer in love and rapture." [17]

With the deterioration of his health and with all the stresses that Wagner was under, his nerves stretched often beyond endurance and he lashed out more and more often at Cosima. Nietzsche's sister described his "uncontrollable fits of rage," which were directed at Cosima. Although Cosima "never gave him the slightest cause for such outbursts, he often turned on her, and the equanimity with which she endured the unjustifiable attacks heightened my admiration for this remarkable woman," Elizabeth Förster-Nietzsche continued. "On the whole, it must be admitted that being the wife of a genius is not the easiest position in the world." [18] But Wagner was creating a whole new world of music and Cosima had proved her willingness to sacrifice far more than a few scenes for it.

It was the summer of 1876 before all the major obstacles were overcome and the opening of the Bayreuth Festival could at last take place. Rehearsals had been going on whenever possible since the previous summer. The Wagnerian concept was a wholly new one to the world of opera. It was not only that his music was totally unlike the Italianate style that had heretofore prevailed; it was also that he envisioned a totality of extramusical and dramatic aspects, wherein not only scene and costume were of essential importance but most of all the characterizations, the intimate connection between words and music, between movement and sound, which would make the drama leap into vivid reality. Exhausted as he was, much as he felt his age and illness, Wagner struck fire from his artists. For he himself could outdo any and all of them in his portrayal of a mood or a moment of characterization and he made his intentions live before their eyes so tellingly that they could not help but grasp them.

Not so simple were the temperaments and jealousies of the various artists. Cosima participated in everything and spent a great deal of her time in diplomatic soothing of the highly strung musicians. She attended rehearsals and often, if Wagner could not be there, it was she who tried to convey his wishes. Both Wagner and Cosima were strained to the breaking point when the Festival was finally ready.

It was a great moment, the realization of Wagner's dream that he had held to for a quarter of a century in the face of what would have been, for a lesser man, superhuman obstacles, and which even for him nearly proved so. It was an audience of Kings and Princes, of music lovers and musicians, of the elite of Europe who came to that first summer at Bayreuth. Ludwig,

King of Bavaria, attended the final rehearsals and in his strange way traveled to and from the theater in a closed carriage, avoiding all ceremonies and the crowds who had hoped to greet him.

As if the work of preparation and realization had not been enough, receptions had to be organized and given; dinners, luncheons, entertainments of all kinds. When it was all over, the last note sounded, the final guest departed it was clear that the Festival had represented an artistic triumph of enormous proportions, and an equally large financial debacle. If Wagner could have foreseen, during the arduous years of preparation, that between the first Festival and the second there would be a time lapse of six years during which it would look more than once as though the whole project would have to be abandoned; had he known that one day he would say to Cosima, "Every stone in that building is red with my blood and yours!" Had he foreseen all this, he and Cosima might never have found the courage to create Bayreuth.

This time it was once again, in the end, the King of Bavaria who came to the rescue, in spite of Wagner's heroic efforts to pay off the whole debt himself. Cosima had been active behind the scenes and had written to the King asking his favorable consideration for a plan to salvage the situation that had been suggested to her by a prominent Bayreuth banker. The Bayreuth Festival had taken too big a toll of health and fortune. It could not be allowed to perish now.

CHAPTER XIV

AMONG THE MANY PEOPLE who had come from far and wide to attend the first Bayreuth Festival, there was one notable absence —Marie d'Agoult. She had died a few months earlier, slipping finally away almost without a stir as far as Liszt and Cosima were concerned, as though she had merely taken a short further step away into the mists which had for so long stood between her and them. Cosima had last seen her when her mother came for a visit to Triebschen, the year after her marriage and not long after the Franco-German War. It was surprising that things went as well as they did in view of the ardent opposing nationalism of the two. "She likes being here," Cosima wrote. "I feel very much a stranger to her—yet her great culture makes her very agreeable. We talk a great deal about everything . . . Yet everything went around as if in a circle, all our troubles were revived and our conversations brought little comfort." When Marie left, however, Cosima went on, "I was deeply affected as I embraced her for the last time, and the whole sadness of her life came over me." [1]

Liszt learned of her death through the newspapers. His sentiments, to some extent for the benefit of the Princess to whom he wrote them, were a pitiful memorial to the mother of his three children. "Without being hypocritical I would not know how to weep more at her death than at her life . . . Madame d'Agoult possessed eminently a gift, even a passion for falseness —except in certain moments of ecstasy, the memory of which she could not stand later! For the rest, at my age condolences are not less embarrassing than congratulations. The world goes on—one exists, keeps busy, sorrows, distresses oneself, creates illusions, changes ones mind and dies as one can!" [2]

Cosima was too engaged with all her activities and responsibilities to mourn long and she hid whatever feelings she might have had in order not to distress Wagner.

Among the many others who were present, one very special person did attend the Festival, someone whom Wagner called his "last gift to the gods." It was the beautiful, brilliant, young, fresh Judith Gautier. And into the bargain she adored Wagner. That he became infatuated with her soon was apparent. She attended the second series at the Festival and sat with Wagner during the performances in an ecstasy of "togetherness," holding hands and weeping together, just as so often he and Cosima had done.[3]

Perhaps Wagner fell so easily into Judith's arms a little because of his jealousy of Liszt, and Cosima's attentions to her father. During the Festival, Wagner wrote Judith a note complaining that he was not going to the reception to be held that night as Cosima was again sacrificing herself to her father. His possessive jealousy toward Cosima was so extreme that he could not see the slightest deflection of her attention away from him without interpreting it as a betrayal. It was, however, something of a betrayal on his part when he wrote Judith that she was the "only ray of love in these days so joyful for some and so little satisfying for me. Oh how I would love to embrace you again, dear, sweet one." [4] Or when he wrote her that her embraces were "the most intoxicating and the proudest events of my life." [5]

Although they did not meet, Wagner's letters to Judith increased in number and in warmth during the year after the Festival, while he was gathering his forces for *Parsifal.* For a long time, Wagner had been caught up in the concept of *Parsifal* and the day that he told Cosima he had actually started the libretto was one of the happiest of her life, for she knew then that Bayreuth may have taken its toll of his health but it had not destroyed his creative impulse.

There is no question that Cosima knew all about the affair with Judith. Although for a time Wagner arranged that a local barber act as "post office" for their letters, he later wrote Judith that he had shown all his correspondence with her to Cosima. But Cosima was aware that in spite of Judith she herself was the breath of life to Wagner. He could not do without her for a single moment and even to Judith he wrote of the peace and shelter he had found since he knew Cosima. During the year and a half of Wagner's infatuation with Judith, Cosima held steady to her course, writing continual friendly letters to the young Frenchwoman on her own account and never showing an iota of her personal torment. She could not have been the woman she was had she not been hurt and jealous. She was by far too proud and passionate a nature for that. But her love for Wagner, her understanding of his special needs as an artist enabled her to rise above this shallow betrayal.

Cosima had always had a mystical feeling that through her own suffering she might earn joy and fulfillment for those she loved. "The only feeling to which my heart clings as a refuge is that, although I wish all whom I love more good fortune than is their due, I have never wished that things should go better for myself. The more deeply I suffer the stronger grows this strange pleasure which I feel in pain. I would gladly accept the condition that, as the mists of the earth become fruitful rain, so also the tears that come from my eyes might descend as a blessing for the children." [6]

Besides all the romantic effulgences, Wagner's letters to Judith were filled with commissions that he asked her to fill for him in the sumptuous Paris shops. Wagner's luxurious tastes and his need to be surrounded with special furnishings had only increased as his health and nerves deteriorated. He sent Judith fantastic orders for elaborate fabrics, of satin and velvet, highly concentrated essences of perfume, and so on. He needed more than ever to be buffered against the actual physical world that beat upon his sensitivities. It was especially when Wagner was composing that he needed this insulation from the outside world and that he was in a state of heightened reactivity to his surroundings.

The progress of *Parsifal* was a source of great solace to Cosima. When Wagner completed the Prelude and played it to her on her Saint's day—the day of St. Cosmas—she remembered how he had told her that he was only writing it for her and for the children, for he was bitter and disillusioned with the world.

Wagner's infatuation with Judith was not of any real importance, and Cosima may even have been able to find it in herself to feel that it was good for Wagner to have found this last flash of youthful excitement.

Judith perhaps took the whole thing a little more seriously, judging by what she told a friend: that it was she who should have been by Wagner's side, his wife, his "female," his real other self—as Wagner had told her in his vivid language. She must have received quite a shock when, after a little more than a year and a half of ardent correspondence, Wagner wrote her that Cosima would now take charge of all the commissions he had been asking of her. It was his last letter to her. Cosima took over without missing a step. The only thing that really mattered was *Parsifal* and the saving of the Bayreuth project, something which, after 1878, looked possible at last.

The Bayreuth climate did not help Wagner's health at all, and they began seeking relief in the warmth and sun of Italy where they had always traveled with a large household—maids, governesses, tutors, and the children. The years had not taught Wagner economy, and Cosima was often distressed over their personal finances, but he was completely unable to limit in any way the luxurious habits that he had grown completely dependent on.

In spite of all the other demands on her, Cosima was a devoted and attentive mother. There was a real closeness between the children and the parents. Wagner was often gay and lively with them. He teased the girls and sometimes even managed to interrupt their lessons so that they could go out and play with Siegfried if he was lonely. In this last period of his life, Wagner found full outlet for his family feelings, which were very strong. He enjoyed all the little celebrations, the birthday parties, and most of all the elaborate scenes that Cosima would arrange for Christmas and for his birthday in which all five children would often depict roles from his operas. Cosima was endlessly inventive in this regard.

Cosima was extremely strict, sometimes even harsh with the children in all questions of deportment and education. She wanted to do for them what had not been done for her, most of all to give them the steady assurance of parental love and presence. Her letters to Daniela overflow with affectionate terms and loving words, but she laid great emphasis on moral training and spoke often of the high ideals and lofty purposes she hoped they would follow. No one had done that for her, she told

Daniela. She had been taught how to behave, but no one had tried to inspire her.

Cosima carried over to her children many of the exigent demands she made on herself. Her old habit of hiding that from which she suffered most, the sense of pride before the world was something she expected her children to carry on. "I do not know whether it is due to any lack of tenderness in me," she wrote a friend, "but, really, the only anxiety that I feel about my children is lest they do not meet the vexations of life with sufficient calm pride. As for the vexations themselves, God, they are in the atmosphere itself, and to lament much about them has never been my way. The only thing that I have longed for with all my might is to know that my children are of the same mind as I am about this. Should I have the trial of seeing that they bear the painful things of life with common mediocrity, without distinction or greatness, I admit, my incomparable friend, that this would be the hardest thing in my life, and I ask myself anxiously today, whether and how I would survive it." [7]

Cosima cherished a dream for Daniela, the eldest, whereby she hoped in some small way to lessen her own feelings of guilt toward Bülow: Daniela would become the solace and companion to her father. Cosima hoped to bring the girl up so that she could atone for some of the injury that Cosima had done Bülow. "Take the serious and firm resolution to devote yourself to him from the time you are of an age to do it," Cosima wrote Daniela, "to dedicate your youth to him and all your faculties, and to stifle all the inferior qualities in yourself which would render you unworthy of this mission. Your first duty is to love him more than anyone and to prepare yourself to help him in the sorrows of life." [8]

Wagner found it difficult to understand why Bülow should

hold himself aloof and he sometimes upset Cosima very much by his inability to comprehend how impossible it would be for Hans to behave otherwise. Wagner wanted to invite him to the Festival performances, and there are even indications that he was eager to have Bülow participate actively in them. Bülow, as an old-time Wagnerian, suffered acutely at not being able to go to Bayreuth, let alone to take a hand in the performances. Like a man without a country, he moved restlessly about. A trip to America in the Festival year did nothing to relieve his tormented feelings, although at one point he wrote Cosima that he wanted to become a citizen of the United States and would make his home there permanently. That was impossible, for Europe, and especially the magnet of Bayreuth, drew him irresistibly back again.

After the first Bayreuth Festival, Bülow seemed to go through a more than usually deep crisis of nerves and morale. Liszt was desolate about it. "Rarely has emotion so suffocated me as at reading your letter," he wrote Bülow. "It is heart-rending—and of a sublime goodness of heart. If tears could write themselves, my answer would be long; but weeping is not manly: I forbid it to myself and do not want to despair. It would be an ingratitude toward that Providence which has given me a friend like you. My grief is not less than yours . . . Let us conquer; wounds of fate can serve as spurs; obstacles can become means." [9]

Cosima was kept continuously informed of all the details of what was happening with Bülow. She was overjoyed when things went well for him; and she despaired when, as so often was the case, he had disappointments or his health broke down. "At the moment when I was lighting the lamps of the theater," she wrote Daniela, "I received from your grandfather an envelope, containing a letter from your father, with such a sad and depressed tone, after ten months of suffering and of forced inactivity, that it seemed to me that there was nothing else that I could do but to weep and to pray. God is great and compassionate and if I pray and weep well, every day, it is true, He will allow me to continue to work and to seem to be gay in order not to sadden my family." [10]

Cosima's dream of dedicating Daniela's life to be a compensation to Bülow for her own guilt toward him inevitably ran into trouble from the start. Very occasional letters had passed between Cosima and Bülow on the subject of the children during the years and when, at last, Cosima felt that the time had come for the nineteen-year-old Daniela to see her father again, she wrote Bülow suggesting a meeting. His reply was hardly conducive for an early success to her plan. The following year, Cosima tried again to arrange the meeting. Her idea was that Daniela attend a music festival at Meiningen, where Bülow was to conduct Beethoven's 9th Symphony, the work that Wagner had conducted on the occasion of the foundation-stone celebration. "Frankly," Bülow wrote her, "the outlook of seeing your oldest daughter appear on the 19th in order to indulge in a comparative study of the performance of the 9th Symphony with the means of a small city and of the great festival of May 22, 1872, pleases me—little." [11]

Bülow was still bitter over the past and one of the things that stuck in his throat was the contrast between the luxury and scope of Daniela's life in the Wagner family, and the simpler means and arrangements that he could offer. As a fantastic gesture of pride, of loyalty, of sheer "Bülowism," he even went so far as to give a series of concerts, for the benefit no less—of Bayreuth! He had set a goal for this munificent gesture of forty thousand marks, and in order to make up the entire sum he added twelve thousand from his own savings, severely depleted at that time after some heavy losses on an English tour.

Wagner returned the money to Bülow with "the request that

this be invested for you," Cosima wrote Daniela, "as I have given to the theater the inheritance from my mother." [12] So Bülow was not allowed even the gratification of this largesse!

It was Liszt who finally arranged the meeting between Daniela and her father, for Cosima had determined not to try again after Bülow's last outburst. Typical of Bülow, he was utterly charmed by his daughter. "What an adorable child," he wrote Cosima. "What a soul you have formed! . . . I thank Providence to have reserved this unspeakable joy for me, this happiness which is so sweet that all the bitterness, regret, remorse which is intermixed cannot alter it. Teach me, great, generous, noble woman, what could be the fatherly duties that I could fill toward this dear creature who captivated my soul in a single instant! Thanks, thanks, thanks! I owe you an incomparable happiness, melancholy as it is." [13] It was all so like Bülow, whose intrinsic nature was noble and good, but whose nerves and irritability made every-day life a torment for himself and for those around him. The letter expressed his best, his real feelings, but even with Daniela, he was not always able to control himself and their relationship usually prospered more at a distance than in proximity.

It was not long after their first meeting that another bombshell exploded for Hans. Wagner wanted to adopt Daniela and Blandine and give them his name. As there had never been any distinction made in the Wagner household between Wagner's children and Bülow's, Cosima and Wagner had considered for some time making legal what had for many years been actual. The question of Isolde was a strange one, in that Bülow persisted in seeming to regard her as his child, referring always in his letters to Cosima to "our three daughters" and including her in all his plans for the financial arrangements for Daniela and Blandine. It does not seem possible for him to have believed that Isolde was his daughter, so that his persistence in maintaining the farce could very well have been a pointed dig at the deception which had been practiced on him and which had never been openly admitted. But when the idea was broached that Wagner adopt the two daughters he knew very well and truly his own—Bülow blew up. All the only partially healed wounds opened again. When nothing was accomplished by letter, he asked for a meeting with Cosima which was finally arranged. Needless to say, it accomplished little either and it was extremely painful for them both. Bülow was so little able to control himself that he asked Cosima to stay on another day so that he could try to present his position more calmly. "I attempted to restrain his violent surges of emotion and to overcome his injustice toward Daniela. An impossible task!" Cosima wrote in her diary. Her return to Wahnfried was a sad one, she went on, but she was more than ever convinced that it was there her home lay and that she should live only for Wagner and for the children. But the old poison still rankled in her heart. "After this meeting I set foot in our house once again with the feeling that a new life was beginning for me—desolate, yet peaceful, happiness in his happiness alone, but bearing deep in my heart the consciousness of an inexpiable wrong. May God help me to enjoy the one without ever forgetting the other." [14]

Bülow was in such distress that he turned for a time even against Liszt, and in a moment of bitterness about it he wrote that "for a long time—to my great regret—we understand each other on nothing, absolutely nothing." [15] The plan for adoption was dropped, but it had awakened many of the old memories. There was even a certain coolness for a time again between Liszt and his daughter. He was so deeply attached to Hans that he could not help but try to support him in every way he could. In his last years at Weimar, Liszt kept only two photographs on his table—one of the Princess and one of Bülow. He did not mind Hans' difficult nature at all; in fact he almost enjoyed it.

"Perfection is not of the world," he wrote the Princess. "I admit that Bülow's too often disparaged imperfections remain for me ultrasympathetic because of their noble tempering." [16]

Certainly Liszt enjoyed some of the unrestrained temperamental fireworks in which Bülow often indulged, especially when it was Liszt himself he was defending. "During the past two weeks," Liszt wrote the Princess from Weimar, "Bülow has been exercising a sort of terrorism here on some twenty pianists of both sexes. He has told them categorically, in a gathering at my house, that with the exception of three or four among them, they were unworthy to receive my lessons, and too poorly taught to profit from them. Almost all have already played in public concerts in Berlin, Hamburg, Frankfurt, Naples, London, and pretend to the celebrity of a Rubinstein or a Mme. Schumann! Judge for yourself their disconcertion at Bülow's harangue! For the rest, his sarcastic vein does not stop at the sacred college of pianists . . . The fact is that my very dearest Bülow breaks with the compromises and subterfuges of puerile and courteous civility. His prodigious mind, and the superb qualities of his admirable character and his indelible nobility complicate his habitual relationships more and more. Certainly not with me, but with the large and small of the *tutti quanti*—perpetual aggression becomes his method of sociability!" [17]

Liszt for some years had been dividing his time between Rome, Weimar, and Pest. At Pest he had been given a position as honorary director of the Academy of Music. He had returned too to Weimar, although he had not envisioned that when he left, thinking to marry the Princess, and he lived there for a few months every year. It was to Weimar that pupils flocked to him from all over the world. He taught them with great patience and never took a penny in payment. An apartment for him was kept at the Hofgarten, simple but more than adequate to his modest demands. A third part of each year he spent in Rome, where the Princess lived in almost total isolation and retirement.

The years had not been kind to her or to her strange character, and the long-existing ties that bound her and Liszt together often hurt and chafed him. Only occasionally did he allow himself to complain. "How would I not be mortally sad?" he wrote her once. "Your immense and pessimistic intellectual work that has gone on for thirty years, superimposed on your almost continual physical and moral suffering, has made you contract habits of haughtiness of spirit and even of violent hardness toward your neighbor." [18]

She scolded and dominated him and made his life so miserable sometimes that he even occasionally left her letters unopened. And yet she loved him terribly, and he always remained devoted, in his way, to her. In Rome she lived in a third-floor apartment without elegance, without taste, a simple, furnished apartment. Everywhere there were books, papers, notes in complete disorder, and she, reclining on a chaise longue with a vase of heavy-scented flowers beside her, and the air was thick with their perfume partially masked by the smoke of the strong cigars which she smoked incessantly. Doors and windows were sealed shut and even Liszt was forced to wait for ten minutes in the anteroom in order to insure that he brought not a breath from the outside.

Although Cosima's plans for Daniela and her father did not work out, Daniela spent a great deal of time with Liszt and often visited him both in Weimar and in Rome. She suffered from the Princess as much as Cosima had done, but not with as much justification, as Cosima was careful to point out, although she sympathized and understood what Daniela had to go through.

Finally, and at long last from Cosima's point of view, twelve years after the divorce, Bülow remarried. His second wife was

Marie Schanzer, a daughter of one of the directors of the War Ministry in Vienna, and an actress whom Bülow had met while he was music director at Meiningen. Another step, equally or even more important was that he had found another outlet for his musical loyalties—in Brahms! Since the earliest days there had been a vicious hostility between the Brahms circle and the Wagner-Liszt Music of the Future. Certainly, this adoption by Bülow of the Brahmsian banner was another indication that the old wounds that Wagner had dealt him were still rankling. The person who suffered most from this was Daniela, who was not at all happy with this Brahmsian attachment. Bülow dismissed her reaction as "Bayreuth fanaticism."

As far as Cosima was concerned, however, she was not fooled into thinking that Hans remarried or not, with new musical loyalties or not, was now happy and that the burden of blame that she carried toward him could be lifted from her. She hoped and prayed that he was happy, but she did not feel that her own guilt was expiated.

During the summers at Wahnfried and the long winters spent in Italy, Wagner worked steadily at *Parsifal.* It was a time almost of a second honeymoon in the relationship of Cosima and Wagner. Judith was long since forgotten, and he was as full of attentions and declarations of love as he had been in the earliest days. "I need nobody but you," he told Cosima. "That is why I staked everything on winning you." [19] And he told Siegfried that Cosima was the "only one being who has been indispensable to me and without whom I could not have lived." [20] He joked with her that they should really have married off all the children long ago and then they could "both linger for hours on end in an arbor on a sunny riverbank. That is what I picture to myself. We found each other too late! We should have been united much sooner." [21]

These were happy moments, lovely to live through and to

store in memory. They were made more poignant by the cloud that hung over Cosima all the time now—the obvious, terrible deterioration of Wagner's health. She could no longer pretend. She could no longer hope that climate or rest or anything could help. On one occasion she was called suddenly to his room by the maid, who said that he had been seized with a violent spasm of the heart. Cosima described how "I hurried to him and saw what affected me so violently that I fainted. I soon collected myself again and returned to Richard from the bed where they had laid me. His condition gradually quieted and he became electrified and started joking again. But he is very fatigued. Yesterday we talked again about our end, and I wanted to do anything, anything if only to be worthy to die with him. He said we had to live which was far harder. But my fainting spell today gave me hope." [22]

The summer of 1882 saw *Parsifal* complete and ready for performance. The rehearsals were not as arduous as those for the *Ring* had been, and Wagner had worked everything out very carefully in advance, but he was totally exhausted at the end. In all, there were sixteen performances of *Parsifal* that summer at Bayreuth, and this time the Festival was not only a musical triumph but a financial success as well.

The Festival summer saw the first wedding among the five children—that of Blandine to Count Gravina. It saw also the further deterioration of Wagner's health, so that Cosima said, "How gladly would I take him in my arms and bear him far away from it all." [23]

As soon as possible after the Festival was over, they left for Venice where they moved into the Palazzo Vendramin on the Grand Canal. It was a large apartment of some twenty rooms, needed because of the number of people who always surrounded Wagner. Cosima and the four children—Blandine came later and spent the month of October with her husband—tutor, maids, governess, cook, and a continual horde of visitors.

Liszt was one of them and stayed nearly a month, including Cosima's birthday for which Wagner had prepared a surprise—the performance of his early symphony. Wagner, if anything, was more jealous than ever of Liszt. His poor health had increased his nervous irritability to the point that it was almost more than Cosima could bear. But later, when he would be overcome with contrition at his outbursts, she found it almost worse, for there was nothing that he could do to her that she felt was deserving of an apology.

Cosima carried all the burdens alone of the children, with their needs and illnesses, the household demands, the endless correspondence, the visitors and guests, the planning and maintaining of all the physical arrangements for living that Wagner required. She had constantly to try to keep his spirits up, to enter into his plans for the future which, on the days when he felt well and optimistic, stretched out twenty years ahead. Yet at the same time she watched him fail, more rapidly now, knowing that the final coda was being played out, that every day existed on borrowed time, and she was determined not to lose her composure, not to lose her control.

When Liszt left during the second week of January, Wagner's heart spasms were increasing constantly in intensity and number. Early in February he made plans for an excursion with Siegfried but at the last moment he did not feel up to going.

On the evening of February 12, Cosima wrote in her diary and described how Wagner played a scene from *Rhinegold.* The next morning Wagner again felt somewhat unwell. "I must take care of myself today," he told his servant. Siegfried had never heard his mother play the piano until that morning of February 13 when she very softly played Schubert's *Lob der Tränen.* Wagner sent word that he would not come to lunch as he was not feeling well. Cosima went to him but he preferred to remain alone, as was his habit when his attacks came. A maid was stationed outside his door. Wagner suddenly rang his bell twice and to the maid who hurried in to him he asked that she bring his wife and the doctor at once.

Cosima rushed to Wagner, who was hunched over on a small settee and she took him in her arms. It seemed to her that he fell asleep there and she did not move until the doctor arrived, nearly an hour later, to tell her that her beloved was dead.

How many times had she lived through this moment in her imagination? How many times had she prayed not to be separated from her love even in death. Twenty-five hours later she was still prostrate by his body, having refused nourishment or rest or comfort.

She did not really come to life even when they finally persuaded her to leave him. She cut her beautiful long silver-blond hair and laid it in the coffin with him who had so loved it in his life. Faithful friends and her daughters made all the arrangements, and the tragic journey home to Bayreuth started.

A gondola took the funeral cortege to the train. There was only one stop—in Munich where a brief ceremony took place. It was nearly midnight when the train arrived at Bayreuth. People had congregated at each station all along the way and here now at home crowds of people and masses of flowers were everywhere. But Cosima did not notice. She did not even notice when her rings slipped from her fingers because her fingers had shrunk so in the four days without any kind of nourishment, and was probably equally unaware when they were later returned to her.

Cosima did not attend the huge public funeral. There were only two wreaths on the coffin—both from Ludwig—one from him as King, the other from him as friend.

The coffin was brought back to Wahnfried, where Wagner long since had chosen and planned his tomb. At dusk, the ceremonies were over and everyone went away. Only then did Cosima appear, leaning heavily on the arm of a friend. She watched while the coffin was lowered into the vault and prayed that she would soon follow her husband there. It was to be forty-seven years before her prayer was granted.

CHAPTER XV

COSIMA LIVED. But for long weeks after Wagner's death it seemed almost as though she tried to will herself to die. The strains and pressures of the last years, the painful, helpless watching as Wagner's health deteriorated, the unremitting self-control, the activity and efforts that had been required of her, all of which had brought her near to the breaking point even before Wagner's death, took their full toll now. Indomitable, indefatigable Cosima was broken with grief, withdrawn from everyone and everything. She lived in her sorrow and in her hope that, like Isolde, she would soon find her release in a love-death. "My daughter Cosima is doing everything possible not to survive Wagner," Liszt wrote months after Wagner's death. "From what I am told, for I neither have nor ask direct news from her, she spends hours every day by Wagner's tomb, in spite of all contrary pleas. A decisive vocation!" [1]

Liszt had accepted Wagner's death philosophically as a man who felt that his own age would mark him soon to follow. Bülow, however, had almost collapsed. Even his second wife, Marie, was surprised at the violence of his reaction when she told him of the death of the man who had been his greatest friend and his betrayer. The news had such a shattering effect on him that she realized for the first time to the full, "how passionate was the love he still felt in his innermost heart for Wagner, in spite of everything." [2]

Bülow too heard that Cosima's own life was endangered by the extent of her grief and her lack of will to live. *"Soeur, il faut vivre,"* he telegraphed her. But nothing reached Cosima's innermost spirit during the weeks of prostrated grief. Only the children saw her. Only the children held her in any way to life.

The task that Cosima had set herself when she left Hans, the mission that she had assumed with so much sacrifice and so many tears was accomplished, and heroically accomplished. "Before the eyes of my soul I see not what you are losing, but what you possess at this hour," Nietzsche wrote her. "Few human hearts can say with such profound feeling as yours: 'What I have done for this single man has been my entire duty—it has also been my entire recompense.' You have lived for a single aim, to which you have sacrificed everything. Above your love of this man, you have grasped the loftiest things that *his own* love and hope ever conceived. You have served these things. You have joined yourself and your name to them forever;—to those things which do not die with a man, even though they are born with him. Few souls have the will for such an act; and among these few who else would have had the *capacity* for it? That is why I lift up my eyes toward you . . . as the woman my heart respects above all whom it has known." [3]

With Wagner's death, Cosima felt that her "entire duty" was done and she doubted that she had either the will or the strength to do more. It was a long time before Cosima accepted the fact that her life was not over, that there were still burdens for her to assume, still tasks for her to accomplish. They were no less arduous than before and this time she would be alone, the final arbiter, the prime source of will. Slowly at first, reluctantly even, Cosima moved toward her new mission.

It was the children and her concern for them that nurtured the first flicker of return to life in her. Although she had not followed her beloved to the grave, something in her did die with him, and the Cosima who raised herself from despair was not the same Cosima as before. Something had crystallized in her, hardened into an unchangeable mold. Her ideas, her thoughts, her attitudes, her feelings had all taken on their final cast and would not alter one iota again. Aside from her love and concern for her children, which were very real, Cosima's new life still had only a single dedication—Wagner, manifest now in two aspects: to preserve the image of Wagner as she saw him in all his full genius, free from what she feared would be unworthy attacks and misinterpretations; to continue the work of Bayreuth. Wagner had long been the center of her universe and he would remain so, but now it was a universe that was fixed and immutable, in which nothing could or should be changed. The Master's word was final in every sphere and his final word had been uttered.

Cosima's first act was to try to gain possession of as many as possible of the masses of letters that Wagner had written during his lifetime, some six thousand of which are still extant. Her experience with what enmity and hostility toward him could do made her determined to control, as completely as she could, the vast material that had come from his pen and that she feared might be twisted and used out of context to attack his memory. Even to Liszt the demand went out that he return Wagner's letters forthwith and also his copy of the privately printed autobiography which was to be published only more than twenty-five years after Wagner's death. Cosima felt strongly that nothing intimate should be made public. According to her definition, this related to personal exchanges of an intimate nature as long as one of the persons involved was still alive. Obviously, she was not able to assemble or to control everything pertaining to Wagner, but the control she did exert and the mass of material she did gather are proof of the energy with which she pursued her goal in this regard. There are not many public figures and not a single composer about whom there are so many documents of one kind or another as there are about Wagner. Very little of his life was hidden from public view. The controversies that he aroused from his earliest years inspired an interest, often a hostile one, in these materials which, in view of the undeniable weaknesses of Wagner's personality, were often sensational. Cosima, who saw way beyond all of his very obvious defects and who had a highly developed sense of privacy, took on the role of keeper of the records, choosing if and when they would be made public.

The first meeting about the Bayreuth Festival occurred only a few weeks after Wagner's death, when his wishes were made known about the performances of *Parsifal* for the seaon that was only months away. Cosima was present, at least in body, but totally silent, still in a half-dream of grief. It was to Adolf von Gross that Wagner had written his instructions. Wagner was not mistaken in his choice of Gross, who served Cosima and Bayreuth, as he had Wagner, with intelligent and selfless devotion as long as he lived. The first *Parsifal* performance after Wagner's death took place, as Wagner had planned, in the summer of 1883. Cosima was still sunk in grief, but she at least kept herself informed as to the progress of the rehearsals and the performances.

As Wagner grew older, as he felt his health failing, he had fallen into ever greater despair about the future of Bayreuth. He felt that there was not a single person, neither singer, nor conductor, nor stage designer, nor manager, nor even stagehand on whom he could depend to do things exactly right, who truly understood what he wanted and could be counted on to carry on without him. There is no questioning his real distress over this. How was it that he did not see in Cosima everything and more than he was looking for? Did he feel that her still existent shyness, of which perhaps only he was aware, would make it impossible for her to act decisively without his presence to bolster her? Was her role in his eyes, the aspect in which he saw her, only that of the devoted handmaid, the selfless disciple, the wholly feminine, following only where he led, able to express herself only through him? Or had she become such a part of him, was her determination not to survive him so strong, that he found it impossible to imagine her without himself? Certainly he knew how difficult life would be for her without him, and he evidently did not dream that alone she could direct the work of Bayreuth with its myriad problems—musical, financial, personal, and political.

Cosima's assumption of this new task did not happen all at once, nor was it easy for her, especially at first. For a long time the thought of going out into the world again, of seeing people and of being seen, was out of the question for her. To be looked at, talked about, observed was impossible even to consider. And yet the Festival drew her like a powerful magnet. How could she watch over the Bayreuth performances, keep alive what Wagner wanted at a time when she was still unable to face the world? How could she bear to listen in full public view to Wagner's music again, that music which represented to her the highest and most real aspect of the man? Her solution was an ingenious one. She had a secret hideaway made for herself in the theater from which she could hear everything and see most of the stage but where no one could observe her.

It was from this hidden box that Cosima first began to take up the reins of musical direction at Bayreuth. Between each act, at every pause, at the end of each rehearsal and performance Cosima would send her comments and suggestions to the conductor. Written on small scraps of paper, these notes contained the most detailed and specific directions about tempo, balance, accents, nuances, besides more general comments on interpretive meaning. There was no detail too small to escape her observation, and no note of the score with which she did not show herself intimately familiar. In one place she would disagree with a change in tempo and indicate that there should be sharper accents, especially in the sixteenth notes and triplets. In another she found the timpani too heavy. Here the entrance of the flutes should be more delicate and there she found a passage for strings not always cleanly played. She constantly emphasized the proper balance between singers and orchestra. She kept a score beside her and covered it with her comments, sometimes words of praise but more often critical indications. And it was not only the musical aspects with which she dealt, but technical and stage directions too. Her notes gave myriad indications for the singers, including such familiar ones as not to pay too much attention to the public but more to the character to whom the particular singer was supposed to be singing.

Cosima's musical abilities had been apparent already when she was a child and in the Berlin days before her marriage, we saw how impressed Bülow was with her pianistic gifts and that he even favored a professional career for her, which Liszt vetoed. The step from that early level to what she was doing now, however, was an enormous one. It was clear that she had not only absorbed from Wagner the over-all musical views and impressions, but that she had assimilated technical and interpretive details to an astonishing degree. Nevertheless, no matter how penetrating and skillful her direction was, it is hard to see how any conductor could function under the constant barrage of suggestions that came from her hidden box. Hermann Levi, who had conducted the *Parsifal* performances while Wagner was alive, showed himself to be a model of patience and forebearance.

Cosima set the tone from the start and made her position clear. This woman who even some years later could write about her inborn shyness and how the difficult conditions of her life had increased it, nevertheless overcame whatever hesitancies or inhibitions she might have had and acted with such force that there was no question that she had taken over full authority at Bayreuth. She admitted in a letter to a friend that this had not been easy for her.

"I cannot write you the timidity, even the shyness with which I approach the remarks on the artistic production of the works that I revere; and I would have been completely silent were it not that the love of the dear artists gave me courage and raised me up to a complete freedom and ease." [4]

For the first three years, the Festival presented only *Parsifal,* but Cosima determined to expand this and hoped in the end to produce all of Wagner's operas. It was a bold and far-reaching plan. The first opera to be added to the repertoire was the one that lay especially close to her heart—*Tristan and Isolde.* She planned it for the summer of 1886, the ten year anniversary of the Festival opening. By this time Cosima no longer directed things from her hidden box, but worked directly with everyone just as Wagner had. Like him, she took the singers through their roles, illustrating, gesturing, acting it out for them until they grasped what she wanted.

Here was the new Cosima, a woman of overpowering determination, a quality that had not been lacking in her before, but which was now manifested in a different way. She herself summed it up, perhaps, better than anyone. When she was asked why she had not made use of her musical and directional talents during Wagner's lifetime, she gave the concise answer, *"Da diente ich"* (Then I served). Here was the massive change in Cosima. She no longer served, although her life was still dedicated to the service of Wagner. She was the leader now, the one who dominated and directed.

Opposition to Cosima was enormous, partially that a woman, and one some people still termed a Frenchwoman, should take over the reins of the Festival. But Cosima was far too accustomed to hostility to left this affect her in any way. More serious were the legal attacks, questions of inheritance, of performing rights, even of her marriage. The bitterness that Wagner had aroused so widely fell wholly on Cosima now, and Wagner's enemies prepared for the kill. It was soon clear, however, that in Cosima they had more than met their match in every engagement.

Certainly Cosima was amazingly successful in all she set out to do and she maintained throughout a complete singleness of purpose. Bayreuth had once been referred to as the grave of friendships, and Cosima, as Wagner had done before her, counted loyalty to the cause as the one important virtue. This was not surprising in view of her feelings about Bayreuth, which were of an almost religious nature. She felt that the voice of God could be heard there as in no other place.

We see here in Cosima, carried to an extreme, the exclusivity of feeling that was so apparent in her mother. She had long before developed the blind, burning passion for a cause that is the necessary concomitant for its success. She herself had sacrificed everything for this cause. No wonder that the small sacrifices she felt she demanded of others seemed trifling in comparison with what she had been ready to do and had done, and that she had no patience at all with anyone who balked at doing what she wanted.

A humorous illustration of Cosima's dictatorial determination is told by Walther Siegfried in his book about her. A certain young singer at Bayreuth wanted to make one of her entrances with arms outstretched, a gesture that Cosima found out of keeping with the nature of the role. The singer, in league with her teacher who agreed with her, determined that she would obey Cosima at the rehearsals, but that at the performance she would enter with the forbidden gesture. But she reckoned without Cosima. Imagine her surprise when the evening of the performance came and she tried to lift her arms to find that the sleeves of her costume were carefully sewed to her sides. Cosima, had not been fooled for a moment by the apparent docility of the young singer and had made sure that her own wishes would be carried out as she had indicated.

Anyone as well versed in the arts of diplomacy as was Cosima is bound to arouse a certain amount of doubt, even of distrust. Cosima had such a way with people, her tact, her manner of getting what she wanted was so perfect that it was inevitable that her sincerity would be questioned. She herself mentioned that one of her greatest assets in dealing with the complex problems of Bayreuth was her ability, which was manifested throughout her life, not to show her deepest feelings. Cosima's manner was too perfect, her command of the social arts too subtle not to arouse a certain amount of questions and hostility about "this Frenchwoman." At this period of her life, however, Cosima no longer cared what attacks were made on her and paid very little if any attention to them any more. All she cared about was the fulfillment of her final mission.

If Cosima had her enemies, she had her friends and allies too. Just as Wagner had been able to do, she drew to her side a group of enormously devoted, loyal friends who saw in her the *Meisterin,* the bearer of the tradition of the great master himself, and they were ready to do anything for her. It was not only as Wagner's heir, however, that she commanded this devotion but equally so in her own right. The duality that her mother had seen in Cosima in her early youth was as apparent here as ever it had been, and she continued to arouse the greatest affection and admiration as well as hostility.

There was never any artistic compromise as far as Cosima was concerned. Her standards were high and her demands inflexible in her attempt to achieve Wagner's artistic ideal. She allowed no modifications at all in anything that he had indicated. Everything must remain exactly as he had approved it, to the very last detail, and she knew that she understood and could interpret his wishes as no one else could.

The "new" Cosima that emerged after Wagner's death and whose image became more and more fixed as she grew older, had been a long time in the making. The early years when she had determined to learn to accept her fate, the middle years when she had sublimated everything to the personality of Wagner had done nothing to destroy or alter the basic image and force of her character. The impress of a personality as powerful as that of Wagner, in whom she believed with every aspect of herself, left her completely satisfied in her sublimation to him. All the unsureness, all the conflict and self-doubt that had plagued her youthful years were resolved under the certitude that Wagner represented the supreme truth. Although she maintained a feeling of guilt toward Bülow for as long as she lived, nevertheless there was never the slightest doubt in her mind that she had done the right thing in leaving him and joining her life to Wagner's. She knew that it was not self-interest but devotion and sacrifice that had prompted her act. Wagner had made his need of her too clear, and she had seen too well what she had been able to accomplish ever to doubt the validity of her decision. Living as she had done in such intimate intellectual and emotional contact with Wagner's supreme self-confidence, identifying completely with him as she did, basking in the appreciation and admiration that he showed her, Cosima had no room for doubts or questions. She had understood the great man as no one else had ever been able to do; she had helped him when no one else would or could; without her none of the accomplishments of the last years would ever have been achieved. "Never before has there been anything like us two," Wagner had told her not long before his death, and the supremely self-centered artist assured her that: "You and I will live in the memory of men." [5]

Cosima had faced the world in her relationship to Wagner, and she had faced it down. Shocking as her conduct had seemed to the conventional world, cast out as she had been, Cosima succeeded in transforming her position from one of dishonor to one that commanded universal respect. The striking similarity between Cosima's actions and those of her mother ended here, for Cosima had succeeded in everything where Marie d'Agoult had failed. And her success was crowned by a general acceptance, even approval, of everything she had done. Even those most intimately concerned and hurt by the whole situation had ended by coming completely around. Liszt, who had been so unalterably opposed to Cosima's behavior, forgave her everything. "Cosima surpasses herself," he had written of her in 1872, after the breach between them was healed. "Let others judge and condemn her—for me she remains a soul worthy of the *gran perdono* of St. Francis and admirably my daughter!" [6] Bülow never wavered in his admiration for Cosima and he retained the highest respect for her as long as he lived. "Frau Wagner herself is a lofty being. For me she is an angel," he wrote his friend Bechstein shortly after Wagner's death.[7] Marie d'Agoult who had not injected herself actively into the picture during the crisis of Cosima's relationship with Wagner, gave perhaps the most poignant approval of all to her daughter. On her visit to Triebschen in the spring of 1871, she began to weep one evening when Wagner was playing the piano. "Triebschen made a great impression on her," Cosima wrote later. "She said it was life as she herself had dreamed it." [8] With all this, it is small wonder that Cosima's ego flourished and that when she was ready to emerge from under Wagner's looming shadow, she burst forth in splendid conflagration.

The new Cosima did not appeal to everyone, and one can feel that even Liszt was among those who, after Wagner's death, began to find her emergent personality somewhat oppressive. Possibly he had had enough of dominant and domineering women.

When Wagner died, Liszt had offered to come if Cosima wanted him, but she let him know through Daniela that it was not necessary and that he should spare himself the ordeal of the huge public funeral. Cosima did not see her father again until three years later, when she journeyed to Weimar, except for a few seconds when he was brought to her darkened, secret box during his visit to the Bayreuth Festival in 1884. It seems strange, in view of her former admiration of her father, that she should have delayed so long in seeing him, that she seemed determined to avoid him. The children were in constant touch with him, but Cosima remained silent and distant. Liszt had written once ten years before, when there had been no letters from Cosima for more than two months, that "we understand each other without phrases!" [9] Did he understand this strange detachment now for three years after Wagner's death? Probably he did, although it is difficult for us today to understand it. He was ill and old and tired, and anyone who loved him knew that he would not live much longer. Had Wagner finally succeeded in changing even Cosima's feelings toward her father? Certainly, Wagner's jealousy toward Liszt made him lash out to Cosima about his old friend in violent attacks against every aspect of his personality and his work. Did Cosima at last take over even this from Wagner? Or was it that she was so emotionally exhausted and drained that a meeting with Liszt might have stirred memories which she did not have strength to face? Perhaps it was unbearable to her to see Liszt alive and to know that Wagner was dead.

It was the spring of 1886 before Cosima finally visited Liszt in Weimar and told him of Daniela's engagement to Heinrich Thode. The wedding was to be in July, and she asked Liszt to be present. Although Liszt was not at all well and had not planned to visit the Festival that summer in spite of the first performance there of *Tristan,* he went for the wedding and, after visiting friends nearby for a few days, returned for the *Tristan* performance. He had caught a severe cold by then, which had been increased by the draft from a window thoughtlessly left open in the railway carriage by a pair of young people who had no idea who the tired old Abbé sitting huddled in the corner was. Ill as he was, Liszt sat through the entire *Tristan* performance. Six days later he died, not at Weimar, not at Rome, not even at Wahnfried, but in a small bedroom in lodgings in a house around the corner from Wahnfried. Receptions for visiting notables to the Festival were not cancelled; performances went on as planned. Perhaps Liszt would have wanted it that way, for he had once said that he did not wish to "trouble others to follow me to the cemetery, when I can no longer serve them in any way."

There was a funeral procession, nevertheless, to the modest local cemetery, the arrangements for which a group of Liszt's pupils, who had arrived to pay their last respects to the master they loved so well, found not at all to their liking. It was Alexander Siloti who spoke up with considerable vehemence and declared that the pupils would follow directly behind the family in the procession and not in third place after the opera personnel. Liszt's pupils were nearer in spirit to him than all the inhabitants of Bayreuth, Siloti declared in no uncertain terms.

Word came back from Cosima at once that she agreed to this.

Other cities had wanted to claim him—Weimar, his home for many years and the place which had seen so much of his service to music; Pest, which wanted to honor its eminent native son; Rome, where a final resting place had been planned for the ardent believer near where his Princess too would lie. Cosima never wavered a moment. She was determined that Liszt would be buried in Bayreuth, at the shrine of everything that represented the good and the great for her. And so Liszt, whose life had been so affected by dominating women, found even his final resting place chosen by his strong-willed daughter who brooked no opposition. What the Princess in Rome thought of it can be surmised. Seven months later she, who had bound her life inextricably to his, followed him in death.

With the death of her father and of the Princess, almost the last links that bound Cosima to her youth were severed. Bülow outlived Liszt by only eight years. Brilliant, successful, and important as his position was, he grew increasingly bitter toward everyone and everything, including finally even a reaction against his former "idolatrous worship" of Liszt.

As the years passed, Cosima settled within herself some of the inhibitions she had developed in her later years toward her father. Had she looked at herself objectively, and with her former sharp sense of humor, she might have laughed at seeing in herself some of the things that Wagner had fulminated against in Liszt, especially his "social" aspect. There is no question that Cosima thoroughly enjoyed the unusual scope of her social life and the highly placed contacts that she had, just as much as Liszt had ever done in his glossiest days. Her many trips around Europe, where she attended performances of works both of Wagner and of Liszt, and the active social life at Bayreuth during the Festival time were greatly enlivened for her by the great names who were eager to see the *Meisterin.* The shy, inhibited little girl of the rue Casimir-Périer delighted in the power of her position. She was on top of the world, of her world, and she never relinquished the certainty that Wagner represented everything of value in her time.

Cosima continued to delight in using her mind and enjoyed making pronouncements of all kinds based on Wagnerian concepts. She had long since modified her earlier, emotional views of Schopenhauer in line with Wagner's admiration of him, and in her later years her ideas did not vary very much, if at all, on anything. Her heroes remained Goethe, Schopenhauer, Luther, and anyone who represented what to her was the true German spirit. Nietzsche had long since earned her scorn. She found reading *Thus Spake Zarathustra* a "torment." "You poor wretched Zarathustra!" she wrote. "Have you really not paid any attention to Homer, Shakespeare, Goethe, Beethoven? Or have you only stolen from them and then denied their very existence in yourself?" [10] She changed her reaction completely even toward *The Birth of Tragedy,* about which she had been so ecstatic in the early Nietzsche days when she had written him that in it he had "evoked demons whom I believed obedient to the Master alone." Now she claimed, "It is indeed as though written by someone intoxicated and it affected me that way." [11]

Cosima left nothing to Nietzsche, not even his ability to express himself in his own language, in spite of his poetic gifts and his exceptionally brilliant qualifications as Professor of Philology. "But Neitzsche himself speaks no German," she stated. "These chopped-up sentences in their desolate monotony belong to I do not know what language." [12] It is fortunate, and yet a little strange too, that Nietzsche, who treasured his Ariadne in his secret heart, never realized where his attacks on Wagner had placed him in Cosima's feelings. He had committed the one unforgivable sin and after it could not be permitted any valid existence at all.

There was only one truth, as far as Cosima was concerned, only one reality, and that was Wagner. In her taking over unquestioningly of every attitude and every idea of his, she never saw, or never allowed herself to see, any of the narrow bigotry and fundamental limitation of so many aspects of his thinking. She brooked no question, no contradiction, no criticism, and woe betide anyone who did not see Wagner and all his works as she did.

Cosima, in spite of being the daughter of one artist and the wife of two, never forgot her early training under the rigid Madame Patersi. There was nothing free and easy in the way she maintained the conventions and Cosima demanded the strictest observance of all the formalities of aristocratic behavior. She ruled Bayreuth like a queen and moved about Europe with a truly imperious air.

Cosima had an overpowering influence over her children as long as she lived. It was only Blandine, who had married young, who enjoyed any real independence of Cosima and Bayreuth, although the relationship with her mother remained a close one. Eva, the gentlest and most loving of them all, dedicated her life to her mother. She did finally marry, at the age of forty-one, Houston Stewart Chamberlain, who had been one of Cosima's most ardent disciples for twenty years. They lived at Bayreuth inevitably, and her marriage in no way altered Eva's self-sacrifice to Cosima. Daniela, too, never really moved out of Cosima's orbit, and after her divorce, rather late in life, she returned to Bayreuth and to attendance on her mother. Isolde had the most tragic fate of all. Her marriage to Franz Biedler when she was thirty-five was perhaps not the one she had hoped for, but she was intensely loyal to her husband. Although she had shared in the inheritance from Bülow, and was legally considered as his child, she wanted to establish herself as Wagner's daughter, which she unquestionably was. Her reasons for this were complex, having to do with her husband's musical ambitions and with her wish to secure the future of her child. In the end she brought suit to have herself declared Wagner's child. As there was no way of actually proving this claim, her petition was disallowed. The old wounds were opened once more, but the only result of all the agony was that Cosima never let Isolde's name be mentioned in her presence again, although that first love child had always been her favorite among the girls. Isolde was less in awe of Cosima, less hampered in every way, and was the only one who dared to tease her mother and laugh her out of her stiff attitudes.

It was Siegfried, of course, who represented Cosima's hopes and dreams and although as a boy and young man, he had been drawn more to architecture than to music, in the end he could not resist what he knew would make Cosima happier than anything else in the world—that he become a musician. Cosima spent years grooming him for the task she envisioned for him. When she felt he was ready she did what no one had believed she could ever bring herself to do—she relinquished the full control of Bayreuth to her son. Siegfried, too, married late, and Cosima was already eighty years old when his first son was born and she could know that the Wagner name and the Wagner heritage would be preserved.

The last ten years of Cosima's life were spent in total blindness and in a misty world that vacillated between past and present, dream and reality. When she was ninety it occurred to her to ask how old she was. "Am I really?" she laughed when she heard. Her four grandchildren used often to play in her room. Daniela and Eva divided the day between them in attendance on her. Occasionally an old friend or an important visitor would be admitted to her.

Cosima lived out her final years, moving still in her memories and her dreams—all passion spent, all drivings stilled, quietly at peace at last until her death, in 1930, in her ninety-third year. Her last words, spoken on the day before her death in that low, rich voice of hers summed it all up: "Glorious," and then a little later, "Sorrow."

NOTES

CHAPTER I

1. Alexander Siloti: *My Memories of Liszt.* Edinburgh: Methven Simpson Ltd., P. 32.
2. *Correspondance de Liszt et de la Comtesse d'Agoult (1833–1840); publiée par* M. Daniel Ollivier. Paris: B. Grasset, 1933. P. 58.
3. As quoted in Frederick Corder: *Ferencz Liszt.* New York, London: Harper & Bros., 1925. P. 39.
4. *Letters of Franz Liszt;* collected and edited by La Mara. London: Grevel & Co., 1894. Vol. I, p. 8.
5. Richard Graf du Moulin Eckart: *Cosima Wagner.* Munich: Drei Masken Verlag, 1929. Vol. I, p. 10.
6. Frederick Corder: *Ferencz Liszt.* P. 56.
7. Hans von Bülow: *Briefe und Schriften. Herausgegeben von* Marie von Bülow. Leipzig: Breitkopf & Härtel, 1898. Vol. III, p. 186.
8. Balzac: *Beatrix.* Philadelphia: 1898. P. 208.
9. *Ibid.,* p. 356. Liszt showed one of his rare flashes of real meanness and the degree of hostility that had built up in him by that time toward Madame d'Agoult when he wrote of Balzac's book: "Madame de Rochefide is a portrait drawn by a master hand; it is so accurate a photograph that I, who thought that I thoroughly knew this woman, with her way of courting notoriety as much as other women shun it, was amazed, and actually understood her far better after reading the book." Balzac's picture of Liszt was no more flattering than that of Madame d'Agoult.

10. Comtesse d'Agoult (Daniel Stern). *Mes Souvenirs,* 2nd ed. Paris: Calmann-Levy, 1877. P. 349. *"Six pouces de neige sur vingt pieds de lave,"* not, *"six pieds de glace sur vingt pieds de lave,"* as most translations would seem to have it.
11. *Ibid.,* p. 198.
12. *Ibid.,* p. 195.
13. Comtesse d'Agoult (Daniel Stern): *Mémoires (1833–1854); avec une introduction de* M. Daniel Ollivier. 11th ed. Paris: 1927. Autorisé par Calmann-Lévy Editeur. P. 242.
14. *Ibid.,* p. 237.
15. *Ibid.,* p. 237.

CHAPTER II

1. Comtesse d'Agoult: *Mémoires.* P. 21.
2. *Correspondance de Liszt et de la Comtesse d'Agoult.* Vol. I, p. 90.
3. *Ibid.,* Vol. I, p. 83.
4. *Ibid.,* Vol. I, p. 108.
5. Comtesse d'Agoult: *Mémoires.* P. 41.
6. *Correspondance de Liszt et de la Comtesse d'Agoult.* Vol. I, p. 132.
7. *Ibid.,* p. 135–6.
8. Comtesse d'Agoult: *Mémoires.* P. 68.
9. Official document from Basilica Cattedrale di Como. This shows without doubt that Cosima was born at Como and not at Bellagio as has so often been stated. Also, that her birthday was the twenty-fourth and not the twenty-fifth of December, although she always celebrated it on Christmas Day. According to a letter of Wagner to Judith Gautier, Cosima was born at midnight. Marie d'Agoult, in a letter to Liszt dated Christmas 1840, gives Cosima's birth date as December 24.
10. *Correspondance de Liszt et de la Comtesse d'Agoult.* Vol. I, p. 203.
11. *Letters of Franz Liszt.* Vol. I, pp. 20–1.
12. *Correspondance de Liszt et de la Comtesse d'Agoult.* Vol. I, p. 231.
13. Comtesse d'Agoult: *Mémoires.* P. 147.
14. *Ibid.,* pp. 149–50.
15. *Correspondance de Liszt et de la Comtesse d'Agoult.* Vol. I, p. 235.
16. *Ibid.,* Vol. I, p. 239.
17. *Letters of Franz Liszt.* Vol. I, pp. 33–4.
18. *Correspondance de Liszt et de la Comtesse d'Agoult.* Vol. I, p. 254.
19. *Ibid.,* Vol. I, p. 262.
20. *Letters of Franz Liszt.* Vol. I, p. 31.
21. *Correspondance de Liszt et de la Comtesse d'Agoult.* Vol. I, p. 267.
22. *Ibid.,* Vol. II, p. 60.
23. *Ibid.,* Vol. II, p. 338.
24. Comtesse d'Agoult: *Mémoires.* P. 184.

CHAPTER III

1. Du Moulin Eckart: *Cosima Wagner.* P. 32–3.
2. *Correspondance de Liszt et de la Comtesse d'Agoult.* Vol. II, p. 98.
3. It is sometimes supposed that all the children spent the summers with their parents at Nonnenwerth. However, Liszt wrote a letter stating that "Blandine spent several months at Nonnenwerth in '43 with her mother and me." And in July of 1843 he wrote from Nonnenwerth to his mother: "Take care of the children; let them not want for anything." This would indicate that only the eldest daughter joined her parents on this single occasion.
4. Jacques Vier: *La Comtesse d'Agoult et son temps.* Paris: A. Colin, 1955. Vol. II, p. 140.
5. Du Moulin Eckart: *Cosima Wagner.* Vol. I, p. 45.
6. *Ibid.,* pp. 36–7.
7. *Correspondance de Liszt et de sa fille Madame Émile Ollivier, 1842–1862; publiée par M. Daniel Ollivier.* Paris: Grasset, 1936. P. 45.
8. Du Moulin Eckart: *Cosima Wagner.* Vol. I, p. 52.
9. *Franz Liszts Briefe an seine Mutter.* Leipzig: Breitkopf und Härtel, 1918. P. 87.
10. Du Moulin Eckart: *Cosima Wagner.* Vol. I, pp. 53–5.
11. *Ibid.,* p. 57.
12. *The Letters of Franz Liszt to Marie zu Sayn-Wittgenstein;* translated and edited by Howard E. Hugo. Cambridge: Harvard University Press, 1953. P. 47.
13. *Ibid.,* p. 89.
14. Cosima Wagner: *Franz Liszt, ein Gedenkblatt von seiner Tochter.* 2nd ed. Munich: F. Bruckmann, 1911. P. 18.
15. Du Moulin Eckart: *Cosima Wagner.* Vol. I, p. 62.

CHAPTER IV

1. Richard Wagner: *My Life.* New York: Dodd, Mead & Co., 1911. Pp. 608–9.
2. Marie Fürstin zu Hohenlohe: *Erinnerungen an Richard Wagner.* Weimar: Hermann Böhlaus, 1938. Pp. 13–4.
3. Du Moulin Eckart: *Cosima Wagner,* Vol. I, pp. 748–9.
4. *Cosima Wagners Briefe an ihre Tochter Daniela von Bülow, 1866–1885. Herausgegeben von* Max Freiherr von Waldberg. Stuttgart and Berlin: Cotta, 1933. P. 233.
5. *Correspondance de Liszt et de sa fille Madame Émile Ollivier.* P. 93.
6. Robert Bory: *Liszt et ses Enfants.* Paris: C. Editions Buchet Chastel, 1936. P. 53.
7. *Correspondance de Liszt et de la Comtesse d'Agoult.* Vol. II, pp. 403–4.
8. Bory: *Liszt et ses Enfants.* P. 59.

9. Franz Liszt: *Briefe an eine Freundin.* Leipzig: Breitkopf und Härtel, 1894. Pp. 42–3.
10. Du Moulin Eckart: *Cosima Wagner.* Vol. I, pp. 94–6.
11. *Correspondance de Liszt et de sa fille Madame Émile Ollivier.* Pp. 138–40.
12. *Ibid.*, p. 144.

CHAPTER V

1. *Briefwechsel zwischen Franz Liszt und Hans von Bülow. Herausgegeben von* La Mara. Leipzig: Breitkopf und Härtel, 1898. Pp. 152–3.
2. *Early Correspondence of Hans von Bülow.* New York: D. Appleton & Co., 1896. P. 53.
3. *Ibid.*, p. 51.
4. *Ibid.*, p. 52.
5. *Ibid.*, p. 55.
6. *Ibid.*, p. 55.
7. *Ibid.*, p. 69.
8. *Ibid.*, p. 70.
9. *Ibid.*, p. 94.
10. *Ibid.*, p. 123.
11. *Correspondence of Wagner and Liszt.* New York: Scribner & Welford, 1889. Vol. I, p. 87.
12. Richard Wagner: *Briefe an Hans von Bülow.* Jena: E. Diederichs, 1916. P. 125.
13. Correspondence of Wagner and Liszt. P. 69.
14. *Ibid.*, p. 74.
15. *Early Correspondence of Hans von Bülow.* P. 123.
16. *Breifwechsel zwischen Franz Liszt und Hans von Bülow.* P. 162.
17. *Early Correspondence of Hans von Bülow.* P. 227.
18. *Othello,* Act I, scene 3.
19. Bory: *Liszt et ses Enfants.* P. 132–4.
20. *Early Correspondence of Hans von Bülow.* P. 248.
21. *Correspondance de Liszt et de sa fille Madame Émile Ollivier.* P. 157.
22. Marcel Herwegh: *Au Printemps des Dieux; correspondance inédite de la Comtesse d'Agoult et du poète Georges Herwegh.* Paris: © editions Gallimard 1929. P. 183.
23. *Correspondance de Liszt et de sa fille Madame Émile Ollivier.* P. 174.
24. *Briefwechsel zwischen Franz Liszt und Hans von Bülow.* Pp. 208–9.
25. Bory: *Liszt et ses Enfants.* P. 212.

CHAPTER VI

1. Franz Liszt: *Briefe an eine Freundin.* P. 4.
2. *Ibid.*, p. 98.
3. Herwegh: *Au Printemps des Dieux.* P. 167.

4. *Ibid.*, p. 179.
5. *Ibid.*, p. 181.
6. Wagner: *My Life.* Pp. 668–9.
7. Hans von Bülow: *Briefe und Schriften.* Vol. III, p. 114.
8. Richard Wagner: *Briefe an Hans von Bülow.* Pp. 83–4.
9. Marie von Hohenlohe: *Errinerungen an Richard Wagner.* P. 20.
10. Du Moulin Eckart: *Cosima Wagner.* Vol. I, pp. 130, 129, 160.
11. Bory: *Liszt et ses Enfants.* P. 169.
12. *Ibid.*, p. 165.
13. Herwegh: *Au Printemps des Dieux.* P. 223.
14. Richard Wagner: *Briefe an Hans von Bülow.* P. 93.
15. Du Moulin Eckart: *Cosima Wagner.* Vol. I, p. 428.
16. *Ibid.*, pp. 870; 974.
17. As quoted in Ernest Newman: *Life of Richard Wagner.* New York: Alfred A. Knopf, 1946. Vol. III, p. 299.
18. *Hans von Bülow Neue Briefe. Herausgegeben und eingeleitet von* Richard Graf du Moulin Eckart. Munich: Drei Masken Verlag, 1927. Pp. 409–10.
19. Richard Wagner: *Briefe an Hans von Bülow.* P. 107.
20. *Briefwechsel zwischen Franz Liszt und Hans von Bülow.* P. 269.
21. *Ibid.*, p. 269.

CHAPTER VII

1. Du Moulin Eckart: *Cosima Wagner.* Vol. I, pp. 180–1.
2. Bory: *Liszt et ses Enfants.* P. 225.
3. Herwegh: *Au Printemps des Dieux.* P. 230.
4. *Correspondance de Franz Liszt et de sa fille Madame Émile Ollivier.* P. 268.
5. *Ibid.*, p. 271.
6. Richard Wagner: *Briefe an Hans von Bülow.* P. 153.
7. Herwegh: *Au Printemps des Dieux.* P. 237.
8. *Ibid.*, p. 238.
9. Hans von Bülow: *Briefe und Schriften.* Vol. XI, p. v.
10. *Briefwechsel zwischen Franz Liszt und Hans von Bülow.* P. 291.
11. Wagner: *My Life.* P. 707.
12. *Correspondance de Franz Liszt et de sa fille Madame Émile Ollivier.* P. 235.
13. *Correspondence of Wagner and Liszt.* Vol. II, p. 119.
14. Ernest Newman: *The Life of Richard Wagner.* Vol. III, p. 108.
15. *Correspondence of Wagner and Liszt.* Vol. II, p. 308.
16. *Correspondance de Franz Liszt et de sa fille Madame Émile Ollivier.* P. 211.
17. Franz Liszt: *Briefe an eine Freundin.* P. 145.

18. *Franz Liszts Briefe an die Fürstin Carolyne Sayn-Wittgenstein. Herausgegeben von* La Mara. Leipzig: Breitkopf und Härtel, 1902. Vol. II, 195, 198–9.
19. Fay: *Music Study in Germany.* Chicago: A. C. McClurg & Co., 1887. P. 206.
20. Richard Wagner: *Briefe an Hans von Bülow.* Pp. 160–1.
21. Wagner: *My Life.* P. 792.
22. *Franz Liszts Briefe an die Fürstin Carolyne Sayn-Wittgenstein.* Vol. II, pp. 209–10.
23. *Breifwechsel zwischen Franz Liszt und Hans von Bülow.* P. 289.
24. Wagner: *My Life.* P. 830.
25. Herwegh: *Au Printemps des Dieux.* P. 230.
26. Wagner: *My Life.* P. 832.
27. Du Moulin Eckart: *Cosima Wagner.* Vol. I, pp. 213–14.

CHAPTER VIII

1. Wagner: *My Life.* P. 840.
2. *Ibid.,* p. 838.
3. *Ibid.,* p. 876.
4. *Ibid.,* p. 876.
5. Richard Wagner: *Briefe an Hans von Bülow.* P. 209.
6. *Ibid.,* p. 218.
7. *Franz Liszts Briefe an die Fürstin Carolyne Sayn-Wittgenstein.* Vol. III, p. 36.
8. Richard Wagner: *Briefe an Hans von Bülow.* P. 226.
9. *Briefwechsel zwischen Franz Liszt und Hans von Bülow.* P. 320.
10. *Ibid.,* p. 321.

CHAPTER IX

1. *König Ludwig II und Richard Wagner Briefwechsel. Bearbeitet von* Otto Strobel. 5 vols. Karlsruhe: G. Braun, 1936, 1939. Vol. I, p. 40.
2. *Ibid.,* Vol. I, p. 57.
3. *Franz Liszts Briefe an die Fürstin Carolyne Sayn-Wittgenstein.* Vol. IV, p. 4.
4. *Ibid.,* Vol. III, p. 78.
5. *König Ludwig II und Richard Wagner Briefwechsel.* Vol. I, p. LIV.
6. *Ibid.,* Vol. I, p. LIV.
7. *Ibid.,* Vol. I, p. LII.
8. *Ibid.,* Vol. I, p. LXII.
9. As quoted in Ernest Newman: *The Life of Richard Wagner.* Vol. III, p. 483.
10. Peter Cornelius: *Ausgewählte Schriften und Briefe.* Berlin: Bernhard Hahnefeld, 1938. P. 398.

CHAPTER X

1. Peter Cornelius: *Ausgewählte Schriften und Briefe.* P. 395.
2. *Ibid.,* p. 394.
3. *König Ludwig II und Richard Wagner Briefwechsel.* Vol. I, p. 284.
4. *Ibid.,* Vol. IV, p. 126.
5. Richard Wagner: *Briefe an Hans von Bülow.* P. 239.
6. *König Ludwig II und Richard Wagner Briefwechsel.* Vol. IV, p. 141.
7. *Franz Liszts Briefe an die Fürstin Carolyne Sayn-Wittgenstein.* Vol. III, p. 117.
8. *König Ludwig II und Richard Wagner Briefwechsel.* Vol. IV, p. 140.
9. *Ibid.,* Vol. IV, p. 140.
10. *Ibid.,* Vol. II, p. 35.
11. *Ibid.,* Vol. IV, pp. 146–7.
12. Peter Cornelius: *Ausgewählten Schriften und Briefen.* Pp. 401–2.
13. *König Ludwig II und Richard Wagner Briefwechsel.* Vol. II, p. 54.
14. Du Moulin Eckart: *Cosima Wagner.* Vol. I, pp. 290–2.
15. Hans von Bülow: *Briefe.* 7 vols. Leipzig: 1899–1908. Vol. IV, p. 145.
16. *Ibid.,* Vol. IV, p. 132.
17. *Hans von Bülow Neue Brief.* P. 216.
18. *König Ludwig II und Richard Wagner Briefwechsel.* Vol. II, p. XXI.
19. *Ibid.,* Vol. II, p. XXII.
20. *Franz Liszts Briefe an die Fürstin Carolyne Sayn-Wittgenstein.* Vol. III, p. 159.

CHAPTER XI

1. *König Ludwig II und Richard Wagner Briefwechsel.* Vol. II, p. 235.
2. *Ibid.,* Vol. II, p. 235.
3. *Ibid.,* Vol. II, p. 244.
4. *Ibid.,* Vol. V, p. 80.
5. *Lettre de F. Liszt à sa fille la Baronne H. de Bülow à Munich, 2 Novembre, 1868.* From Charnacé Collection, Versailles Public Library.
6. Du Moulin Eckart: *Cosima Wagner.* Vol. I, pp. 422–3.
7. *Ibid.,* Vol. I, p. 423.
8. *Ibid.,* Vol. I, p. 451.
9. *König Ludwig II und Richard Wagner Briefwechsel.* Vol. V, pp. 115–8.
10. *Hans von Bülow Neue Briefe.* Pp. 477–83.
11. From Charnacé Collection, Versailles Public Library.
12. *Correspondence of Wagner and Liszt.* Vol. II, p. 308.
13. Du Moulin Eckart: *Cosima Wagner.* Vol. I, p. 529.
14. *Marie von Mouchanoff-Kalergis (geb. Gräfin Nessolrode) in Briefen an ihre Tochter. Herausgegeben von* La Mara. Leipzig: Breitkopf und Härtel, 1911. P. 281.

15. *Ibid.*, p. 225.
16. Du Moulin Eckart: *Cosima Wagner*. Vol. I, p. 448.
17. *Ibid.*, Vol. I, p. 442.
18. *Ibid.*, Vol. I, p. 444.
19. *Ibid.*, Vol. I, p. 513.

CHAPTER XII

1. E. F. Podach: *The Madness of Nietzsche*. London & New York: Putnam, 1931. P. 143.
2. Nietzsche: *Ecce Homo*.
3. *Die Briefe Cosima Wagners an Friedrich Nietzsche. Herausgegeben von* Max Freiherr von Waldberg. 2 vols. Weimar. Nietzsche Archiv, 1938, 1940. Vol. I, p. 69.
4. As quoted in *The Portable Nietzsche,* selected and translated by Walter Kaufmann. New York: The Viking Press, 1954. P. 8.
5. *Die Briefe Cosima Wagners an Friedrich Nietzsche*. Vol. I, p. 14.
6. *Ibid.*, Vol. I, p. 12.
7. *Ibid.*, Vol. I, p. 18.
8. *Ibid.*, Vol. I, p. 14.
9. *Ibid.*, Vol. I, p. 30.
10. *Ibid.*, Vol. I, p. 33.
11. *Ibid.*, Vol. I, pp. 25–6.
12. Letter to Gast as quoted in Karl Jaspers: *Nietzsche*. Tuscon: The University of Arizona Press, 1965. P. 83.
13. *Die Briefe Cosima Wagners an Friedrich Nietzsche*. Vol. I, p. 33.
14. *Ibid.*, Vol. I, p. 9.
15. *Ibid.*, Vol. I, p. 22.
16. *Ibid.*, Vol. I, p. 31.
17. Du Moulin Eckart: *Cosima Wagner*. Vol. I, p. 501.
18. *Die Briefe Cosima Wagners an Friedrich Nietzsche*. Vol. I, p. 57.
19. As quoted in Edward J. O'Brien: *Son of the Morning, a Portrait of Friedrich Nietzsche*. New York: Robert O. Ballou, 1932. P. 78.
20. *Die Briefe Cosima Wagners an Friedrich Nietzsche*. Vol. II, p. 40.
21. *Ibid.*, Vol. I, p. 65.
22. Du Moulin Eckart: *Cosima Wagner*. Vol. I, p. 538.
23. *Die Briefe Cosima Wagners an Friedrich Nietzsche*. Vol. I, p. 70.
24. *Ibid.*, Vol. II, p. 17.
25. Nietzsche: Foreword to *The Birth of Tragedy*.
26. Marie Von Bülow: *Hans von Bülows Leben, dargestellt aus seinen Briefen*. 2nd ed. Leipzig: Breitkopf und Härtel, 1921. Pp. 250–2.
27. *Die Briefe Cosima Wagners an Friedrich Nietzsche*. Vol. II, p. 40.
28. Letter to Gersdorff as quoted in E. J. O'Brien: *Son of the Morning*. P. 115.
29. *Die Briefe Cosima Wagners an Friedrich Nietzsche*. Vol. II, p. 35.
30. As quoted in Karl Jaspers: *Nietzsche*. P. 44.

31. Nietzsche: *Ecce Homo.*
32. As quoted in Karl Jaspers: *Nietzsche.* P. 45.
33. *The Nietzsche-Wagner Correspondence, edited by Elizabeth Förster-Nietzsche.* New York: Boni and Liveright, 1921. P. 311.
34. *Nietzsche contra Wagner.*
35. Nietzsche: *Thus Spake Zarathustra.*
36. As quoted in Karl Jaspers: *Nietzsche.* P. 44.
37. Friedrich Nietzsche: *The Case of Wagner.* New York: MacMillan & Co., 1896. P. 9.
38. As quoted in Karl Jaspers: *Nietzsche.* P. 377.
39. As quoted in *Ibid.,* p. 226.
40. Nietzsche: Poetic Fragment: *Naxos (1885).*
41. Nietzsche: *The Lament of Ariadne.*
42. As quoted in E. F. Podach: *The Madness of Nietzsche.* P. 143.

CHAPTER XIII

1. Du Moulin Eckart: *Cosima Wagner.* Vol. I, pp. 616–7.
2. *König Ludwig II und Richard Wagner Briefwechsel.* Vol. II, p. 74.
3. *Ibid.,* Vol. II, p. 334.
4. Du Moulin Eckart: *Cosima Wagner.* Vol. I, p. 605.
5. *Franz Liszts Briefe an die Fürstin Carolyne Sayn-Wittgenstein.* Vol. IV, p. 7.
6. *Ibid.,* Vol. III, pp. 349–50.
7. *Ibid.,* Vol. III, p. 350.
8. *Ibid.,* Vol. III, p. 349.
9. Alexander Siloti: *My Memories of Liszt.* P. 58.
10. *Franz Liszts Briefe an die Fürstin Carolyne Sayn-Wittgenstein.* Vol. III, p. 360.
11. Du Moulin Eckart: *Cosima Wagner.* Vol. I, p. 621.
12. *Ibid.,* Vol. I, p. 629.
13. *Ibid.,* Vol. I, pp. 630–1.
14. *Ibid.,* Vol. I, p. 627.
15. *Franz Liszts Briefe an die Fürstin Carolyne Sayn-Wittgenstein.* Vol. III. P. 336.
16. Du Moulin Eckart: *Cosima Wagner.* Vol. I, p. 644.
17. *Ibid.,* Vol. I, pp. 708–9.
18. *The Nietzsche-Wagner Correspondence.* P. 247.
19. Du Moulin Eckart: *Cosima Wagner.* Vol. I, p. 955.
20. *Ibid.,* Vol. I, p. 964.
21. *Ibid.,* Vol. I, p. 964.
22. *Ibid.,* Vol. I, p. 962.
23. *Ibid.,* Vol. I, p. 974.

CHAPTER XIV

1. Du Moulin Eckart: *Cosima Wagner.* Vol. I, pp. 555–6.
2. *Franz Liszts Briefe an die Fürstin Carolyne Sayn-Wittgenstein.* Vol. IV, p. 131.
3. Richard et Cosima Wagner: *Lettres à Judith Gautier. Presentées et annotées par Leon Guichard.* Paris: Gallimard, 1964. P. 63.
4. *Ibid.,* p. 59.
5. *Ibid.,* p. 63.
6. Du Moulin Eckart: *Cosima Wagner.* Vol. I, p. 758.
7. *Ibid.,* Vol. I, pp. 935–6.
8. *Cosima Wagners Briefe an ihre Tochter Daniela von Bülow, 1866-1885. Herausgegeben von* Max Freiherr von Waldberg. Stuttgart and Berlin: Cotta, 1933. P. 34.
9. *Briefwechsel zwischen Franz Liszt und Hans von Bülow.* P. 398.
10. *Cosima Wagners Briefe an ihre Tochter Daniela von Bülow.* Pp. 53–4.
11. *Hans von Bülow Neue Briefe.* P. 523.
12. *Cosima Wagners Briefe an ihre Tochter Daniela von Bülow.* P. 171.
13. *Hans von Bülow Neue Briefe.* P. 524.
14. Du Moulin Eckart: *Cosima Wagner.* Vol. I, pp. 944–5.
15. *Hans von Bülow Neue Briefe.* P. 526.
16. *Franz Liszts Briefe an die Fürstin Carolyne Sayn-Wittgenstein.* Vol. IV, p. 276.
17. *Ibid.,* Vol. IV, p. 292.
18. *Ibid.,* Vol. IV, p. 306.

CHAPTER XV

1. *Franz Liszts Briefe an die Fürstin Carolyne Sayn-Wittgenstein.* Vol. IV, p. 395.
2. As quoted in Ernest Newman: *The Life of Richard Wagner.* Vol. IV, p. 713.
3. As quoted in Edward J. O'Brien: *Son of the Morning.* P. 243.
4. Letter to Frau Rosa Sucher as quoted in Max Millenkovich-Morold: *Cosima Wagner.* Leipzig: Philipp Reclam jun., 1934. P. 338.
5. Du Moulin Eckart: *Cosima Wagner.* Pp. 975, 812.
6. *Franz Liszts Briefe an die Fürstin Carolyne Sayn-Wittgenstein.* Vol. III, p. 366.
7. Letter of Hans von Bülow as quoted in Walther Siegfried: *Frau Cosima Wagner.* Stuttgart: Union Deutsche Verlags Gesellschaft, 1930. P. 65.
8. *Die Briefe Cosima Wagners an Friedrich Nietzsche.* Vol. I, p. 72.
9. *Franz Liszts Briefe an die Fürstin Carolyne Sayn-Wittgenstein.* Vol. IV, p. 134.

10. *Cosima Wagner und Houston Stewart Chamberlain im Briefwechsel, 1888–1908. Herausgegeben von* Paul Pretzsch. Leipzig: Philipp Reclam jun., 1934. P. 610.
11. *Ibid.*, p. 613.
12. *Ibid.*, p. 609.

INDEX